LYING EYES

AND THE HITMAN FOR HIRE

Emer Connolly

Gill & Macmillan

Gill & Macmillan Ltd
Hume Avenue
Park West
Dublin 12
with associated companies throughout the world
www.gillmacmillan.ie

© Emer Connolly 2008
978 07171 4625 3

Typography design by Make Communication
Print origination by O'K Graphic Design, Dublin
Printed in the UK by CPI Mackays, Chatham

The paper used in this book is made from the wood pulp of
managed forests. For every tree felled, at least one tree is
planted, thereby renewing natural resources.

A CIP catalogue record for this book is available from the
British Library.

1 3 5 4 2

CONTENTS

PROLOGUE | A BRIGHT SUMMER'S DAY IN KILKEE

It was a bright summer's day in Kilkee. The tourist season was in full swing and the popular seaside resort was buoyant. The sky was clear, the sea was blue. Much to the oblivion of the tourists who strolled around the town, the latest sitting of the town's District Court was taking place. Squad cars converged on the tiny run-down courthouse and, inside, the three rows of benches were full. The court list in Kilkee—which only sits nine times in the year—is short, generally lasts no more than a couple of hours, and consists mainly of public order cases, road traffic charges and the odd licensing dispute.

But on the morning of 26 June, 2007, things were rather different. A sense of anticipation prevailed in the air. The television crews and photographers were lined up. A tip-off very early that morning confirmed my requirement to head to the west Clare town. This was the morning that Sharon Collins would make her first court appearance, but, significantly, hers was no ordinary crime. This was the moment that gardaí, who were investigating allegations of a conspiracy to murder a wealthy Ennis family, had waited for. An extensive and complex nine-month investigation had finally brought charges of conspiracy to murder and there were two people standing accused—Ennis housewife Sharon Collins (then aged 44) and Egyptian poker dealer Essam Eid (then aged 51). An unlikely pair!

Although a posse of photographers had rounded on the courthouse, no other journalists waited in anticipation for the arrival of Collins and Eid. Though other reporters in the region would later zone in on the story, as events unfolded at Ennis Circuit Court that morning.

In Ennis, Eid had been due to go on trial, charged with extorting €100,000 from Robert Howard, but that charge—along with a burglary charge and two charges of handling stolen property—was dropped by the prosecution that morning. He was then released and immediately re-arrested, charged with conspiracy to murder and brought the 35-mile journey west to Kilkee.

This caught the attention of the journalists sitting in the Circuit Court, who swiftly took to the road and followed the car in which Eid was travelling.

Sharon Collins, too, was on her way to Kilkee court and some time after midday, she was brought into the courtroom. Pretty, with blonde hair to her ears, she looked as baby-faced as the female garda who accompanied her—despite being up to 20 years her senior. Garda Annette Ryan accompanied Collins to the court and she was immediately taken to a room off the main courtroom to speak to her solicitor, Mary Larkin. Her arrival, and that of Essam Eid at the courthouse, sparked a flurry of excitement among the waiting photographers and television crews, but they were afforded little in terms of useful images as both had coats covering their heads. Collins was dressed casually in jeans and a top and as she sat in the courtroom, tears streamed down her pale face. Shock was in evidence around the packed room and my initial thoughts were laced with amazement that this seemingly meek woman could be involved in a devious plot to kill.

Alongside her sat her elderly mother Bernadette Coote, who was well turned out, heavily made up, hair pinned up in a bun and wearing a long cream-coloured coat.

Essam Eid, who sat flanked by two gardaí, took one look at Collins and was heard to mutter, 'I was cheated.'

Why the reaction? Because, ironically, this was the first time that Collins and Eid had met face to face. Their lives had intersected, but not in person, until that very moment in the tiny Kilkee courtroom. That morning, both were charged with conspiracy to murder brothers Robert and Niall Howard, between August and September 2006. They would later be charged with conspiracy to murder Collins's multi-millionaire partner PJ Howard, who is also Robert's and Niall's father.

The day was brimming with ironies as Collins made her first court appearance in a town she despised. As a child, she was taken there by her grandmother with her sisters, but grew to dislike the town strongly and never became attached to it. Tearful memories of this bright summer's day in a Kilkee courtroom will only add to her dislike of the seaside resort.

On the other hand, the town has held many happy memories for her targets—PJ Howard has had an affinity with Kilkee since he was a child, while his sons Robert and Niall have both grown very fond of the place. They spend most weekends socialising in the town, and own a holiday home and boat there.

The case before Judge Joseph Mangan got underway, when Detective Garda Jarlath Fahy said he had arrested Sharon Collins at 8.59 that morning. In reply after both charges, she said, 'I never did that.' Detective Sergeant Michael Moloney said that Eid had had nothing to say in reply to the charges put to him, at Lifford, Ennis, that morning.

Both were remanded in custody, but Collins's solicitor said she would be applying for bail in the High Court, at the earliest opportunity. She applied for free legal aid for the mother-of-two.

Superintendent John Scanlan, who headed the investigation, had also travelled to the court. He pointed out that Collins owned property, although her 'situation may have changed somewhat in the course of this investigation'.

Ms Larkin said the rent was paying the mortgages on Collins's properties.

Supt Scanlan replied, 'I'd have concerns whether she would be a suitable applicant for free legal aid.'

The application was deferred for two days at Ennis District Court, when, after hearing Collins would be 'very lucky' if she has 'anything left' after the case was over, Judge Mangan granted her free legal aid.

Eid's solicitor John Casey said he was not objecting to an application by the State to remand his client in custody.

No sooner had Collins and Eid left Kilkee on their way to Limerick prison, than news spread like wildfire in her home town of Ennis of the stirring events, as shock set in among locals. While she was known to have enjoyed the high life, few could believe what had happened in court that morning. Nobody wanted to believe the allegations against Collins. Many of the intriguing questions asked around the streets of Ennis that summer's day would present astounding answers over the following 13 months as the name Sharon Collins would, eventually, go down in history.

01 | A POWERFUL OPENER

It was a powerful opening speech that gripped the nation. By the time senior counsel for the Prosecution Tom O'Connell sat down at 3.39 p.m. on Thursday, 22 May 2008, after delivering a two-and-a-half hour speech, it was clear that this story was going to be a major talking point across the country for weeks to come.

Mr O'Connell had told an engrossed jury that the case was most unusual and contained many elements, including confabulation, lies, a lethal poison, a plot to wipe out a family and dozens of exchanges between 'hitman' and 'lyingeyes' email addresses.

Opening speeches for the Prosecution generally give an outline of the allegations and this was done in great detail by Mr O'Connell, in a speech which would later be referred to by Essam Eid's senior counsel David Sutton as 'long and enthusiastic'.

The previous morning, Wednesday, 21 May, both the accused, Sharon Collins and Essam Eid, had appeared before Mr Justice Paul Carney in courtroom number 1, in the Round Hall of the Four Courts. She was on bail, while he was in custody. Collins was neatly dressed, in a black trouser suit and white crisp shirt, while Eid wore a white shirt, red and blue striped tie and black jeans.

Collins was represented by the Kilrush-based solicitor Eugene

O'Kelly, who instructed Paul O'Higgins, senior counsel; Michael Bowman, junior counsel; and Joanne Kirby, junior counsel. Eid was represented by Ennis solicitor John Casey, who instructed David Sutton, senior counsel; Michael Collins, junior counsel; and Mark Nicholas, junior counsel. The State was represented by Tom O'Connell, senior counsel; Úna Ní Raifeartaigh, junior counsel; and Stephen Coughlan, junior counsel, instructed by Helen Kealy of the office of the Director of Public Prosecutions.

The ten charges in the case were read out and both defendants pleaded not guilty. Collins faced six charges and Eid faced seven. Three of the charges, conspiracy to murder, referred to both accused.

Collins and Eid pleaded not guilty to conspiring to murder PJ, Robert and Niall Howard, within the jurisdiction of the Central Criminal Court, between 1 August 2006 and 26 September 2006. Collins pleaded not guilty to soliciting Essam Eid to murder PJ, Robert and Niall Howard, within the jurisdiction of the Central Criminal Court, on 15 August 2006.

Eid also pleaded not guilty to making an unwarranted demand for €100,000 from Robert Howard, on 26 September 2006 in exchange for not killing PJ, Robert and Niall Howard, at Ballaghboy, Doora, Ennis.

Eid also denied entering as a trespasser a building known as Downes and Howard Ltd, Unit 7A, Westgate Business Park, Kilrush Road, Ennis, and stealing a computer, a laptop, computer cables, a digital clock and a poster of old Irish money, on 25 September 2006.

He also pleaded not guilty to handling stolen property: keys to Unit 7A, Westgate Business Park; a digital clock; a poster of old Irish money; and computer cables, at the Two Mile Inn hotel, Limerick. Eid also denied handling a stolen Toshiba laptop computer at Ballaghboy, Doora, Ennis, on 26 September 2006.

Prior to swearing in a jury for the case, Tom O'Connell delivered a brief outline of the facts of the State's case to the jury panel. He explained that the alleged targets of the conspiracy were PJ Howard and his two sons Robert and Niall. 'PJ Howard is a businessman who lives in Ennis, at Ballybeg House, Kildysart

Road. He is involved in the property business and operates through the names Downes and Howard Ltd and Waymill Ltd.'

He said that Mr Howard operated his business from Unit 7A Westgate Business Park, Kilrush Road, Ennis, while he spends part of the year in Spain.

He explained that PJ Howard's wife, from whom he had been separated, died in 2003. In 1998, he had met Sharon Collins and the two had lived together but were not married, adding, 'but Ms Collins was keen to get married'.

He said it would be alleged that Sharon Collins solicited Essam Eid to kill PJ Howard and his two sons. Robert, he said, was PJ's eldest son, lived at Ballaghboy, Doora, Ennis, and worked in PJ's property business, continuing 'The third target was Niall Howard, son of PJ Howard, who worked in the family business.'

He then explained to the jury panel that Sharon Collins hailed from Ennis and that her maiden name was Coote. She was living with PJ Howard for a period of eight years, 'until these offences occurred'.

'In essence, the Prosecution case is that she organised a proxy marriage through the internet, without PJ's knowledge. Subsequently, she contacted Mr Eid on the internet, using various computers, on www.hitmanforhire.net. He advertised himself as Tony Luciano. This was done through a website, email address, not in her own name, in another name,' said Mr O'Connell.

He said that Essam Eid was an Egyptian national, living in Las Vegas, where he worked as a poker dealer in a casino. He travelled to Ireland on 24 September 2006 and stayed at the Two Mile Inn hotel, Limerick, and allegedly burgled the Downes and Howard family business on 25 September.

After hearing this outline of the State's case, a jury of eight men and four women was sworn in. They were told the trial would last about four weeks, in courtroom number 16 in the Four Courts, before Mr Justice Roderick Murphy. The jury was then directed to the small courtroom number 16 on the second floor, where space was limited.

Mr Justice Murphy told the jury that it would benefit the Prosecution and Defence if they could have 'a bit of time without

your presence' and the jury was sent away until the following
morning.

Prompted by Sharon Collins's senior counsel Paul O'Higgins,
the judge had issued the first of what would become several
warnings to the jury, relating to the media coverage of the case.
'You try the case on each of the counts, in relation to the evidence
in the court, not what others are going to say, not what is in the
press,' said the judge, at 1 p.m. on 21 May.

The following morning, in the cramped conditions of the
courtroom, Mr O'Connell began his opening speech to the jury.
Both defendants sat at the back of the courtroom, separated by
just a few people. A few yards to their right, the three men at the
centre of the case—PJ, Robert and Niall Howard—sat closely
together, alongside their public relations consultant, Caimin
Jones.

At 11.49 a.m., Mr O'Connell rose to his feet and began his
lengthy speech, laced with bizarre, almost incredible allegations.

He began by telling the jury that the case was 'rather complex,
with evidence gleaned from computers.' He said it would be
alleged that Sharon Collins and Essam Eid conspired together to
murder Robert, Niall and PJ Howard, 'the whole family in fact',
and that this conspiracy was hatched between 1 August and 26
September 2006. 'Conspiracy is in essence an agreement between
two or more persons to do an unlawful act. It will be the State's
case that the conspiracy was indeed to kill these three persons.'

He said the next three offences charged Sharon Collins only
with soliciting Essam Eid to murder the three Howard men, on 15
August 2006.

'What solicit means is to urge or incite someone to do
something. It's the State's case that Sharon Collins solicited Essam
Eid to carry out these murders,' he explained.

He said that Essam Eid was accused of demanding money with
menaces, in that he made an unwarranted demand for €100,000
from Robert Howard, in exchange for not killing the three men,
at Ballaghboy, Doora, Ennis, on 26 September 2006.

'The place in question was the home of Robert and Niall
Howard, who live together. On that particular evening, Mr Eid

turned up on their doorstep, told them he had a contract to kill them and their father and said, "Well if you give me €100,000 I won't do it because I don't want to do it"', he said.

Mr O'Connell said it would also be alleged that Essam Eid entered the Howard's family business the previous evening, 25 September, as a trespasser, and took a number of items. 'He had the keys. This was not a forced entry. The keys were given by Sharon Collins,' he said.

The prosecutor continued that the State alleged that Essam Eid handled stolen property in Room 208 of the Two Mile Inn hotel, Limerick, on 27 September, while he was also accused of handling a stolen Toshiba laptop, at Ballaghboy, Doora, on 26 September. 'When Essam Eid turned up on the doorstep [of Robert Howard's home], he had a laptop which he had stolen from the business premises. He produced the laptop and handed it over to Robert Howard,' he said.

Next, Mr O'Connell went into the backgrounds of the people at the centre of the case. He explained that Sharon Collins had met PJ Howard, who was separated, in 1998. She had quickly moved into his house with her two sons and they had ended up staying there. 'Mr Howard's wife died in 2003. After her death, Ms Collins was anxious and agitating to get married to Mr Howard. It seems he didn't wish to marry her as it would complicate inheritance matters. He wanted whatever fortunes he had to go to his two sons,' he said.

He explained how Sharon Collins had worked in PJ Howard's business at 7A Westgate Business Park, Kilrush Road, Ennis. 'She was quite good apparently, according to Mr Howard, on computers, having been apparently self-taught.'

'She had been married previously, annulled and subsequently divorced. She was keen to get married to Mr Howard. She was very much concerned with inheritance and frequently visited various websites interrogating the computer about her position. Apparently, a marriage was arranged at her instigation, to take place in Rome in 2005. PJ pulled out of it, but they went to Sorrento where they pledged themselves to each other, but no marriage took place,' said Mr O'Connell.

He said that after they had returned home, Sharon Collins had told people they had got married and they had held a wedding reception in Spanish Point in November 2005. The same year that Sharon Collins had 'conceived and organised through the internet a proxy marriage under Mexican law. This was done without the knowledge of PJ Howard.'

She had paid had $1,295 for a certificate testifying to the proxy marriage and arranged for the certificate to be sent to her accountant in Kilrush, Co. Clare, where she had later collected it.

On 22 February 2006, she had gone to Cork, where she had obtained a passport under the name Sharon Howard, by using the proxy marriage certificate.

'It's the State's case she intended to use the marriage certificate to stake a claim in PJ's estate on the deaths of him and his two sons. It could be inferred by using the documents, she was trying them out to see if they would pass official scrutiny,' said Mr O'Connell.

The prosecutor then moved on to the key email evidence that would be presented during the course of the trial, the discovery of which had led to the charges being brought. He told the jury that the three key dates were 2, 8 and 16 August 2006. He said it would be alleged that Sharon Collins had set up the email address lyingeyes98@yahoo.ie on 2 August 2006. A shocked courtroom then heard the first of many startling allegations that would be made throughout the trial. 'It is the State's case that this was done for the purpose of hiring an assassin or hitman,' he stated.

'The email address was set up from an Advent desk computer which had been in the business premises at Downes and Howard at 7A Westgate Business Park. That computer was stolen from the premises by Essam Eid,' said Mr O'Connell.

Those fortunate enough to have seats in the cramped courtroom were shell shocked by the suggestion that this neatly dressed, petite blonde could have considered such a thing. Mr O'Connell continued with his speech.

He stated that the email address lyingeyes98@yahoo.ie had established contact with an email address hire_hitman@yahoo.com on 8 August 2006, through the website www.hitmanforhire.net.

'It will be engraved in your memories by the end of the case. It is the State's case that Essam Eid operated that email, using the alias Tony Luciano. Emails were sent from that email address, signed Tony Luciano. The services offered by 'hitmanforhire' were contract killings,' he told the jury.

Several emails were exchanged between the two email addresses after 8 August and, on 15 August, a contract had been made between 'the person behind 'lyingeyes' and 'hitman' to kill PJ and his two sons, at the price of $90,000; $50,000 was the normal price, but because there were three, $90,000'.

He said that, on that day, Sharon Collins had made a down payment of €15,000, on foot of the contract.

'She sent the €15,000 in cash on that date by FedEx courier services, from Shannon,' he said. She had withdrawn €13,000 from her own account at AIB Bank in Ennis, while the other €2,000 had come from her Credit Union account.

Mr O'Connell said that Sharon Collins had sent the money from Shannon to Teresa Engle at a Las Vegas address.

'This was Essam Eid's home address at that time. Teresa Engle appeared to be his wife at the time. She had gone through a marriage ceremony with Essam Eid. She's a witness in the case. She lived with Essam Eid in Las Vegas at that address, with his previous wife Lisa Eid,' he said.

According to the Prosecution, Teresa Engle had visited Ireland at the end of August 2006 with a friend of Essam Eid—Ashraf Gharbeiah—and had then travelled to Malaga, where PJ Howard owns an apartment. Mr O'Connell said that on 24 September 2006, Essam Eid had travelled to Ireland and had booked into Room 208 at the Two Mile Inn hotel in Limerick and had allegedly burgled the Howards' business premises in Ennis, on 25 September.

'It was an inside job. There was no evidence of any forced entry. Whoever entered the premises that night had the keys to the premises and also had the alarm code. It would seem the purpose of the burglary was to get rid of incriminating evidence. The following day when gardaí carried out a search of Room 208, they found the keys to the office premises. It is the State's case these were provided by Ms Collins. They were left in Ennis to be picked up and used then to remove the potentially incriminating computer,' said Mr O'Connell.

He then moved on to 26 September, when Robert Howard had received a call on his mobile phone. It was 10.30 p.m. and Robert was at his home at Ballaghboy, Doora, on the outskirts of Ennis.

The caller had said to him, 'Hello, I'm Tony,' and added, 'I heard you lost a few computers.' The caller had said he had a computer and would be at Robert's house in five minutes. Within five minutes, Robert had answered the door and a man, calling himself 'Tony' had been there. He had handed Robert a Toshiba laptop computer and had said that someone had wanted Robert, his brother Niall and their father PJ dead. He had said he had been offered €130,000 to kill them, but that he didn't want to do it.

'Robert will say he had various sheets of paper in his hand, containing personal information on PJ Howard. He proposed that Robert would buy out the contract that he had to kill the three of them,' said Mr O'Connell.

Robert Howard would say that 'Tony' had had two photographs in his hand, which had been printed from a computer and that he had taken them from him. One was a photograph of PJ Howard and Sharon Collins, in which she was wearing a red dress, taken at a Christmas party in Dromoland Castle; the other was of PJ Howard on his boat in Spain. Robert Howard had then gone into his house where he had spoken to his brother Niall. Shortly afterwards, 'Tony' had pulled away in a car, having been at the house for about 20 minutes.

The following morning, 27 September, Robert had received a phone call and after a series of telephone conversations, he had arranged a meeting at the Queen's Hotel in Ennis, for 5.15 p.m. that day, when he was to hand over money to two women at the toilets. A garda surveillance operation had been set up and Essam Eid and Teresa Engle had been arrested. Later, in an identification parade, Essam Eid had been identified by Robert and Niall Howard as the man who had been outside their door the previous night.

A room in the Two Mile Inn hotel had been searched and keys

and other items had been found. 'These events triggered an extensive garda investigation,' said Mr O'Connell. He said that the trial would hear from the FBI, who had carried out investigations in Las Vegas, mainly at the home of Essam Eid, while details of computer and telephone traffic would also be presented.

The prosecutor said that Sharon Collins had denied being part of a conspiracy.

'She claimed she was the victim of a blackmail. The State says this was a lie. She admitted sending €15,000 cash to Mr Eid's address in Las Vegas. She admitted filing pictures Essam Eid had in his possession. She admitted obtaining a proxy marriage certificate that was unknown to PJ Howard,' he said.

He said that Essam Eid had claimed to know Sharon Collins and had claimed to be her lover. He had told gardaí that she had paid for a ticket for him to visit Ireland. An Irish soldier trawling the internet had come upon the 'hitman' website and after email exchanges, 'Tony Luciano' had rung him and had asked him if he could get him a gun in Ireland. The soldier had panicked and had said it wasn't him who had sent the emails.

At this stage, the courtroom was gripped and the momentum was flowing. But few of those in attendance were prepared for what was to come next. There was a poisonous element to the case.

Mr O'Connell calmly proceeded through his speech, telling the jury that on receipt of intelligence from the FBI, gardaí had carried out a search of Essam Eid's cell in Limerick prison in April 2007. There, they had found a contact lens case, which had showed traces of 'a very dangerous poison, ricin'.

As swiftly as Mr O'Connell had introduced the ricin element, he moved away from it and proceeded to the next part of the evidence. He said that Matt Heslin, an accountant, had done some work for Sharon Collins. In August or September 2005, she had told him she was going to have a proxy marriage to PJ Howard in Mexico and had asked him if she could have the documents of the marriage sent to him and he had agreed. Around this time, the marriage documents had arrived at Mr Heslin's office in Kilrush and he had given them to Ms Collins.

'She said she didn't want Mr Howard's sons to see the documents. These documents were used to obtain a passport. That was done in February 2006. Sharon Collins herself turned up at the passport office, wishing to renew her passport. She had an original marriage certificate, one in Spanish, one in English,' said Mr O'Connell.

He said that the passport office had taken photocopies of the certificate and, on 8 March 2006, had issued a passport in the name of Sharon Howard.

In advance of going through some of the relevant emails, Mr O'Connell told the jury, "Lyingeyes' is Sharon Collins.'

He said that at 1.14 p.m. on 2 August 2006, a search for 'hitman' had been carried out on an Advent desktop computer at the Downes and Howard business premises at Westgate Business Park. One minute later, www.hitman.us (a website selling T-shirts) had been accessed and this web page had been visited at 1.16 p.m. It had been accessed again later that afternoon, and, at 4 p.m., the user had visited the yahoo login page. At 4.01 p.m., the user had accessed the inbox of sharoncollins@eircom.net and had read emails.

'Someone using it knows Sharon Collins's password and is using her email,' he said.

Various activity had taken place in sharoncollins@eircom.net and, at 4.47 p.m., yahoo searches had been carried out for inheritance rights. At 5.17 p.m., the user had logged in to the lyingeyes98@yahoo.ie email account and, at 5.42 p.m., an email had been sent from sharon collins@eircom.net to lyingeyes98@yahoo.ie.

'Somebody sitting at the computer in the office, knowing Sharon Collins's password—and there was very limited access to the office—sends an email from her email address to 'lyingeyes'. That site had only been set up that day. The person sending the email knew that email had been set up that day and was testing the site,' said Mr O'Connell.

He said that the internet activity had continued and, at 5.44 p.m., the inbox of 'lyingeyes' had been opened and had contained three emails, including one from Sharon Collins and another from killers@hitman.us (this was an email from the T-shirt website, presumably responding to a query).

Six days later, on 8 August 2006, the login page for 'lyingeyes' had been accessed, at 11.23 a.m. There had been no unread messages. At 11.34 a.m., sharoncollins@eircom.net had been accessed. "Lyingeyes', within 10 minutes, is being accessed by someone in the office. Sharon Collins's email address is also being accessed,' said Mr O'Connell.

Later that day, at 1.02 p.m., the user had accessed the inbox of sharoncollins@eircom.net. At 1.05 p.m., the user had signed in to lyingeyes98@yahoo.ie. That evening, at 9.53 p.m., the user had again accessed sharoncollins@eircom.net and five minutes later, at 9.58 p.m., the user had run a search on yahoo, for 'assassins for hire'. About this time, the user had accessed a webpage www.hitmanforhire.net, which explains how to order a hitman for contract.

Mr O'Connell then referred to another date, 16 August 2006.

'That's the day after the money was sent,' said Mr O'Connell. He said that the user of the Advent computer in the office at Westgate Business Park had logged in to lyingeyes98@yahoo.ie, at 12.23 p.m. There were no unread messages. The user had then carried out a search of FedEx courier service. The FedEx website had then been opened and a 12-digit tracking number had been entered. This showed that a shipment had been sent on 15 August 2006 to an address in North Las Vegas and that the estimated delivery date had been 17 August 2006.

'The significance is that the person using 'lyingeyes' knows the tracking number. 'Lyingeyes' is checking the progress of the package. Sharon Collins personally went to FedEx and the next day in the office of Downes and Howard is checking the tracking number of the package sent to the US. The inference is that 'lyingeyes' is Sharon Collins,' said Mr O'Connell.

The courtroom remained silent as Mr O'Connell then referred to the Toshiba laptop computer, which had been stolen from the business premises and had then been given to Robert Howard on the evening of 26 September 2006. Gardaí had analysed the computer and had discovered that it had been used in the early hours of the morning, just hours after the office burglary.

Between 2.22 a.m. and 2.36 a.m. on 26 September, a number of web-based email pages had been accessed —hire_hitman@yahoo.com, tonyluciano2001@yahoo.com, essameid@yahoo.com and tengle2005@yahoo.com.

'That shows the State would invite you to draw the inference that Essam Eid is 'hitmanforhire', Tony Luciano. He had the computer. It was stolen and he had the keys. It's an inference you can draw. It's open to you,' said Mr O'Connell.

Before breaking for lunch, Mr O'Connell told the jury that when Sharon Collins had been in Spain with PJ Howard, she had frequently used computers in internet cafés.

After the courtroom filled again after the lunch break, Mr Justice Murphy could clearly see that there was not enough space for the legal teams, gardaí, members of the public, the accused, the witnesses and the sizeable media presence. He said that the trial would continue in courtroom number 16 for the remainder of the week and he would endeavour to find a more suitable room for the remainder of the case. Courtroom number 2, in the Round Hall of the Four Courts, was acquired and from the following Monday, the trial moved to that more spacious room.

Mr O'Connell continued with his opening speech just before 2.30 p.m. He made reference to a third computer, an Iridium laptop, that had been seized at Ballybeg House on 26 February 2007, when Sharon Collins had been arrested. He pointed out that only a limited number of people would have had access to both the computer at Ballybeg House and the computer at Westgate Business Park. He spoke about emails that had been retrieved from the Iridium laptop. One email, sent on 8 August 2006 from 'lyingeyes', had said, 'Hi, we were just talking. As you can imagine, I'm extremely nervous about sending this message. There are three; two in Ireland and one in Spain.' The email had said that one was aged 27 and the other 23. One was a 'big guy', while the other was 'not so big' and they both worked in the same place. 'I do not want it to look like a hit. I want it to look like an accident,' the email had added. The email had suggested a boating accident as the two do a lot of boating. The 'third' had been described as being 57 years of age and 'not very fit'.

'It's imperative it does not look like a hit. He has got a lot of health problems,' the email had said. It had suggested that the death of the 57-year-old would look like a 'suicide or perhaps natural causes', without causing suspicion. The sender had also enquired about the cost and the amount of deposit required, before asking, 'How would I know you wouldn't disappear with the money and not do the job. Who could I complain to?'

A message from 'hitman' to 'lyingeyes' was sent at 11.12 p.m. on 8 August 2006 and had said, 'Hello, well we discuss about your situation and we assume that these people is your two stepson and your husband. Maybe we are right and maybe we are wrong. We can do two male first and after cool-off we will do the third one.'

It had stated that the cost would be $50,000 per person, but 'cause three bird in one stone' the total would be $90,000, which could be sent via FedEx money order or paid by cash or cheque. The email had added, 'You get your money back if we are failed or we didn't do the job. Tell us more info. about our target. Thanks, Tony Luciano.'

Mr O'Connell said that an email sent from 'lyingeyes' to 'hitman' from the Iridium laptop on 8 August 2006 had said, 'I've been away. At this stage, I realise you probably wouldn't be able to get the job done by 18th August. You are right about my relationship to the men in question. I know it must seem terrible of me, but my back is to the wall and I don't have much choice. I would prefer it if it was just my husband, but because of the way he has arranged his affairs, it would be way too complicated if his sons were still around. The price you quoted seems very fair. My husband is in Spain and lives on the top floor of a tall building while he's there. If he were to hear that his sons had a fatal accident, he might suddenly feel suicidal and just jump off the building. Is that too far fetched, do you think? Is it possible for it to look like an accident and not a hit?' Mr O'Connell told the jury that this email had been signed 'S'.

He then referred to an email that had been sent from 'hitman' to 'lyingeyes' on 11 August 2006, which had been signed 'Tony

Luciano.' It stated, 'We have already reservation at hotel called Greenhills at Ennis Road, Limerick, the 18th of August. We will do it on the 19th. We decided to send two woman and a man to do that job and I will do third one myself in Spain. We will poison the two guys. We will use the two woman to get close to them.'

An email from 'lyingeyes' to 'hitman' was sent on the same date, 11 August 2006, and was also retrieved from the Iridium laptop at Ballybeg House. That email had stated that the 'two guys' usually go to Kilkee at weekends and socialise in the Greyhound Bar. It had asked, 'What do you plan? Putting poison in their drinks? I would be in Spain with my husband when the job would be done. I could get the keys of his apartment to you and arrange a time to be out. I would be a suspect if anything looks suspicious, especially when I'd be the one to inherit. Many people think I'm with him for his money anyway. He's a bit older than me.' The email, signed 'S', had continued that 'lyingeyes' was going to Spain the following Wednesday, adding, 'We will definitely do business. I've no conscience about my husband. He's a real asshole and makes my life hell, but I do feel bad about the others. I realise it is necessary or there is no advantage to getting rid of my husband, other than not having to look at his miserable face again.'

Another email, from 'lyingeyes' to 'hitman', also sent on 11 August 2006, had said, 'I definitely have photos of my husband and I think I have one of the guys. I think I could get €13,000, not money that would be missed. Kind regards, S.'

An email from 'hitman' to 'lyingeyes' sent at 8.55 p.m. that evening had said, 'Here's the deal. You can send $15,000 by Wednesday.' Another $30,000 was to be paid on 18 August and the $45,000 no later than 72 hours after the job was done. 'This is our contract or you will be our target. Sorry to say that, but this is our policy.'

On the same date, 'lyingeyes' had written to 'hitman', from the Iridium laptop, looking for advice. 'Another thing I need advice with is, I used the computer at work to search for a hitman. If the cops seize the computer, could they find evidence of my search?'

'Hitman' replied, 'My plan is we will get close to your two

stepson. After, I will fly to Spain by myself. If you arrange to give me the key I will take him out to his boat and we will do it there. That's why I have to have some money by Wednesday.'

The following day, Saturday, 12 August 2006, 'hitman' had emailed 'lyingeyes' saying, 'That's what I said. We need €15,000 by Wednesday. About your husband, let him jump. I want to do it the same day when he gets the bad news.'

On the same day, 'lyingeyes' had written, 'The apartment is on the top floor of a 14-storey apartment block' and again on 12 August 2006, 'hitman' had written, 'Don't ever use the work computer. You have to delete everything.'

'Lyingeyes' had replied, 'Yeah, I'm worried about that. I was told by a guy in the computer company that services our computers that even if you delete stuff, it can be still accessed. It must look like suicide for him. Or natural causes. This is vital. The body can't disappear. S.'

'Hitman' had replied, 'We are professional people here. Even if they offer us €10 million, we carry out contract. I want to ask you does your husband have a gun. I want you to stay with him until you leave Spain with his body. Don't leave him. It will be suspicious.' In that email, 'hitman' had also asked for 'lyingeyes'' phone number in Spain.

The following day, 13 August 2006, 'lyingeyes' had emailed her mobile number to 'hitman'. Mr O'Connell said that on 15 August 2006, three text messages were sent from the number that 'lyingeyes' had given to 'hitman' to a phone that Essam Eid had admitted to gardaí was his number. Also in that email, 'lyingeyes' had written, 'I've been trying to think of an excuse for removing the computer from the office.'

Also on Sunday, 13 August 2006, 'hitman' had written to 'lyingeyes', 'Let me know when we can talk. Just send FedEx through your company. Don't write any name.'

'Lyingeyes' had replied, 'OK then, I'm 90 per cent decided to go ahead with it.'

Later that day, 'hitman' had mailed a phone number to 'lyingeyes', saying, 'You can call me any time Sharon.'

'Lyingeyes' had replied, 'I'm assuming your people will put that substance in the guys' drink.'

'Hitman' had replied, 'I was in Malaga before and I know how to get there. I am so excited to talk to you on the phone. Tony Luciano.'

The following day, Monday, 14 August 2006, 'hitman' had written to 'lyingeyes' saying, 'If you can't send the money today, forget about it. Now it's up to you. Sorry, the pressure is on me. By the way, you have a nice voice. Sorry to say that.'

'Lyingeyes' had replied, 'I'm at work right now, have to behave as normal and when I'm sent to the bank later, I will sort out the money. Don't worry. I'm going to do it. I've decided.'

Mr O'Connell said that this was a crucial email, showing the decision had been made. 'That's the final decision. It's signed 'Sharon', said Mr O'Connell.

'Hitman' had replied and had supplied an address in Las Vegas, to which the money would be forwarded. 'I will talk to you later sweetie,' the email had said.

'Lyingeyes' replied, saying, 'I've decided to parcel up the money. I will probably put something else in with it to make it look like a present. I'll also put in the photos and the keys.'

On Tuesday, 15 August 2006, 'lyingeyes' had written to 'hitman', saying, 'I'm not sure which photos were which, while I was sending them. You will be able to tell which one is my husband. I'm the devil in the red dress.'

Mr O'Connell told the jury that in that photograph, Sharon Collins was wearing a red dress, sitting on PJ Howard's knee, at a Christmas party in Dromoland Castle, Co. Clare. He said that on 15 August 2006, 'the decision was made and the money was sent by Sharon Collins'.

Journalists scrambled to take notes on Mr O'Connell's powerful, lengthy opening speech, particularly his references to the emails exchanged between 'lyingeyes' and 'hitman'. The level of detail grabbed everybody's attention. While the gardaí sitting in the courtroom were aware of exactly what Mr O'Connell was going to say, those who did not know the inner details of the case were captivated by the content of the emails.

The prosecutor then moved on to the relevant dates in September

2006. He explained how the office of Downes and Howard had been burgled on 25 September 2006. The following evening, Robert Howard had received a visit to his home, on the outskirts of Ennis. This had prompted a garda surveillance operation to be set up on 27 September at the Queen's Hotel in Ennis, where Essam Eid and Teresa Engle had been arrested.

'After the burglary and the demand for cash, Robert Howard spoke to PJ Howard. PJ was on a boat. Sharon Collins was with him. Later that night, Sharon Collins told PJ for the first time about Maria Marconi, who was tutoring her to become a novelist and she said that Maria Marconi had visited Ennis. There was no trace of Maria Marconi. The Prosecution treats this as a lie. She has disappeared off a computer, even though she said she had been in almost daily contact. The Prosecution regards this as a fabulous lie. That day, suddenly Sharon Collins told him about Maria Marconi. She's a phantom, according to the Prosecution,' said Mr O'Connell.

He said that the burglary had been investigated by gardaí and Room 208 at the Two Mile Inn hotel in Limerick had been searched. Among the items that had been found in the room were computer cables, keys, a digital clock, a poster of old Irish money, two wigs, two masks and a pair of gloves. Mr O'Connell said the keys fitted the locks of the Downes and Howard office at Westgate Business Park. 'Later that night, gardaí conducted an identification parade at Ennis Garda Station,' he continued. He said that Essam Eid was picked out, in that parade, as the man who had demanded money from Robert Howard.

He said that Sharon Collins had made a statement to gardaí in October 2006. She had been arrested on 26 February 2007 and the Iridium computer had been seized from Ballybeg House. At that stage, the Advent computer, from the Downes and Howard business premises, was still missing. Then, as a result of intelligence from the FBI, gardaí had gone to the back of the Two Mile Inn hotel in April 2007. A maintenance worker, Christy Tobin, had found the computer in a bag under bushes in 2006 and had put it into a boiler room. Gardaí had conducted an analysis of the hard drive of that computer.

In April 2007, gardaí had obtained a search warrant and had searched a cell at Limerick prison for ricin, also on foot of intelligence from the FBI.

'During the course of the search, a contact lens case was recovered in Essam Eid's cell, which was kept under the bed. It was located and taken for testing by the army. It was found to contain the ricin poison,' said Mr O'Connell. He said that it had then been examined in the UK, and this test had showed the presence of ricin.

Mr O'Connell then referred to garda interviews with Sharon Collins, which he described as 'voluminous'. He said that on 2 October 2006, she had told gardaí a story about Maria Marconi. She had said she had met her at the Downes and Howard office in mid-June 2006 and had taken her on a trip around Clare, taking in Lahinch and Kilkee. She had said she had left Maria Marconi on her own in the reception area of the office. She had allowed her to use the computer at the reception.

'She claims she received emails on 8 August, that she'd pay €20,000 so that an attachment would not be sent to her husband. That was an email she had sent to Maria, saying things about PJ Howard that she didn't want PJ to see,' said Mr O'Connell. Sharon Collins had told gardaí that she had contacted Maria, who had told her that her computer had been stolen. 'She [Sharon] claimed she got phone calls from a private number, but the caller hung up. She thought it was connected. She says she sent money by FedEx. She denies that she knows Essam Eid and states that she no longer has an email address for Marconi,' said Mr O'Connell.

He said that in her first interview after her arrest in February 2007, Sharon Collins had admitted using the Iridium laptop computer at Ballybeg House. She had admitted having keys and the alarm code for the Downes and Howard business premises, but could not identify anyone in Ireland who would know Maria Marconi. He said she had admitted sending money to a Las Vegas address and claimed she had been ringing Maria Marconi after she had sent the money and that the calls had been diverted.

'She denied having anything to do with 'lyingeyes' and agreed that emails from 'hitman' seemed to refer to PJ's family,' said Mr

O'Connell. He said she had also admitted sending letters to the Director of Public Prosecutions.

Sharon Collins had been arrested for the second time, on 25 June 2007. She had accepted that the email account sharoncollins @eircom.net was hers. Questioned about a Mexican proxy marriage, she had said she had got a marriage certificate, but had claimed she had burned it. PJ didn't know about it until June 2007. She had said she had taken steps to change her name by deed poll to Howard. In April 2006, she had had a row with PJ over personal matters and had told Maria Marconi about this in an email. 'The attachment was about this and she was afraid if PJ found out, it would end their relationship and that was why she sent the money,' added Mr O'Connell.

He then moved on to the garda interviews with Essam Eid. Eid said he had agreed to take part in an identification parade at Ennis Garda Station.

'He claimed to know Sharon Collins. He said he used to date her. He last met her in June [2006] on a boat in Malaga. Sharon Collins knew he was coming to Ireland and paid for his ticket using a credit card,' said Mr O'Connell. He said that Essam Eid had denied involvement in the burglary and had denied trying to extort money from Robert Howard. He had admitted travelling to Ireland on 24 September 2006 with Teresa Engle.

'He then changed his tune and denied having certain communication with Sharon Collins. He claims he knew Sharon Collins in different circumstances,' said the prosecutor. He said that a lot of what was said by Sharon Collins and Essam Eid was 'confabulation and lies'.

He went on to tell the jury that the Prosecution had a number of reasons to believe that Sharon Collins is 'lyingeyes'. 'She had access to the computer at Ballybeg House and the computer in the office. The only other people who had access to those computers were PJ, Robert and Niall Howard and they were the targets. 'Lyingeyes' was set up by Sharon Collins,' he said. He pointed out that the context in which the €15,000 was paid was outlined in email traffic and the tracking number was checked.

'On the 16th of August, 'lyingeyes' knew the tracking number and who knew it? Sharon Collins, because she sent the package. Essam Eid was found in possession of photographs of Sharon Collins and PJ Howard. Sharon Collins admits putting them on a computer. She identified herself as "the devil in the red dress", he said.

'Traces of ricin were found in a contact lens case in the cell of Essam Eid. That, in a context where poisoning had been discussed as one of the methods of assassination. The case against Mr Eid, the Prosecution says, is an overwhelming one.' He said these beliefs had been formed on a number of grounds, including that Essam Eid had admitted staying in Room 208, the Two Mile Inn hotel, Limerick; that he had been picked out by Robert and Niall Howard in the identification parade as the man who had demanded money; the discovery of the ricin in his prison cell; and the evidence of Teresa Engle and the soldier who had accessed the 'hitman' website.'

As Mr O'Connell's speech eventually came to a close, he told the jury, 'It has taken rather long to open it, unusually, but because of the complexity of the case, it is essential.'

It was 3.39 p.m. and after Mr Justice Murphy again advised the jury to refrain from reading the newspapers relating to the case, the stuffy courtroom quickly emptied as everybody filed out, in pursuit of fresh air, full of wonderment, after hearing such a bizarre and gripping opening speech.

02 | A BIZARRE TRIAL

FROM the moment Sharon Collins had been charged, there had never been any doubt that this case would capture the public's imagination, not only in her home town of Ennis, but far beyond the county of Clare. And it didn't fail to deliver on the early promises. The anticipated interest prompted the trial to be moved from the wholly unsuitable courtroom number 16 to the more spacious courtroom number 2. This was a necessity, given the large number of people who watched the proceedings daily as each and every one of the 95 witnesses took the stand.

Although much of the first four weeks of the trial were taken up by legal argument, heard in the absence of the jury, once the case ignited, there was no going back and it received wall to wall coverage every day, such was the fascination across the nation.

This chapter will deal with some of the more intriguing evidence produced over the course of the trial. On 1 July, the arrival of Gerry Ryan to give evidence created much excitement in the public gallery, while a friend of Collins's, John Keating, created a stir amongst the Prosecution when he divulged certain information in the witness box. He was called three times during the trial.

Dublin soldier Brian Buckley told how he came into contact with the 'hitman' website, while Collins's two sisters Suzette and Catherine also gave brief evidence during the trial. While PJ Howard's evidence is dealt with in Chapter 12, the testimony of the other two 'targets', his sons Robert and Niall, appears later in this chapter. Tempers frayed from time to time during the sometimes tense trial, not only among the lawyers, but also in the jury box. This chapter also gives in-depth detail of the garda sting which resulted in the arrest of Essam Eid and the eventual chief Prosecution witness Teresa Engle, on a September's evening in Ennis town centre.

On Tuesday, 1 July, RTÉ 2FM broadcaster Gerry Ryan and his producer Siobhán Hough were called by Sharon Collins's legal team to give evidence. The State's case had not closed at this stage, but Tom O'Connell, SC for the Prosecution, did not object to the witnesses being called out of turn, as they were due to leave Dublin airport at 12.45 p.m. that day.

Michael Bowman BL for Sharon Collins, told the jury that Mr Ryan and Ms Hough had made arrangements to travel out of the country, prior to being issued with witness summonses. Mr Ryan's brief appearance—he spent just eight minutes in the witness box—was the single biggest crowd-puller during the evidence over the entire case, as several members of the public called in especially to see the popular presenter giving evidence. Wearing a black pin-striped suit, a light striped shirt and silver striped tie, Mr Ryan confidently walked up to the witness box at 11.11 a.m. He was asked several questions by Mr Bowman and most of his answers were brief. He explained that he hosted a daily radio programme on 2FM, which covered topics of the day, along with personal interest subjects. The programme had a broad listenership and some of the listeners wrote in to the programme. Mr Ryan said that he personally had not come into contact with a letter emailed to his show by Sharon Collins on 4 April 2006, from her email account sharoncollins@eircom.net.

'To the best of my recollection, no such document was received, not to me,' he said. He said that gardaí had never made any inquiries with him in relation to the letter.

He explained that he receives up to 2,000 emails for his show per month and a filtering system was in place whereby some letters are broadcast and others are not. The producer of the *Gerry Ryan Show*, Siobhán Hough, told the court that she had no recollection of receiving Sharon Collins's letter. She spent less than three minutes in the witness box. The trial was told that neither Mr Ryan nor Ms Hough were seeking costs for travelling to the court to give evidence.

Earlier in the trial, on 17 June 2008, the court had heard details of the letter Collins wrote to the *Gerry Ryan Show*, in which she had complained about her partner, saying he regularly used prostitutes and transvestites and had encouraged her to take part in strange sex.

Detective Garda Peter Keenan said the email had been found on the hard drive on the Iridium laptop seized by gardaí at Ballybeg House, the home Collins shared with PJ Howard. On the cover note of the email—from sharoncollins@eircom.net to grs@rte.ie —she had said she found herself living in an unbearable situation with very few real options. She continued that she was writing the letter to the radio programme in the hope that hearing it on air may push her into making the move that frightened her so much. She had written that she was sharing very intimate details of her life and had requested that she would not be identified. In the attached letter, only some of which was retrieved, she had said her partner's black moods and tantrums were unbearable:

Nothing I do is ever enough. His black moods are unbearable. Tantrums can be thrown at any moment and never in my life have I come across anyone who uses the kind of appalling language that he does. He has a holiday home abroad and likes us to spend as much time there as possible. However, the main attraction for him there is the sex industry. He uses prostitutes and transvestites regularly, but what he really wants is for me to engage in what he describes as 'strange sex.' It's never-ending. He will wake me early in the morning or during the night, asking me when I'm going to do 'something'. What he means is, when am I going to pick up a stranger and have sex with him or when will I have a threesome with a male escort and himself. He has even told me that he would love it if I would work as a prostitute and that this would really turn him on. I find the idea beyond repulsive. He has insisted on many occasions that we go to swingers' clubs while abroad and has been unbearable to live with afterwards as I do not want to partake in what goes on there. I've witnessed things that I sincerely wish I never had to see. Don't get me wrong, I'm no prude, but I simply do not see myself this way.

She had written that she was only interested in a monogamous relationship, but that her partner had said this was boring and made her a 'stick-in-the-mud'.

I haven't done any of the things he wants me to, nevertheless, every single time we have sex, I have to describe to him in detail what I would do if I were with another man. This, it seems, is necessary for him to keep an erection. If I don't do this, he will blame me for losing his erection and there would be another black mood to tolerate.

She had also said, however, that it would never come across that he was as she had described, as anyone seeing them together would never think that he was like that.

However, the Prosecution believed that it was 'completely unnecessary' to bring in Gerry Ryan as a witness for Sharon Collins. In summing up the Prosecution case at the end of the trial, Úna Ní Raifeartaigh BL asked, 'Why on earth was Gerry Ryan brought into the court to say he didn't see it [the email Collins wrote to his show]? As a lawyer it serves no purpose. Does it matter whether it made its way to Gerry Ryan or not? What matters is she wrote it. In any event we got the confirmation from the RTÉ [technical] witness, but no, the defence had to pull in Mr Gerry Ryan who said, "I get so many emails but I didn't see this one." That is feeding the ego of Sharon Collins. She likes to be centre of attention. She wants Gerry Ryan in there giving evidence, even though it bears no relevance'.

However, in his closing speech, Mr Bowman said that was an unfair comment. 'Much play has been made and unfairly so about Gerry Ryan coming in to give evidence. There is no issue about Siobhán Hough. It's been painted as an unnecessary stunt. I can't see why it's fair to say it's feeding the ego of Sharon Collins.'

He said the email, composed by Sharon Collins to the Gerry Ryan show, had only been partially retrieved and that the Prosecution had no interest in retrieving the full document. 'They didn't take a statement from Gerry Ryan. They were happy for us to go to that effort and bring in Gerry Ryan,' he said.

The John Keating evidence took a turn that had not been anticipated by the Prosecution. He gave evidence for the Prosecution on 5 June. Mr Keating, a builder with an address at Garryowen Road, Limerick, told the trial that he was contacted by the Howards to change locks at the Downes and Howard office at Westgate Business Park in Ennis, at the end of September 2006. However, under cross-examination by Paul O'Higgins, SC for Collins, he said that he had met Sharon Collins on 16 August of that year. He said they had met at Ballybeg House at around 10.30 that morning. There was a leak in the house and they had discussed building a conservatory in an effort to stop the leak. He said Collins had then driven him to her mother's house, off the Kilrush Road in Ennis, where they had stayed for about 40 minutes. They had discussed building an extension to her mother's house. They had visited Collins's previous house at Maiville on the Kilrush Road. He said that house was rented at the time and Collins had been thinking of building an extension, in the shape of two-self contained apartments and she had wanted Mr Keating to have a look at it. They had also called to Brian Pyne's tile shop near the Downes and Howard office at Westgate Business Park, as she had wanted to look for tiles for a house that Niall Howard was building on the Kilrush Road in Ennis. He said that Collins had also gone into the Downes and Howard office for about five or 10 minutes and they had then returned to Ballybeg House, arriving at around 12.40 p.m. or 12.50 p.m. He said he had returned to his home in Limerick and had arrived at about 1.30 p.m. Mr Keating said he was sure of the date, as he had returned from a trip to the UK two days earlier, on 14 August 2006.

This evidence was significant as on 16 August, it was the Prosecution's case that 'lyingeyes' had sent emails to 'hitman' at a time Mr Keating claimed he had been in Collins's company, driving around Ennis.

Ms Ní Raifeartaigh then brought this to the attention of the court, in the absence of the jury. She said that an issue, relating to an alibi, had been raised, of which the Prosecution had no idea. She said it was the Prosecution's case that three dates were crucial in relation to computer activity; 2, 8 and 16 August 2006. Shortly after 12 noon—when Mr Keating said he had been in Ms Collins's company—the person using 'lyingeyes' had appeared to be using a computer.

'Without notice to the Prosecution, the defence has produced evidence seeking an alibi for Ms Collins,' she said.

She said if it could be proved that Collins was not on the computer that day, it would go a long way towards an acquittal. 'This is clearly an attempt to set up an alibi,' she said. She asked that Mr Keating be stood down and that the matter be investigated by the Prosecution.

Mr Justice Roderick Murphy said the Book of Evidence contained eight lines relating to Mr Keating's evidence. He noted that during cross-examination, Mr Keating was very precise in relation to his dates.

'Clearly this evidence [relating to 16 August] was not contained in the witness statement in the Book of Evidence. An application is being made to the court now to have this witness stood down to allow gardaí to make their investigation, on the basis they should have had notice because it deals with the setting up of an alibi,' said the judge. He said he would accede to the application by the Prosecution that Mr Keating be stood down and the matter be dealt with. He said the Prosecution had the right to re-examine Mr Keating at a later stage.

The issue was later mentioned in court on 30 June, again in the absence of the jury. On that occasion, Tom O'Connell said he wished to recall Mr Keating. He pointed out that Mr Keating had been interviewed by gardaí, after he had given evidence on 5 June.

'The defence can't play tricks and put up an alibi and prevent the Prosecution from cross-examining the alibi,' said Mr O'Connell.

He said there were three different types of ink used in entries written in Mr Keating's diary for the date of 16 August 2006, while there would also be evidence from Stena Line that he hadn't travelled to the UK on the dates that he said he had. Mr Justice Murphy noted that Mr Keating could recall what he had been doing in August 2006 based on his diary and on certain family events. He said he would accede to Mr O'Connell's application to recall Mr Keating to the witness box.

The jury was then recalled and so too was Mr Keating as he sat in the witness box for the second time during the trial. He again told of having spent the morning of 16 August 2006 with Collins driving around Ennis. Mr O'Connell put it to him, 'You refer to her as Sharon. Do you know her?'

Mr Keating replied that he had known her since 1995 and she had introduced him to the Howards, from whom he had got a lot of work. He was then asked to explain to the jury when he was first asked to recollect the events of 16 August 2006.

Mr Keating replied, 'Gary Collins [Sharon Collins's eldest son] contacted me a few weeks before I was last here and asked me if I could recall the events of 16 August. I found my diary in my van.'

He said he had travelled with Stena Line from Rosslare to Fishguard, in his car, on 27 July 2006 and had returned to Ireland on 14 August. However, Mr O'Connell said Stena Line had checked those dates and there had been no record of him travelling. Mr Keating replied that he had phoned Stena Line the previous day and had been told that a new computer system was in place and records for the time in question were not available. Mr Keating then told the court that he had felt intimidated after he had given evidence on 5 June after certain things were said to him by gardaí. He said that after he had left the courtroom that day, Detective Garda Terese Flannery had said to him, 'We'll be getting handcuffs for you here, John.' He said this had shocked him.

'I felt intimidated that day, what was said to me outside that door,' he told the court. He said that having given evidence on 5

June, he had been questioned by gardaí for over three hours and had been scared.

'I didn't know whether I was going to be arrested, after what was said to me. I didn't know. It was scary,' he said. However, Mr O'Connell put it to him that what had been said by Detective Garda Flannery was intended as a joke.

Detective Garda Flannery then took the witness stand and refuted the allegation. She told the court that her role in the trial was to liaise with the witnesses. She said that she had gestured— by putting her hands up—to a number of witnesses, including Mr Keating, that they were being rounded up at lunchtime that day. 'I didn't mention handcuffs. I wanted to bring them across the road,' she told the trial. She said there had been three other witnesses present that day. Asked by Ms Ní Raifeartaigh was there 'some kind of threat arising out of the evidence he gave that day', the garda replied, 'Not at all. I did make that gesture, but I didn't mention John.'

Mr O'Connell put it to Mr Keating that his diary entries for 16 August were written in three different inks. 'You used three different pens,' he said.

The witness replied, 'I've loads of biros, loads of biros at home and in my van.' He said he could use several biros at any one time.

'You made them up, the entries in your diary,' said Mr O'Connell.

'Excuse me, I didn't make them up,' was Mr Keating's response.

The court then heard from Detective Inspector Michael Moore who forensically examined Mr Keating's diary, on 10 June 2008. He said that he had been asked to examine the entry for 16 August 2006 and was asked if more than one ink had been used and if they had been used at the same time.

'The only conclusion I could make was that at least three different types of ink were used for the entries of the 16th of August, 2006,' he told the court.

Caitriona O'Connell, a duty supervisor with Stena Line, then told the court that their records had been searched for John Keating, with a view to establishing if he had travelled with the company on 27 July and 14 August 2006. She said she had found nothing in relation to Mr Keating.

'I searched on the computer database and could find no record of this gentleman,' said Ms O'Connell.

However, this was not the end of the matter as the John Keating issue was again raised on Thursday, 3 July, when he was, for the third time, called to the witness box. He told Mr O'Higgins, sc for Collins, that he had been very confident about the dates in August 2006. He said that after giving evidence earlier that week—on Monday, 30 June—he had travelled to the Stena Line offices at Dublin Port. He said he got there at 5.15 p.m. 'I wanted confirmation that I travelled on those dates,' he said. He said he had been told that dates further back than 12 months could not be searched and that a representative of Stena Line would have to contact a colleague in the UK to look into the matter. He said he had then telephoned the Stena Line office on the Tuesday morning, but nobody was available to speak to him. Later that day, he had telephoned again and was told that the records would be posted to his address from head office in Sweden. He was told by a representative from the company that she could not discuss it over the phone and could not email or fax it to him. Keating said he had not yet received the letter.

Mr O'Higgins then told the court that he had received a letter from the Prosecution relating to this. This letter, addressed to Mr Keating, confirmed that he did, in fact, sail. The letter stated that Mr Keating had earned points on his loyalty card for the outward and return journeys and points are only added if a passenger boards and the boat sails. Mr O'Connell then apologised to Mr Keating.

'Apologies. It shouldn't have happened. It was Stena's fault that I was put in a position to contradict you and I apologise for that. I was misinformed by Stena.'

Later in her closing speech, Ms Ní Raifeartaigh again raised the Keating issue and told the jury the Prosecution did not intend to mislead the court. Mr Justice Murphy also made reference to this element, in summing up the entire evidence. 'You should take into account Mr Keating's very clear evidence and the concession by the Prosecution that he had in fact travelled. It's a matter for you, the diary of the 16th of August,' the judge told the jury.

PJ Howard's two sons Robert and Niall attracted much public attention during the trial, publicity they would not have been accustomed to. Like their father, the two young men are intensely private and live their lives away from the spotlight in their home town of Ennis.

Their evidence centered mainly around the visit by a man called 'Tony' to their home on 26 September 2006, demanding money to cancel a contract on their lives and their father's life. Robert's evidence commenced on the third day of the trial, Friday, 23 May, continued on 26 May and concluded the next day, in between various legal arguments. He took the stand after the first two witnesses in the trial—Garda Mark Walton and Garda Paul Crowley—had given evidence relating to maps and photographs of Co. Clare and of the buildings at the centre of the case.

Robert Howard told the court that he had gone to work on the morning of 26 September 2006. He noticed that the Chubb lock on the door of the company office was not locked, while the alarm for the premises was not on. He had noticed that his own Toshiba laptop was missing, along with an Advent desktop computer. Also taken was a poster of old Irish money, a digital clock and computer cables. His father and Sharon Collins were in Spain at the time. That evening, he had been at his home at Ballaghboy, Doora, on the outskirts of Ennis, when he had received a call on his mobile phone, at around 10.30 p.m. A male voice said, 'I heard you lost a few computers.'

Robert said he had agreed with this and the caller had told him he would be at his house in a few minutes. Five minutes later, Robert had heard a knock on his front door and he had answered the door. He said the caller had said, 'Hello. I'm Tony.'

He said 'Tony' had picked up a blue Toshiba laptop computer from the ground and had handed it to him. Robert had gone back into the house and had told his brother Niall—who had been keeping watch—to ring the gardaí. He had then gone back outside and the bombshell had been dropped.

'He said there was a contract on the three of our lives for €130,000. He said he didn't want to do it. He wanted me to buy the contract out, for €100,000.' Robert said 'Tony' had had paperwork, including directions to his house and to PJ's house and had also had two photographs, the latter of which Robert had taken from him and would not give back. The photographs were printouts from a computer. One was a photograph of PJ and Sharon Collins, while the other was a photograph of PJ on his boat in Spain.

Robert said he had returned to the house to see if the gardaí were on their way and when he had returned outside, 'Tony' was leaving in a car. He said he had tried to phone him and had then got into his jeep and had tried to follow 'Tony's' car, but he had lost him at the crossroads a short distance away. He described him as having been 5' 11" in height, in his mid-40s, clean-shaven with sallow skin, and wearing spectacles, a baseball cap and a tracksuit. He said he had thought the man had had an Algerian accent, even though he had told him he was Italian and they had spoken for about 20 minutes.

Less than two hours later, at 12.30 a.m., he had again received a call from 'Tony' who had been interested to hear if Robert had started getting the money together for him. 'I said I had, yes. He said he'd give me a ring tomorrow,' Robert said.

True to his word, 'Tony' had phoned Robert a number of times the following day. During one telephone call, at 12.15 p.m., he had asked Robert what time he would finish work that day and again had asked him if he had started getting the money together. 'Tony' had suggested a meeting at the bus station in Ennis, but Robert had opted for the Queen's Hotel, in the heart of Ennis town.

During this time, Robert had remained in contact with the gardaí and he had headed to the Queen's Hotel for his 5.15 p.m. meeting. While there, he had received another phone call from 'Tony', at 5.40 p.m., telling him to go to the bathroom where he would meet a lady and she would count the money. Although reluctant to do this at first, Robert had phoned Detective Garda Jarlath Fahy, who had advised him to go and meet the woman. Robert did this and described the woman as having been in her late 40s or early 50s. He had seen her walking past him in the bar a few minutes earlier. She had dark hair and wore a leather jacket.

'She said, "Have you got the envelope?" I said, "Have you got the computer?" At that stage, a garda in plain clothes walked past the lobby and she took off,' recalled Robert Howard in court. He had received no more calls from 'Tony' after that.

He said that he had felt 'very frightened' and had taken steps to protect himself. He had put in a call to Ennis Security Services, but the events had happened so quickly, that he didn't go ahead with it. The director of that company, Kevin Cooper, later told the trial that Robert had phoned him, in a nervous state, claiming that he had been threatened and asking him to provide security. This was the evening of 26 September 2006. They were to meet the following day at the Howard's family business at Westgate Business Park.

'He said, "I just want someone to be around me and mind me. Someone made a threat." He said that the offices had been broken into. He seemed very nervous,' said Mr Cooper. However, Mr Howard had not followed up and had never contacted him again.

Robert Howard was asked if he had set up the email account lyingeyes98@yahoo.ie and he replied, 'No, I did not.' Asked did he know anybody called B. Lyons—the name in which the 'lyingeyes' email account had been set up—he said that his father's previous partner's name was Bernie Lyons. She had died in 1998. He said his only email address was robert@downesandhoward.com.

Asked if his father had ever married Sharon Collins, Robert replied, 'I know I was given a letter from PJ, stating that no marriage took place when they were in Italy.' This was in 2005 and after the couple had returned from Italy, a 'wedding reception' had taken place in Spanish Point. Asked if he and Niall socialised with Sharon Collins, he replied, 'Yes.'

He told the trial that he had been informed by Detective Garda Fahy on 26 February 2007 that Sharon Collins had been arrested at Ballybeg House that morning. He said he spoke to his father. 'He told me they [the gardaí] had his permission to search his house and take anything they wanted from it,' he said.

While Robert spent almost two hours in the witness box over the three days, his brother Niall's evidence was much shorter and lasted just 35 minutes. He explained how he had kept watch inside the house when 'Tony' had called on 26 September 2006.

Soft-spoken and as equally well groomed as his brother, Niall Howard explained that he and Robert had tried to follow 'Tony' on the Quin Road of Ennis—in Robert's jeep—but said that they had lost sight of him and had gone back home. Robert had then rung PJ, who had been in Spain and had told him what had happened.

'We were very shocked by it all,' he said. He too was asked if he had set up the email account lyingeyes98@yahoo.ie and, similarly, he replied, 'No, I did not.'

Under cross-examination by Collins's barrister Paul O'Higgins, SC, Niall Howard said he had known Sharon Collins since 1998 and agreed that she had looked after PJ when he was ill.

'She was in most respects the position of someone who appeared married to him?' asked Mr O'Higgins, to which Niall Howard replied, 'Yes.' He said he had enjoyed a close relationship with Sharon Collins and that she had offered him support when his mother had died.

The evidence from Dublin soldier Brian Buckley (23) was also interesting. He told the trial on 13 June that he played computer games for his own entertainment and that he had been looking for cheat codes for a game called 'Hitman' when he had come upon the website www.hitmanforhire.net, which advertised contract killings. He said he had thought it was a joke and said the homepage of the site had featured a cartoon animation of a man with a gun, wearing a hat, sunglasses and holding a pistol, which he had thought was a cartoon drawing.

He said that out of curiosity, he had filled out an application form on the website, but under a false name, Will Buckimer. This was on 29 July 2006.

Less than two weeks later, on 10 August, he had received an email from 'Tony Luciano' to his email address judas69@gmail.com. That email had said, 'I have a job for you if you are interested. Two males in Ireland. One in Spain. asap. Let us know. We will try and call you.'

Mr Buckley told the court that he had received another email from 'Tony Luciano' on 28 August. It had said, 'Please help us out for this. I need some strong poison. One of us will be in Shannon. We cannot shift this stuff for security reasons—you know that—so please help us out. Will pay and I will owe you favourite. Thanks brother. Tony.'

He said this email had made him feel uneasy and he had received several phone calls from a man who had called himself 'Tony Luciano', but he had told him that he had the wrong number.

In her closing speech, Ms Ní Raifeartaigh said Mr Buckley believed that the website was a joke. 'He thought it was a joke. He gets emails and phone calls saying, "We have intended targets, one in Spain and two in the west of Ireland." That's Mr Eid seeing if he can get a local outsourcing of his hit. It's absurd. We are dealing with fools here, but they are dangerous fools.'

Seven defence witnesses were called on behalf of Collins, while Eid did not call any. Two of Collins's witnesses were her two sisters Suzette Liddy and Catherine Donegan. Both of them gave their names in Irish and spoke briefly in court. Between them, they spent less than 10 minutes giving evidence. Neither made eye contact or had any communication with Collins as they walked past her to and from the witness stand on 1 July. Suzette introduced herself as Máire Uí Liduihigh.

She explained how she was married to Seán and had lived in Galway since 1994 or 1995. Asked by Paul O'Higgins if she had stayed with Collins in Ennis in August 2006, she replied, 'No, absolutely not.'

She explained that she was older than the accused. She said Sharon had gone to school in Ennis and had left when she was 18 or 19, having passed her Leaving Certificate.

She said that Sharon had got married at the age of 19 and had had two sons. Asked when the marriage had come to an end, she replied, 'I'm not sure.'

She said her mother's maiden name was Cronin and her father, Charles Coote, was deceased.

'My parents were separated for a long number of years. I'd have been an adult when they separated. I think she would have been an adult as well, possibly a teenager,' she said.

Catherine, who introduced herself as Cáit Uí Donnachán spent two minutes in the witness box, during which she said she was married to Conail.

Asked if she had gone to stay with Sharon in Clare in 2006, she replied, 'No, I did not … I wasn't there in July or August 2006. I'm certain about that.'

Later, Ms Ní Raifeartaigh, in her cross-examination of Sharon Collins put it to the accused that her two sisters had been 'trying to put distance between you, by using Irish names'.

Collins replied, 'I would say they are very embarrassed by the whole affair.'

The seventh day of the trial, Tuesday, 3 June 2008, heard about the extensive garda surveillance operation that had been put in place at the Queen's Hotel on 27 September 2006, when Robert Howard was to meet somebody in connection with the visit to his home the previous evening. The operation had been meticulously planned and had involved eight gardaí, who had been positioned in a 360 degree angle around the premises, while two gardaí had been seated inside the hotel. Five of the gardaí have described their various roles in the operation.

Detective Garda Jarlath Fahy explained that he had been investigating the burglary at the Downes and Howard premises on the night of 25 September 2006. He had also been made aware of the visit by a man calling himself 'Tony' to Robert Howard's home the following night. Detective Garda Fahy had stayed in touch with Robert Howard throughout the day on 27 September and had told the court that as a result of those communications, a surveillance operation had been set up at the Queen's Hotel, which is located just yards from Ennis Garda Station. At around 5.45 p.m., he and Detective Sergeant Michael Moloney had stood in the friary car park, which is across a narrow street to the side of the Queen's Hotel.

'I observed a man acting suspiciously. He seemed to fit the description to what had been outlined to me,' said Dt Gda Fahy.

The man was wearing a beige anorak and jeans and wore glasses. Around this time, he had also seen a woman leaving the Queen's Hotel, who he now knows to be Teresa Engle. She had walked up the nearby Abbey Street and the garda said he had then seen her and Essam Eid walking up Abbey Arcade. At 6.10 p.m., Dt Gda Fahy had arrested Essam Eid on suspicion of handling stolen property. 'I believed him to be the man called 'Tony', he said.

Detective Sergeant Michael Moloney had organised the surveillance operation that evening. While he and Detective Garda Fahy had been located in the friary car park, he said 'the other members of the team were in a 360 degree circle.' He said he had seen a man fitting the description provided to gardaí by Robert Howard. Detective Garda Kieran Kelleher said he and another garda, Albert Hardiman, had taken up position in the Abbey Street car park. They were in view of the hotel. Following communications with his colleagues, Dt Gda Kelleher then walked the short distance towards an area known as 'The Height' at the very centre of Ennis town.

'I was informed that a person was identified in the friary car park. He walked up Abbey Street to 'The Height' and appeared to make a phone call from one of the phone boxes there. He then walked up Abbey Street. He took up position at Knox's Lane. I stayed watching him. After a few minutes, he moved from the Lane to the Abbey Street car park.'

He said he had stopped the man at King's bar, directly across from the Queen's Hotel and Dt Gda Fahy had approached and had arrested him.

'He said his name was Essam Eid. He said he was on holidays in Ireland and that he was staying in the Two Mile Inn hotel outside Limerick. He was just very casual and said very little. He also said that he had a car rented but he didn't know the location of the car. He just said it was over the bridge. I located the car at Harmony Row on the right hand side,' he said.

Garda Beatrice Ryan had also been involved in the operation. She, along with Garda Michelle Holian, had taken up duty in the Queen's Hotel, where they sat at the bar. Shortly after they had arrived, Robert Howard had entered the hotel and had sat close to them.

'I noticed him getting a number of phone calls on his mobile.

After one particular call, he appeared to become particularly nervous,' recalled Garda Ryan. She had then seen a woman arriving. This woman had had long fuzzy dark hair, had worn jeans, a leather jacket and black gloves and was in her 40s. Garda Ryan said she now knew this woman to be Teresa Engle. Garda Ryan had received a phone call from Detective Garda Fahy, informing her that this was the person that Robert Howard had to meet.

'A short time after I received the phone call, Robert Howard got up and made his way towards the bathroom. The lady appeared to follow afterwards,' she said.

Garda Ryan had left it about 10 to 15 seconds and had then followed them out. They had both been standing in the hallway outside the toilets. She had heard Robert Howard say something about a computer but she said she had not wanted to draw attention to herself and had gone into the ladies toilets. She said she had waited for a while and the woman had then gone out on to the street. She had informed Dt Gda Fahy of the situation and had followed the woman onto the street. She had seen her speaking to a man at a laneway, who she now knew to be Essam Eid. She said Teresa Engle had walked to the right and Essam Eid to the left, towards 'The Height'. She had followed Eid up Abbey Street and had seen him going into a telephone box where he had appeared to make a phone call.

Garda Michelle Holian told the trial that she had seen Robert Howard in the bar of the Queen's Hotel. She had known him as a businessman in the town. She said that some 10 or 15 minutes after she and Garda Beatrice Ryan had arrived in the bar, she had seen a woman arriving. 'The reason I noticed her was because she walked around a number of times,' she recalled.

She said that after Robert Howard left to go to the bathroom area, he had returned to the bar and had sat down again. She said throughout his time in the bar, he had received a number of phone calls, one which had prompted him to be anxious.

'He appeared quite agitated. I knew from his facial expression he was quite agitated,' she said.

Later that evening, an identification parade had been set up at

Ennis Garda Station, which had included nine men. Sergeant Noel McMahon gave evidence to the trial of his involvement in conducting this. He said that Essam Eid had agreed to take part in the parade and had taken up position 9. He had brought Robert Howard into the room and Robert had picked out Essam Eid as the man who had called to his house the previous night. Eid had moved to position 5 for the next identification parade. Niall Howard was then brought into the room and he also picked Eid out of the parade.

However, Michael Collins BL for Eid put it to Sergeant McMahon that his client was aged 50 at the time and only one of the volunteers who had taken part in the identification parade had been in his 50s. Mr Collins said that one of the men was in his 40s, four were in their 30s and two were in their 20s. Sergeant McMahon accepted this.

'These were the volunteers that were assembled. There was no objection to them,' he said.

Mr Collins said that Eid had been the only person in the identification parade to have a moustache. 'Mr Eid would have stuck out like a sore toe. There was no-one remotely like him.'

However, Sergeant McMahon replied, 'I don't believe he stuck out. These were the people who were made available to me. There was no objection. I had to work with them. I conducted the parade as it should be conducted.'

The trial also heard from the gardaí who had been involved in a search of Eid's room, Number 208, in the Two Mile Inn hotel, Limerick on the same date. Detective Garda Kieran Kelleher said there had been two large suitcases in the room and a plastic bag, which had contained cable leads for a computer and two keys. Detective Garda Jack Duffy said he had taken possession of several items from the room and these were all presented to the court. They included a white tracksuit top, a blue baseball cap (with the words 'us Open 2000' written on it), three computer cables, a digital clock, a poster of old Irish currency, two keys, two wigs (a black and a blond), a pair of black leather gloves, a black balaclava and a transparent plastic Halloween mask. He said the keys found in the hotel room had 'fitted the lock Robert Howard brought to Ennis Garda Station' on 28 September. 'I believe it was from Robert Howard's business premises at Unit 7A, Westgate Business Park, Ennis,' he said.

In his closing speech to the trial, David Sutton, sc for Eid, said the case had been an enormous one, 'with more witnesses, more rows than I've seen in any other case. I'm sorry if that's what you have had to put up with.'

And while the jury had looked tired on several occasions— given the intense and technical nature of some of the evidence—they addressed their role with due diligence, typified by the amount of time they spent deciding on the verdicts. Except for one occasion, when a juror lashed out at the bench in front of him, the eight men and four women showed great patience throughout the case, which lasted for several weeks longer than had been initially anticipated.

As the case entered its sixth week on Monday, 23 June, tensions were raised, one juror slammed the palm of his hand off the bench in front of him when he could not hear a speaker. Three jurors sitting alongside the agitated juror in the front row muttered to each other, before the forewoman indicated to the judge that the jury could not hear prosecutor Tom O'Connell. The frustration had finally taken its toll in the jury box, but the matter was quickly rectified as Mr O'Connell, who, at the time was reading details of emails exchanged between 'lyingeyes' and 'hitman', immediately turned around to face the jury, for the remainder of that particular phase of the trial.

03 | 'A TISSUE OF LIES'

Given the spectacular reference to the lethal poison ricin in the opening speech, the evidence from Essam Eid's wife Teresa Engle was always going to be dramatic, compelling and of enormous significance. And the star prosecution witness didn't fail to deliver as she coolly told the court that she and her husband had made ricin at their home in Las Vegas and had then brought it over to Ireland.

Ohio native Teresa Engle, one of Eid's two wives, gave evidence over a two-and-a-half hour period on the thirteenth day of the trial, Thursday, 12 June 2008. The jury was told that morning that Ms Engle had been granted immunity from prosecution in the case, on the basis that she would give evidence in the trial and that this decision was unconditional and irrevocable.

At 11.40 a.m., Teresa Engle stepped into the witness box, where she was to remain for most of the day. She was questioned and cross-examined at length, always answering in a monotone. The line of questioning became intense on occasions and she was accused of being a fraudster and a liar, but this did not perturb the American, who remained cool at all times and was categorical in her sometimes bizarre assertions.

During cross-examination by David Sutton SC, representing Essam Eid, she regularly asked him to repeat his questions, saying 'I'm sorry?' on several occasions and claimed he was speaking too quickly.

Wearing black trousers and grey jumper, and with her long, black, bushy hair neatly pinned at the top, she steadied herself in the witness box, before speaking quietly into the microphone in front of her. The entire courtroom waited in anticipation for her words to flow.

Senior counsel for the Prosecution, Tom O'Connell began questioning Ms Engle by asking her if she had spoken to lawyers before she had travelled from the USA to give evidence.

She replied, 'Yes, I did.'

She explained that she had known Eid since 2003 or 2004, having previously been married to a man called Todd Engle three times. She had met Eid at a casino in Detroit, Michigan, when she had been living in Michigan. She had been separated at the time. They had had a relationship together and she had moved to live with him in Las Vegas in June 2006. She said they had got married in Las Vegas and said Essam Eid had previously married another woman, Lisa Eid. The three of them lived together at 6108 Camden Cove Street, Las Vegas, Nevada.

She was then asked if she had ever visited Ireland previously. She said she had, at the end of August or beginning of September 2006. 'I was here to meet Ash [Ashraf Gharbeiah, a friend of Essam]. He was supposed to kill PJ and Robert ... no, Robert and Neil [Niall], the two sons. Essam had a website, www.hitmanforhire.net. He got email from Sharon to do a contract to kill PJ and his two sons, Howard, no, Robert and Neil [Niall]. They corresponded. She sent him a down payment of like €15,000. That would have been in August 2006.'

While these allegations had been made in Tom O'Connell's opening speech to the jury, it was the first time that they had been heard from a key civilian witness, who had been close to one of the defendants.

Mr O'Connell asked her if she had seen any of the emails and she said she had. Asked if Eid had used any other name, she said, 'Yes. Tony Luciano. That was the name used with the website.'

She was then asked about telephone calls and said, 'Sharon had called him several times and he had called her back several times.'

Mr O'Connell asked if she had heard the woman speak on the phone.

She replied, 'I heard her voice. It was a very strong Irish accent. She spoke very fast. He kept telling her to slow down so he could understand her accent.'

Asked what the woman's email address had been, she said, 'The email address was 'lyingeyes.''

She was asked about a package sent to her home in Las Vegas in August 2006 and said, 'There was some kind of goggles for a virtual reality game.'

She said she was at work when the 'deposit' arrived and Eid's other wife Lisa signed for it. 'The money had arrived. The next stage was Essam getting hold of Ash and going through with it, getting it done.'

Mr O'Connell asked her how this was going to happen and was told, 'Ash was supposed to be poisoning the two sons.'

She said she had travelled alone to Ireland at the end of August 2006 and 'Ash' had travelled either the following day or two days later. She had stayed at the Queen's Hotel in Ennis. 'When Ash arrived, I had previously the day before walked around to the business park to see where it was. Me and Ash walked there.' She also explained that she was referring to the Howards' family business, Downes and Howard Ltd.

She said she had known how to find it 'from directions from Sharon' and that 'Ash' had wanted to see exactly where it was.

'He had his own plan. He had several medications that was supposed to cause a heart attack or for somebody to die,' she said, and added that these medications could have been put into liquor.

'He'd been to a grocery store and looked at the liquors there. We walked to the business park and he decided the plan was not do-able. I think he left the next day. I was still booked in Ireland for a few more days and then I went to Spain. I was there for a day or two,' she said.

Sharon Collins, sitting in the dock, looked increasingly uncomfortable as she listened to Teresa Engle's evidence. As she did on several occasions during the trial, Collins wrote furiously on yellow post-its as the witness told her story, and then passed them over to her legal team. But her concerns mounted as the unstoppable Engle continued.

Engle was asked why she had gone to Spain and said, 'I was picking up a key to the apartment in Spain. I was to look around and find info. for Essam, the location, go see the boat.' Asked what apartment she was referring to, she replied, 'Mr Howard's apartment in Spain.'

Mr O'Connell asked her, 'What keys?' She replied, 'The keys to that apartment. They were left for me at the hotel. They were left in an envelope with my name on it.'

She said she also had directions to the apartment on an email from Sharon. Asked what boat she was referring to, she said, 'The Howards' boat,' but said she did not find it.

Teresa Engle said that at the time, she had been in communication with Eid and had been telling him everything. 'There was an internet café Essam wanted to know about. Sharon had told him she'd be at that café to email him,' she said.

Asked why she went to the café, she replied, 'Just to see there was a café there, to verify that. Essam wanted to be sure there was a café there.'

She said she had checked out the area around the apartment and sat at a restaurant down from it, 'just to look and see if I'd see PJ or Sharon. At that point I was starting to get sick. I just couldn't bring myself to go in either.' She said she had become sick, had gone back to her room and had then returned to Ireland for a day or two. Mr O'Connell asked her if there had been a plan relating to PJ Howard at that stage.

She said, 'Not specifically at that point, no, not that I know of.' She said she returned home to the US and was asked what Eid's reaction was.

'He was furious because the plan hadn't been done. He started working on a visa to come to Ireland to do it himself.' She said he had gotten a visa and they had both travelled to Ireland about a month later, at the end of September 2006.

At this stage, the momentum of the evidence, which had been compelling, increased considerably, as she was asked about the poison ricin. To say that the courtroom descended into a stunned silence when the ricin was mentioned would be to put it mildly. Mr O'Connell prompted the reference to the ricin when he asked her, 'Did ye bring anything with ye [to Ireland]?'

She replied, 'Ricin. We made it, Essam and I.'

She said she wasn't sure exactly when they had manufactured it, but was certain about some of the ingredients used. 'He'd got a recipe from the internet, with castor beans, acetone and something else. I can't remember,' she said, clearly.

Asked where they had bought the castor beans, she said, 'I don't know.'

Mr O'Connell asked her, 'Were you involved in the manufacture of ricin?' She replied, 'Yes. I think we oiled the beans, took the skins off, blended it with acetone and something else, put it through a filter, dried it out to become a powder and put it in a contact lens case.'

She said they had dressed in masks and gloves while they were making it and there had been none left over when it had been put into the contact lens case.

Asked again, 'Who manufactured it with you?'

She replied, 'Essam.'

As the jury listened carefully to the dramatic revelations coming from the key witness, the Prosecution then moved on to the 'hitmanforhire' website. Mr O'Connell asked the witness if anybody else had contacted the website, during this time.

She replied, 'Yes. There was another woman. There were several people who contacted it to look for work.'

She was asked if anybody had contacted it from Ireland and said, 'Yes.' But she could not remember when that was. She said that Eid told Sharon that he would need money up front. 'Essam told her the people he had sent before didn't finish the job obviously and he'd be coming himself to finish the job and that he had spent a lot of money on the other people.'

She said that the details of an American Express account had been contained in an email and the name on the card had been PJ Howard. She said that Eid and herself had travelled from Las Vegas to Shannon airport and had hired a car in September 2006. They had stayed together in the Two Mile Inn hotel in Limerick.

She was asked by Mr O'Connell if they had contacted Sharon Collins while they were in Ireland.

She replied, 'Essam was trying to phone her and email her. We went by the business [Downes and Howard Ltd] to look at it so Essam could see everything about it. We had instructions from Sharon that he had to get the hard drive of the computer in the office.'

Sharon had said the keys to the office were under a brick behind a house in Ennis. They had collected the keys and had gone into the office 'to pick up the computer'.

'There was an alarm but we did have the code from Sharon to turn off the alarm.'

Asked if they had taken anything from the office, she said, 'Yes, I got the main computer hard drive and Essam got the laptop and a bunch of cords. We took it back to the room at the Two Mile Inn.'

She said they had brought masks with them from the US, which she referred to as 'Halloween masks', but said that they had not used them. Asked why they had brought them, she said, 'To disguise our faces when we went into the office.' She said they 'took the stuff back behind the Inn [hotel], a wooded area, to hide it.'

She said that Eid had been trying to contact Sharon but this had proved impossible. 'I know he was trying to reach her but I don't think he was able to,' she said.

Mr O'Connell asked her what Eid's reaction had been to this and was told, 'He was quite furious. Then he decided instead to go to Robert and sell him the contract.'

She said he had contacted Robert by telephone. 'He had all the info, where he lived, directions to his house and his phone number, from Sharon,' she said. She said he was offering €100,000 to cancel the contract.

Asked how much the contract had been for, she said, 'I believe it was €100,000 or €125,000. I'm not sure exactly.' She said that Eid had contacted Robert and he had then driven to meet him at his house. She had gone with him and they had brought a laptop, instructions from Sharon and some family photographs. This was late evening, around 10 p.m. or 11 p.m.

She said she had remained in the car, while Eid had got out and gone to the front door of the house. She had seen Robert coming to the door, and had noticed another man inside the side window of the house. Eid had spent up to 30 minutes at the house, she said. He had told Robert there was a contract on the three lives 'and he was offering him the opportunity of buying that contract. He gave him back his laptop. He had shown him details of emails relating to the contracts. Apparently Robert had snatched a couple of pictures away from him and taken them. The following day, he phoned Robert to arrange to meet to get the money from him.'

She said that Robert had agreed to meet Eid at around 4.30 p.m. or 5 p.m. that evening at the Queen's Hotel in Ennis, to give him the money.

'I went to the Queen's Hotel. I was the one who was going to pick up the money from him, near the restrooms,' she said.

Engle told the trial that both she and Eid had arrived at the Queen's Hotel. He had stayed across the street in a little bar. She had met a man who she had thought was Robert Howard. 'I wasn't 100 per cent sure it was him so I said his name 'Robert'. He said, "Yes." I asked him did he have something for me. He said he wasn't going to be giving anything until he got the computer back. I said I didn't know anything about that. He said he wouldn't give any money until he got the computer back.' She said she had then left the hotel and had walked around Ennis before returning to their hired car. Eid wasn't there and she had been about to write him a note, but she had then been arrested.

Mr O'Connell then asked her again about the contact lens case the couple had brought from the US to Ireland.

'That was in Essam's bag, that had his medicines. He had several prescription medication,' she said.

Asked about the keys to the apartment in Spain, she said that after she had been arrested, she had been brought to the courthouse in Ennis. She had wrapped the keys in tissue and put them into the garbage in the women's toilets at the courthouse.

Mr O'Connell then made reference to another incident in the US, where Teresa Engle had been charged with extortion. She said she had pleaded guilty, that there was no plea bargain, and that she was awaiting sentence. (In July 2008, Teresa Engle was jailed for eight months for attempted extortion, at a court in Los

Angeles. She had admitted telling Anne Lauryn Royston that she would be killed unless she paid $20,000 to Eid to call off a hit allegedly ordered by an ex-girlfriend of Royston's partner, in September 2006.)

She was asked where the emails had been received and said it was at their home, Camden Cove Street, Las Vegas.

Teresa Engle's examination by the Prosecution concluded just before lunchtime and the defence team began its tough cross-examinations in the afternoon. First up was Paul O'Higgins sc for Sharon Collins. He made reference to the incident in the US and put it to the witness, 'You told Mr O'Connell that there hadn't been a plea bargain in the case in the US. Can I suggest to you there was a plea bargain and the plea of guilty came in the context of an elaborate bargain?'

He accused her of being a 'fraudster, facing serious charges and trying to cut a deal with the people prosecuting', which she denied.

'To injure a person so that you could extort money from them is not fraudulent?' asked Mr O'Higgins.

She replied, 'I was under Essam's direction.'

Counsel replied, 'Your suggestion that it was done under any direction is self-serving. You were a willing participant in the fraud to which you pleaded guilty.'

She denied this.

He also put it to her that she was 'at the mercy of the FBI' in relation to her evidence before the court, but she also disputed this. 'I agreed to give evidence here without the immunity and against the advice of my own attorney.'

Mr O'Higgins replied, 'Didn't you know well your plea bargain in the US on 23 April 2007 would leave you in a better position in the US?'

She also denied this.

He asked her why her sentencing hearing had been adjourned in the US and she replied, 'So I could spend more time with my family.'

Counsel then said, 'Can I suggest to you it was adjourned because you hadn't given evidence in this case?'

She also denied this.

He put it to her, 'Provided the US Attorney's Office feels you told the truth that no matter what the court feels, it may seek to have your sentence shorter and probably not a jail sentence at all. Aren't you at the mercy of the US authorities as to what evidence you give here?'

She also denied this.

Mr O'Higgins then asked her what else she had agreed to do in the past. 'Have you agreed, for example, to act in an undercover capacity for the US Attorney's office and to tap phones and that kind of thing, if required to do so?'

She replied, 'Yes, I did that.'

He put it to her that she did that out of desperation, because of the serious crime she had committed in the US.

Engle replied, 'I did that because it was the right thing to do, to expose the truth.'

Referring to the other incident in the US, Mr O'Higgins said to the witness, 'Can I suggest to you, you were a participant fully in the scheme in the US, a scheme to extort, a scheme like the circumstances of this case, in some respects? Didn't you go to a lady called Royston with Mr Eid and tell her she'd be killed if ye didn't get money?'

The witness replied, 'Mr Eid's direction, yes.'

He asked her when the Royston affair had happened and she told the court it was in September 2006. Mr O'Higgins quickly commented, 'Right in the middle of the time when you are talking about 'lyingeyes'.'

He then referred to his client, Sharon Collins, who sat alongside her two sons in the courtroom, continuing to write note after note. 'You have referred repeatedly to Sharon as though you somehow knew Sharon Collins, the defendant in this case. Have you ever met Sharon Collins at all?' he asked.

Ms Engle replied, 'No, I have not, at all.'

Counsel then put it to her that she had claimed she had received keys to PJ Howard's apartment in Spain. Engle explained that Sharon had given instructions to Eid, via email, in relation to obtaining the keys.

Mr O'Higgins then questioned her on her earlier evidence,

claiming she had felt sick in Spain and had decided against going into the apartment. 'Before lunch, you said you didn't go into the apartment because you were feeling sick and you couldn't bring yourself to go to the apartment. Can I suggest the reason you didn't was because there was no circumstances of knowing if they were in and in fact there was someone there all the time? No-one has ever seen the keys to the apartment?'

Quietly, she replied, 'They took the keys out of my bag at the station in Ennis, but I told them they were my house keys.'

Mr O'Higgins then suggested that Engle was giving evidence merely hoping to improve her own position. 'All you are doing, far from telling the truth, is seeking to advance your position in the proceedings in the US,' he said.

She quickly replied, 'That's absolutely not true.'

Engle said she had first heard of the name Sharon during the emails in August 2006 and insisted that she had been completely under the influence of Eid. However, counsel took issue with this. 'You are someone who was not under his influence, but a particular with him as a pretty nasty piece of work in what he was doing. You moved into the house as his wife, even though his wife lived there. You were busy in your criminal schemes then and your evidence is your attempts to get out of them. If you satisfy the US Attorney's office, you hope not to go to jail in the US,' said Mr O'Higgins. He accused her of telling lies to the gardaí in Ennis, when questioned initially.

She responded, 'I denied that we had broken in or that I had anything to do with it. I did deny it. What I'm saying now is I agreed to give the truth against my attorney's advice.'

Mr O'Higgins concluded his cross-examination by suggesting to her that her evidence in this trial would have a major effect on her sentence in the US and that she was telling 'a lie'. She continued to deny this.

As Mr O'Higgins sat down after cross-examining the seemingly unflappable Teresa Engle, Eid's barrister David Sutton SC rose to his feet and, for the next 53 minutes, probed the witness. He quickly put it to her that in her initial interviews with gardaí, she told 'a string of lies'.

She accepted that she had denied everything. Mr Sutton stated, 'You tell lies or you say nothing, because you are a criminal and a fraudster. Do you agree with me?'

She replied, 'No, I do not.'

Counsel put it to her, 'You scammed your way out of it by either telling lies or saying nothing and you successfully got off scot-free.'

Her simple response was, 'I'm not lying.'

He put it to her that through a plea bargain in the us, she would get 'little or no jail. That's what's going on here, Ms Engle. Star witness for the Prosecution.'

She refuted this, saying, 'That's not true. I gave my statement and agreed to testify here without immunity and against the advice of my attorney who told me not to speak here.'

However, counsel disagreed, expressing his view that prior to travelling to Ireland to give evidence, she had had her 'paperwork' well in order.

She again disputed this. 'That's not true. I did give my statement and agreed to testify here without the letter of immunity, back in October.'

Mr Sutton then put it to her, 'If you hadn't got arrested in America, you wouldn't be in that witness box. You'd be in Ohio or Las Vegas or wherever. Is that correct?'

She replied, 'No.'

At that stage, the trial had been running for less than an hour after the lunch break, but Engle wanted a break. She quietly made it known to the trial judge, Mr Justice Roderick Murphy, that she wanted to go to the toilet. He allowed her to take a break and the jury remained in their seats in the jury box as she briefly left the courtroom. As the court waited for Engle to arrive back in the witness box, a tearful Sharon Collins sat gazing at the jury, who sat in a stunned silence across the room from her.

After a two-and-a-half minute toilet break, Teresa Engle returned to the courtroom and waited for Mr Sutton to continue firing questions at her. He moved on to focus on her voice, asking her if she would describe herself as a softly spoken person. She said she believed she spoke with an 'average' tone. Mr Sutton quickly pointed out that FBI agents who had spoken to her had described her voice as 'deep rasping, smoker's' and asked her was she putting on a voice for the jury.

'This is my voice,' was her short response.

He then put it to her that she had married Todd Engle three times and then had married Eid. He asked if this type of thing was common in Las Vegas.

'It's quite bizarre,' she accepted.

Mr Sutton then approached the subject of the ricin, asking her how they had made it. She repeated what she had said earlier—they had boiled the castor beans, peeled the skins off and dried it off. She said they wore masks and gloves—similar to rubber gloves—and he then asked her if she had worn a biological warfare suit.

She replied, 'No.'

Mr Sutton yielded smiles from the neutrals in the courtroom when he asked, 'You didn't test it out, on a passing mouse or a porcupine or anything like that?'

Her response was negative and he then asked her on what website the recipe had been acquired. She didn't know.

Mr Sutton then moved on to the internet activity and asked the witness if she had access to the computer at their home and had she used it. She said she did, and that Lisa Eid also used the computer.

She said she also had access to the 'hitmanforhire' website and was asked, 'You are saying Essam was operating that site and you were operating that site?'

She replied, 'I had access to that site.'

Mr Sutton said the front page of www.hitmanforhire.net showed an image of a man with what looked like a Thompson machine gun, used by the late Al Capone. He said the site stated, 'How to order a hitman … Follow these instructions exactly … Pay a deposit … then further instructions … Pay more … '

'Only a fool of the highest order would think this was serious,' he said.

Engle replied, 'I agree. That's why I was so amazed when she sent the money.'

'You had a mug. You had someone who was stupid enough to log on to the website and someone who was stupid enough to send on the money. You must have been delighted?' said Mr Sutton.

She replied, 'I couldn't believe it.'

He put it to her that she had pleaded guilty to a 'shakedown' in Los Angeles, which had happened in similar circumstances in which she got 'some other eejit'.

'You are involved in shaking down, stealing and robbing ... not killing,' said Mr Sutton.

She replied, 'No, that's what it was supposed to be.'

Mr Sutton asked, 'This piece of nonsense was a plot to kill?'

She replied, 'That's what it was.'

Like Mr O'Higgins, Mr Sutton accused her of trying to better her position in the us. 'You are trying to do yourself a favour in America, where you have pleaded guilty to another shakedown. You are dressing this up as a plot to kill for your own convenience and your own advantage,' he said.

However, she remained insistent, telling him, 'No, that was what it was.'

He said there were vulnerable people searching the internet and she had caught one, but she denied that this was the case. 'It was for doing a killing, not a shakedown,' said Engle.

He put it to her that that was 'another lie', but she refuted this. He asked her had she intended to shake down anybody and she said that she had not. But Mr Sutton continued to quiz her on this, suggesting, 'The intention all along was to get money and that was it in the same way it always was in this operation. Every time you do one of these jobs is for money, not to kill people.'

She insisted, 'It is to kill people.'

Mr Sutton quickly replied, 'You are not very good at your job. You've been caught every time, caught in California and pleaded guilty. You were caught here and scammed your way out.'

She said that was not the case, that she did not have to testify in the trial.

He put it to her that she did not have ricin, but she insisted, 'We did have ricin.'

He then asked her how they had been going to use the ricin.

She said she was not sure. She said that 'Ash' had a variety of medications that he was using, but he didn't have ricin.

Mr Sutton then asked her if there had been a plan to put something into a drink. 'Was it to follow the Howards around town and hope they get thirsty and want a drink? You never intended to do any of this. There was no plan, Ms Engle. You are an incompetent criminal, yes or no?'

She coolly replied, 'I was merely participating to the extent that I was controlled by Essam.'

At 3.42 p.m., just over a half hour after she had had a toilet break, Teresa Engle asked if the door of the courtroom could be opened and this was done. She then made it known to Mr Justice Murphy that she wanted to take a walk. However, she agreed to continue when the judge told her that the court would endeavour to finish for the day at 4 p.m.

Mr Sutton resumed his questioning of the witness and asked her if she would agree or disagree that when there was an attempt being made to kill someone that it wasn't a very good idea to go up and tell the person, or meet the person in a centrally located hotel.

She said, 'I'm not sure what he's asking me exactly … I was just doing what Essam told me.'

He asked her what the plan was if the Howards had said 'No' to the demand for money at that stage and she said she didn't know.

Mr Sutton concluded his cross-examination, by putting it to her, 'Mr Eid was not involved in the plot to kill.'

She replied, 'That's ridiculous.'

With that, counsel got the last word in. 'Ridiculous is the word, because everything you have said to the jury and the trial is ridiculous.'

Teresa Engle stepped down from the witness box and flew back to the US. But her crucial evidence was not forgotten and occupied much time during the closing speeches, both for the Prosecution and Defence. According to the Prosecution, her evidence was credible, while she was heavily criticised by both Defence legal teams, in closing their cases at the end of the trial.

On the 28th day of the trial, Thursday, 3 July 2008, Úna Ní Raifeartaigh BL for the Prosecution, made her closing speech in the case. She gave the jury an accomplice warning in relation to Engle. 'If everything she says was true, that makes her an accomplice. You must treat that evidence with particular care and caution. If you accept her evidence beyond reasonable doubt, you are entitled to act on it.'

She said that Teresa Engle had described going into the Howards' office to get a computer and had keys and the alarm code. She reminded the jury how Engle had said one of the computers had been placed in a wooded area behind the Two Mile Inn hotel. 'There was corroboration of that. Mr Tobin took the computer from behind the bushes.'

She said that Engle's evidence in relation to Eid's reaction when he couldn't reach Sharon Collins was important. 'She said he was quite furious. Then he decided to go to Robert and sell the contract. That's the turning point when things started to go wrong for her [Sharon Collins]. If she had answered, these two boys'—pointing to Robert and Niall Howard—'wouldn't be here right now and this would be a murder trial, not a conspiracy to murder trial, but thankfully Mr Eid had a short fuse,' she said.

On the same day, Michael Bowman BL for Sharon Collins made his closing speech. Mr Bowman said that Engle was an interesting woman who 'took the oath and proceeded to tell lie after lie after lie'.

He said she had no regard for the truth and was self-interested, self-serving and a 'convicted fraudster' who had claimed she was a slave to Essam Eid. 'The only person with a criminal conviction that sat in that box was Teresa Engle,' he said.

He said she had claimed that she had seen an email related to an American Express card, but, in fact, no such email had been retrieved.

'She's a bare-faced liar … She departed with a little fanfare,' he said.

On the 29th day of the trial, Friday, 4 July 2008, Mr Sutton, in his closing speech on behalf of Eid, spent a considerable period of time criticising Teresa Engle. He pointed out that she had been questioned by experienced detectives and, in the end, had gone home on a plane. 'Her only purpose for coming back was to give evidence against Mr Eid and Ms Collins. Only for that we would never have seen this woman again,' said Mr Sutton. He said that she again came to the attention of the law, this time in the US, but 'instead of blagging her way out of it or scamming her way out of it, she is caught again, using the same website. Another woman was shaken down for money. Who was at it again but Ms Engle? That was the reason why we were graced with her presence.'

He said she had presented a 'tissue of lies' to the court and was one of the most 'self-serving and conniving pieces of perjury I've heard in an Irish court. A liar and conniver, here to serve her own interests when she was caught like a rat in a trap. She sat here giving evidence like the stone face of a liar. That is what the State was relying on to tie together their case.'

He said that Engle had claimed the intention was murder, but she hadn't a notion about how that was going to happen. 'Was she going to follow the Howard brothers around Kilkee with a bottle in the hope that they would get thirsty? It's at that ridiculous level,' he said.

04 | THE DEADLY POISON RICIN

The discovery of a trace of ricin in a cell in Limerick prison in April 2007 led to widespread media coverage. However, for legal reasons, the man who was suspected to have brought it there was never identified publicly. At that stage, the investigation into alleged conspiracy to murder was in full swing and the last thing that gardaí involved in the case wanted was any public revelations that could potentially hamper their inquiry.

One of the main talking points in the aftermath of prosecutor Tom O'Connell's opening speech in the trial was his reference to the deadly poison ricin. This was the first time it had been raised in the public domain in relation to Essam Eid and its mention in open court led to it being widely reported in the media. The jury was now aware that there was going to be a ricin element to the case and this evidence was greatly anticipated.

However, a dramatic turn of events during the fourth week of the trial left not only the ricin evidence appearing doubtful, but it also left the trial hanging in the balance.

After hearing submissions from the defence, the trial judge, Mr Justice Roderick Murphy ruled on 10 June that the ricin evidence would not be admissible and would not therefore be put before the jury. As a result of this, the jury would have to be discharged, as it had heard about the ricin in the opening speech.

However, Mr O'Connell sought the opportunity to address this. Eventually, after hearing from several witnesses in relation to the ricin, the judge dramatically changed his mind two days later and allowed the ricin evidence to go before the jury.

The dramatic saga began to emerge on the tenth day of the trial, Monday morning, 9 June, when senior counsel for Sharon Collins, Paul O'Higgins rose to his feet in the absence of the jury. He spoke about the examination of the ricin that had been carried out by the Irish army. He said it was clearly not considered to be an adequate examination, as the contact lens case had been sent to the UK for the purpose of further examination. He said he had not got any additional evidence from the State on the test carried out in the UK until May of this year. He said he had been informed that the testing process in the UK had involved the irrigation of the contact lens holder. Therefore, he said, it was unlikely that there were any remaining traces if the Defence wanted to test it. He said this was one of the significant pieces of evidence to be relied on by the State.

'Teresa Engle alleges she was present when ricin was made by Mr Eid in the US. The sample was destroyed and I was given no notice of the fact that this was going to happen,' said Mr O'Higgins.

David Sutton, SC for Essam Eid, said he fully supported Mr O'Higgins' submission. 'The correspondence is more or less the same between us and the State.'

The following morning, the trial judge Mr Justice Murphy addressed the issue and stated that the defence should have been in a position to examine the ricin. In the absence of the jury, the court then heard from retired Commandant Joseph Butler, who was a technical officer in the army ordnance corps at the time.

He said that he had received information to the effect that there was a requirement to carry out a test for ricin in Limerick prison on 25 April 2007. Comdt Butler and Comdt Peter Daly had travelled from Sarsfield Barracks—the army barracks in Limerick—to Limerick prison, where they had met Superintendent John Scanlan and other gardaí, along with prison staff. They had RAMP (Rapid Analyte Measurement Platform) testing equipment, which can be used to test a number of toxins, including ricin, and had proceeded to carry out the tests. He said that the first test had not been successful, because the cartridge had needed to be inserted into the machine within seconds of adding the liquid to the well and there had been too much delay. Four tests had been carried out. The first had been negative, the second swab had been positive for ricin and the third and fourth had both been negative.

He said that they had gone to the prison after lock-up, at around 8.30 p.m. or 9 p.m., equipped with protective gear. He said that Comdt Daly had found a box under the bunk in the cell, which had contained a contact lens case. The case had been opened and it was found to be empty. It had been put into a plastic bag, before being tested. He told the court that the instrument used in the UK would be different to the RAMP test used in Ireland.

Under cross-examination, Comdt Butler said he was 'quite happy' with the results of the tests. He said the major toxins feared from terrorist activity were anthrax, ricin and botulin.

Comdt Daly then took the stand and spoke about his involvement in the search of the prison cell in Limerick. He was responsible for ensuring the safety of everybody involved in the search and this had included dressing in appropriate protective equipment, in case anything became explosive. He said the RAMP test could be used for detecting quite a number of materials and in military use; it is used in the field. He said he had attended a conference at Sarsfield Barracks in Limerick on the evening in question and had then gone to Limerick prison, to Block C. He said that Essam Eid and an Irish national were in the cell. The search had been carried out. The contact lens case had been found in a cardboard box, along with a bottle of clear liquid and items for diabetic treatment. He said he had suggested that the prison cell should remain as it was, that it not be re-occupied. The team then moved back to Sarsfield Barracks. 'My concern was to do with the safety of the people involved. As a result of our test, I had reason to assume there might be ricin in the cell …

Ricin is quite an unusual compound, a highly toxic plant extract. It's an extremely dangerous compound to handle and deal with,' he told the court. 'I advised Superintendent Scanlan a further sample should be taken from a credited lab,' said Comdt Daly.

Mr Justice Murphy went back through the evidence of both Comdt Butler and Comdt Daly and noted they had agreed that the test results carried out in Limerick were preliminary. He said it appeared that the swabs tested in the UK were not now 'testable' because the contents had been irrigated. The judge said it was decided that further tests should be carried out.

At that time, Eid was in custody. 'It's not clear whether he was in custody on the matter before the court or another matter. He was entitled to have physical evidence maintained until the trial,' said the judge. He said the evidence was that there may have been a trace available and it seemed to him that there was an obligation on the Prosecution to have made known to Eid that there had been a preliminary positive result in relation to the presence of ricin. 'It does seem the court should rule it is not permissible to have that matter adduced in evidence,' ruled the judge.

That ruling left the courtroom in shock. The respective legal teams all left the courtroom and grouped together in the Round Hall to discuss the effects this ruling would have on the case, while gardaí involved in the investigation were flabbergasted. If the ricin evidence could not be introduced, then the jury would have to be discharged, as it had been told about it in the opening speech of the trial. Sharon Collins spoke to her legal team outside the courtroom, before confidently strolling back to her seat moments later. She spoke to her solicitor Eugene O'Kelly and smiled and laughed as she chatted to her two sons. Was this going to be her last day sitting in the dock? The judge's ruling was crucial and she knew it.

After a break of 19 minutes, the court re-sat at 3.09 p.m. and Tom O'Connell rose to his feet. The jury was still in the jury room, unaware of what was happening in the body of the court. 'The defence has an application to have this jury discharged. I am asking the court for a transcript. I want the matter adjourned until tomorrow, so that I can look at this,' said Mr O'Connell. He said the judge's ruling had not been anticipated by the Prosecution and it had 'serious implications' for the Prosecution case. He said he wanted to make enquiries specifically to see if any tests could be carried out on any remaining evidence.

'I should have an opportunity to present all the evidence,' he said.

However, Mr O'Higgins said he had been told that material was not available for analysis and that had been repeated in the court. He said that when Mr O'Connell had dramatically opened the case, there had been no concession in relation to the admissibility of evidence and the ricin issue had been referred to three times. 'He was determined to open the issue of ricin [in the opening speech] … I would, in due course, be applying for a discharge. The evidence has been ruled out. Whether it be today or tomorrow, I've no alternative but to apply for a discharge.'

Mr Sutton then stood up and said he would also be applying for a discharge of the jury. He said that Mr O'Connell had spoken about ricin in the opening speech 'and on he went'. He said the Prosecution was now looking for a favour from the court.

Mr O'Connell then said that three sources would speak of the ricin, during the trial—Teresa Engle, the army personnel from Sarsfield Barracks in Limerick and the witnesses from the UK laboratory where it was tested.

'It's my submission that the court should give me an opportunity to see definitively if evidence can be got from the UK lab. If there's material there that can still be examined, I'll make certain applications,' said Mr O'Connell.

Mr Justice Murphy said he would accede to the application to adjourn until the following morning and the application would be deferred until then. At 3.32 p.m. the jury was called out and the judge told them that legal submissions were likely to continue throughout the following day, Wednesday, 11 June. 'I'm sorry your patience has been tried,' said the judge and sent the jury away until 12 June.

On Wednesday, Mr O'Connell applied to the court for permission to call further evidence. He sought to call Superintendent John Scanlan and three witnesses from the UK laboratory to give evidence. 'Superintendent Scanlan will deal with the circumstances of which the material was sent away and the reasons for it and why it was a necessity,' he said.

However, Mr O'Higgins said the court had ruled on the issue and it would be unfair if matters were now asked to be ruled in. Mark Nicholas, BL for Eid,˘ objected to Mr O'Connell's application and asked the judge not to accede to the request.

Mr O'Connell replied, 'There were extraordinary and exceptional circumstances in this case. I want to be given the opportunity to be heard on this matter.'

Mr Justice Murphy noted that Mr O'Connell was seeking to call evidence from Superintendent Scanlan and said, 'The court does not want to exclude evidence wanted to be called by any party.' He said the court should also allow evidence from the three scientists from the UK.

After lunch, Superintendent Scanlan took the stand and told the court that he had been the senior officer in charge of the investigation on 25 April 2007. He had been made aware that the FBI had received confidential information to the effect that the ricin had been transported from the US to Ireland in a contact lens case. That morning, he had been involved in a meeting with gardaí involved in the case at Ennis Garda Station. A warrant had been obtained to search a cell at Limerick prison and the services of the army explosive ordnance disposal (EOD) team—led by Comdt Daly—had been sought. He said at that stage, his own knowledge of ricin had been limited. 'I had no knowledge of ricin poison. I became aware of it, that this was a serious biological poison,' he said.

He said there were 300 prisoners and staff at Limerick prison and the possibility of evacuating the entire prison was discussed, as there were not only safety, but also public health issues. Eventually, it was decided to carry out a search of Eid's cell and this was to be done after lock-down time that evening. 'Because of the toxic nature of this poison, we decided it would be necessary to be suited up,' he said. Those who went to the prison wore biological suits. The search had been carried out after 9 p.m. and Supt Scanlan remained at Sarsfield Barracks. Between 11 p.m.

and 12 midnight, Comdt Daly had contacted him and had informed him that tests had been carried out for the presence of ricin.

'Comdt Daly said it would be necessary for further tests, but he was satisfied his tests would stand up,' he said.

'It was coming close to midnight. It was decided we would seal down the cell and further examinations would take place the following day, to ensure he hadn't retained any of it in his cell and to sanitise the environment. I enquired where I could get further testing done. I had a serious lack of knowledge myself,' he said.

The following day, military personnel had been dispatched to the prison, to further sanitise the cell. More tests of items in the cell had been carried out, but no positive results had been yielded. Superintendent Scanlan said he spent the day of 26 April trying to source a laboratory in the UK. The services of the Home Office laboratories in the UK had been obtained and Supt Scanlan, along with Sergeant John Brennan of Ennis Garda Station, travelled to the UK with the contact lens case on Friday, 27 April 2007.

'It was necessary for me to get further confirmation that this was ricin. The immediate concern was to confirm that this was ricin and to get an understanding for me to make whatever decisions were necessary. Microgrammes of this substance are lethal, if ingested in any way,' he said.

He said he went on a 'voyage of discovery for information', with a view to getting to the 'ultimate position of knowledge'. 'I did what I did in good faith and for the purposes of protecting human life in this State,' said Supt Scanlan. He said when he and Sgt Brennan had arrived in the UK, the scientists had carried out the tests throughout the night. The following morning, he had become aware that a test had proved positive. 'Nothing could be seen with the naked eye. I had no knowledge that this testing couldn't be replicated by somebody else,' he said. He pointed out that there was no facility in Ireland that could carry out the biological tests undertaken in the UK.

Under cross-examination by Mr O'Higgins, Supt Scanlan said the reason the search of the cell had been carried out after lock-up was because the team did not want to send people to the prison in biological suits, before lock-up.

Mr O'Higgins asked the witness if he had been aware of the need to preserve evidence. 'An extra swab could have been taken and preserved in Ireland,' he said.

Supt Scanlan replied, 'Considering the nature of the substance I was dealing with, I had concerns about keeping any of it here in Ireland.'

Counsel put it to him that no steps had been taken to ensure that the evidence sent to the UK would be preserved. The witness replied, 'It was my understanding from that laboratory that they provide services to the English courts and what was necessary would be done properly. I think the steps taken in this instance were the only steps open to me.' Asked if he had taken steps to ensure or enquire that some of what was being tested would be retained, he replied, 'I didn't make any specific enquiry in that regard.'

Mr O'Higgins asked Supt Scanlan why he had not requested that a second swab should be taken by the army on the night it carried out the test in Limerick. He replied that that in essence was a field test and the next appropriate test would be carried out in a laboratory.

The court then heard from Joanna Peet, from the Laboratory of the Government Chemist (LGC) in Middlesex in the UK, which had carried out work for the UK Home Office. She said she had received some preliminary information that an exhibit had been seized in a prison and that it had been tested for ricin. She said her firm received a package and a contact lens holder was inside the final bag of the package. She took custody of the package on the evening of 27 April 2007.

Asked what ricin was, she said it was a lethal toxin, derived from castor beans. She said it could be toxic if ingested, inhaled or injected. When she received the package, it was screened and x-rayed.

Stephen Kippen, who was the manager of LGC also told the court that ricin was a chemical compound produced by castor beans. Asked if it was toxic, he replied, 'Extremely toxic, one of the most toxic compounds known to man.' Asked if it could kill, Mr Kippen replied, 'Oh, [it] can kill a man stone dead.' Asked to explain what he did with the package containing the contact lens case, he said he had taken it from Ms Peet and it was then placed in a safety cabinet. It was unpacked and irrigated. He said the tests had been carried out at 1.40 a.m. on 28 April 2007 and the results had become available at 8.40 a.m. Michael Bowman, BL for Collins, asked Mr Kippen under cross-examination if he would be surprised to hear that it was thirteen-and-a-half months later before the results were disclosed to the defence.

He replied, 'It is not for me to be surprised. I give evidence as matter-of-fact'.

The court then heard from Emma Stubberfield, a microbiologist, who, along with a colleague had tested the samples at a laboratory in Surrey. They had worked in conjunction with LGC. She said she had received the samples at 1.40 a.m. on 28 April 2007 and had started the tests at 2.20 a.m. The first test, on the control sample, had produced a negative result in that there was no ricin present. The second test had showed a very weak reaction and this had indicated the 'possible' presence of ricin, while the third sample had shown a 'strong positive' reaction, which indicated that ricin was present. She said she immediately faxed the result to Ms Peet at LGC.

After Supt Scanlan and the three scientists had given evidence to the court, Mr O'Connell addressed Mr Justice Murphy. He said there had been exceptional circumstances involved. 'A highly toxic chemical was found,' he said. He pointed out that Supt Scanlan had had concerns and had acted on this. If the gardaí hadn't acted and some disaster had occurred in Limerick prison, it would have led to a major public outcry, he said.

'Whatever the situation in relation to Mr Eid, she [Collins] wasn't charged [when the search and subsequent tests were carried out]. In such circumstances, the Prosecution couldn't be said to be under any obligation to inform her that such tests were being carried out. The ruling does not and cannot apply to Ms Collins. In relation to Mr Eid, there are exceptional and extraordinary circumstances,' he said.

However, Mr O'Higgins said the Prosecution case had taken several steps backwards by the evidence presented that day. 'There was no safety crisis at the prison at the time the specimen was sent off for analysis. Of course ricin is a dangerous substance. There is no question about that, but it's plain there was no ongoing crisis,' he said. He said that his client, Collins, had been charged in June 2007, but had not been told until the following May that there had been a positive test for ricin. He said she should have been told this earlier.

Mr Nicholas, for Eid, said that while Mr O'Connell had said there had been extraordinary circumstances, his client had the right to a fair trial. 'There are no grounds on which your Lordship should re-open your ruling made yesterday,' said Mr Nicholas. It was approaching 5 p.m. and Mr Justice Murphy said he would deal with the matter the following morning, Thursday, 12 June.

The decision made by the judge that Thursday morning was going to be crucial, in terms of whether or not the trial would proceed and a tension-filled courtroom heard him make his judgment. He spent more than 20 minutes addressing the issue, during which he ruled that the ricin evidence would be admitted, after all. Mr Justice Murphy recalled that the court, the previous day, had allowed the Prosecution to present further evidence in relation to the ricin issue.

'The court accordingly has considered the evidence of Superintendent Scanlan and the concerns he had from the 25th to the 27th of April 2007, when he received confidential information regarding the possibility of ricin being found in a contact lens case in Limerick prison. It is clear that Supt Scanlan was not familiar, as indeed most people would not have been familiar, with the nature and toxicity of the poison. His evidence was clear that he was concerned about the safety of the staff at the prison,' said the judge. 'Following the search of the cell, he attempted to find a laboratory that would corroborate the preliminary tests. His priority was the safety of all involved and the cell was indeed sanitised. Mr Eid and the other prisoner were allowed to go into the cell.'

He said the evidence from the three scientific witnesses from the UK had been significant in terms of their understanding of the testing that had been done. The evidence given by Comdt Butler, he said, had also been important, as he had described the RAMP test, which had detected ricin. He noted that in the UK, three samples had been tested. The control sample was negative, the second sample showed a very weak reaction, while the third sample showed a strong positive reaction, which had indicated the presence of ricin. 'It does seem to me in the circumstances, the Prosecution, or rather the gardaí, acted quickly, urgently and expeditiously with the evidence that was got and did the tests that were available to them. It does seem to me it was clearly not a right any defendant has to be present when an original sample was taken,' said the judge.

'The court also finds there was no deliberate attempt to deprive the individuals of the possibility to investigate or indeed to deal with the laboratory in England. The court is of the view that the jury is entitled to hear the evidence and possible conflicts that exist. It does seem then that the matter should be dealt with in that the jury should be allowed to hear the evidence. It seems to me that given the evidence I heard, this is a matter that will go to the jury,' said the judge.

The jury was then recalled and the evidence in the case proceeded. While the army and UK witnesses did give evidence over the following days, Superintendent Scanlan was not called to give evidence before the jury on this matter.

Later in the trial, the statement given to gardaí by Dave Heffernan, who had occupied the cell with Essam Eid on the night it was searched, was read to the court by Úna Ní Raifeartaigh BL for the Prosecution.

Mr Heffernan had been sent to Limerick prison as a result of non-payment of fines. In the short statement, he had said that on 25 April 2007, he and Eid had been removed from the cell and the cell had been searched. They had been brought back to the cell the following day. He said that he knew of ricin through the media and from coverage of 9/11 but that he did not know much about it. He said there were two beds in the cell and he had slept on the top one. He stayed in the prison until 27 April, when he was released.

Given that the ricin element was a key part of the case, the trial heard several references to it. On Friday, 13 June, US Special Agent Ingrid Sotelo took the stand. She said she suspected that Essam Eid was involved in the production of ricin, after she visited his home in Las Vegas in October 2006. Agent Sotelo was investigating an alleged extortion in the US and as part of her investigation, she had visited the home that Eid had shared with Engle and his other wife Lisa Eid. She told the trial that she had seen a drum of acetone on a shelf in the garage of the house. She also saw a blender and a coffee carafe, both of which contained white residue. She told the trial that she believed the residue may have been ricin and based this view on interviews she had conducted with Engle. Asked, under cross-examination, why she had not removed those items from the garage, she said that she was based in Los Angeles and did not have jurisdiction in Nevada. She said she had brought this to the attention of the local FBI bureau. She agreed that one of the sources of her knowledge was Teresa Engle and said that Lisa Eid had told her the items weren't hers.

One of the other occasions in which the ricin got considerable mention was during Mr Sutton's closing speech and this was no surprise, given that it was his client, Eid, who had been at the centre of the ricin element. He said the evidence relating to the ricin had been dramatic. He spoke about the specialist clothing worn by those who had carried out the search of the cell in Limerick prison. In contrast, Agent Sotelo didn't wear a 'warfare' suit when she went to Eid's home in Las Vegas, he said, in a country like the US which had become increasingly security conscious, post 9/11. He said that she hadn't removed the blender from the house, adding 'for all we know it may still be there'.

'There is no evidence of any amount of ricin that could kill anybody and if there was, I'm sure we'd hear all about that. There is no such evidence before you and the State repeating it does not make evidence,' he said.

05 | THE TWO SIDES TO SHARON COLLINS

Given Sharon Collins's demeanour throughout the trial, it was no surprise that she decided to take the stand and give evidence. From the very outset, she had strolled confidently around the Four Courts with the outward appearance of a woman who hadn't a care in the world. Her body language said it all. Sharon Collins appeared coolness personified as she chatted daily to her two sons Gary and David and her legal team. In the face of her seemingly calm attitude, curious onlookers in the Round Hall of the Four Courts building expressed huge surprise to learn that this was the woman who allegedly was 'lyingeyes'. Apart from a rare moment, when she shed tears in front of the jury, this woman appeared self-assured and fearless.

And so her moment did arrive. It was 2.50 p.m. on the 26th day of the trial, Tuesday, 1 July 2008 when Sharon Collins's petite figure arrived in the witness box. Clutching a bottle of still water in one hand and a tissue in the other, she perched herself on the chair, sat back and crossed her legs. On instruction, she fixed the microphone in front of her by confidently tapping it and smiled at the jury, asking, 'Can you hear me now?'

That was the first of many smiles that were to come throughout that afternoon, as she beamed at the jury. Oozing confidence and charm, she appeared very comfortable.

Over the two days, she spent 189 minutes in the witness box. Her examination by her own counsel Paul O'Higgins sc was straightforward, but the sparks began to fly when Úna Ní Raifeartaigh, bl for the Prosecution, began an arduous cross-examination.

Collins explained to Mr O'Higgins that she had been interviewed by gardaí on a number of occasions and had set out her position, in great detail, in letters to the Director of Public Prosecutions (DPP). He asked her if she remembered the date, 16 August 2006. She said she did.

She explained that she had contacted John Keating previously about doing work on her mother's house and about building an extension for herself. 'He came to my house on 16 August,' she said.

She said she had been packing her bag for her trip to Spain when he arrived at her house at around 10.30 a.m. They had had tea together and they had then taken the short car journey into Ennis. She said that PJ Howard's son Niall had been building a house on the Kilrush road and, in Ennis, she and John had gone to a tile shop to look at tiles for this house. They had also visited her mother's house. She had explained that her mother was elderly and had lived in a terraced house and was keen to build on a bathroom. She said it was difficult to say what time they had reached her mother's house, stressing, 'I couldn't tie myself. I know he had to be in Limerick at 1.30 p.m. or 1.45 p.m. I'm not sure if he wanted to get away so I wouldn't have him doing too many jobs.'

The smiles continued as Collins explained how she and John Keating had looked at houses similar to her mother's and he had expressed the view that she would not get planning permission for an extension. As she continued to explain her movements that morning, she said they had then visited the Downes and Howard office at Westgate Business Park, Kilrush Road. The office is located about a mile from her mother's home.

'As far as I know, I went in there to pick up PJ's medicine. I rang my mother to tell her that I'd pick her up for lunch and to be ready at the door as I'd be there in 15 minutes,' she said.

Collins said they had returned to Ballybeg House—the home she shared with PJ Howard—and Mr Keating had left straightaway. This was around 12.50 p.m. or 12.55 p.m. 'Home at the time was Ballybeg House,' she explained. She later picked up her mother and they went for lunch in the Old Ground hotel in Ennis town.

Mr O'Higgins then moved to the letters Collins had written to the DPP in 2007. 'These accounts represent the truth in relation to what happened?' he asked.

She replied, 'The truth.'

Asked if she solicited anyone to kill, she said, 'Absolutely not' and shook her head. When asked if she conspired with anyone, she said, 'No I didn't.'

After Mr O'Higgins' nine-and-a-half minute examination of his client had concluded, Ms Ní Raifeartaigh rose to her feet, to begin her grilling. She immediately put to Collins that she had a detailed recollection of events on 16 August 2006.

Collins explained that she had been to Lough Derg on 9 August. She said she had spoken to her mother, who had remembered Mr Keating calling to her house on 16 August. However, Ms Ní Raifeartaigh said, 'It is fabrication from start to finish that you can remember what you were doing in August 2006.'

Collins just smiled and said, 'I can remember.'

She was then asked about the €15,000 she had sent to an address in America. 'I accept I sent €15,000 to an address I was given. I didn't know anything about Essam Eid. I think if I was paying somebody to kill somebody, it would be very obvious to me it would be traceable. I had no idea the guards were investigating anything like this. The guards were investigating a break-in to the office. The information I gave to the guards was related to a blackmail,' she added.

Ms Ní Raifeartaigh then questioned her about her association with Maria Marconi. She put it to her that she only told PJ

Howard about Marconi after the office had been burgled and there had been an extortion attempt. 'You realised the plan had gone wrong and you told him [PJ Howard] about Maria Marconi.'

Collins calmly replied, 'I was trying to see basically if I could write. I wanted to feel my way first. I didn't want to tell PJ [until she could see how she was getting on with the writing]. Several people keep things to themselves. Some people do, some people don't.'

It was put to her that the reason she had told gardaí about sending the €15,000 to a Las Vegas address was because it was 'essential'.

Looking to the body of the court, Collins replied, 'I see Mick Moloney [Detective Sergeant Michael Moloney was one of the chief investigators in the case] down there. I asked him was there any chance of getting the money back.'

Ms Ní Raifeartaigh quickly pointed out that Collins was on first name terms with gardaí, referring to them as Mick, Jarlath and Jack.

Collins was equally swift in her response. 'They sat in my kitchen with me for three to four hours. I'd say, why not?'

She was then probed about telephone calls. It was put to her that there had been traffic between her number and Essam Eid's phone. 'I have traffic with a woman. You are saying it was Essam Eid,' she said. Asked about her interviews with gardaí in relation to the phone calls, Collins had a point to make. 'There were a lot of phone calls mentioned. Thirty-two conversations were put to me when it might have been six conversations, you know, a few minutes each. I attempted to return a call to a blackmailer,' she said.

She was asked if she had been blackmailed by a man and replied, 'I think at the time I couldn't be sure if it was one man or two men … I don't know who was ringing me. It was very hard to know where the call was coming from.'

She said she had never phoned Essam Eid. Ms Ní Raifeartaigh asked, 'You never spoke directly to him after the package had been sent?'

She replied, 'No.'

Collins accepted that some of the language used in the emails was similar to her language, adding, 'but I don't know what was going on, but some of it was definitely not my language'.

She was then asked about the proxy marriage certificate she had bought 'behind PJ's back'. She accepted that she had done this and that she had presented it at the passport office in Cork, where she had obtained a passport in the name of Howard. It was then put to her that the name 'S. M. Cronin' had appeared on an application form on the 'hitmanforhire' website.

'You were asked [by gardaí] would that mean anything to you. You said, not a thing,' said counsel.

Collins replied, 'I told the guards my mother's maiden name was Cronin. I volunteered that to them.'

When asked about this again, Collins confidently responded, 'I'd say, watch the tape,' referring to her interviews with gardaí, before adding, 'I'm absolutely 100 per cent sure I told them that was my mother's maiden name.' Collins later told the court, 'A lot of people in Ennis would know me as the girl of the Cronins. I'm not known by my maiden name.'

Counsel spoke of the 'lyingeyes' email address and referred to the song by the Eagles, called 'Lyin' Eyes'. She put it to Collins that the song was about a beautiful young woman marrying a rich old man and then cheating on him. Collins said she had not been aware of the song, 'Except that a friend of mine pointed it out to me recently that there was a song 'Lyin' Eyes' and sent me the first verse of it recently. I thought if someone composed that email address, it was a bad-minded thing to do.' Collins said that Robert Howard was into old music. 'I am more into Justin Timberlake myself,' she laughed, adding, 'I was quite surprised Robert was into old music. I know from driving his car.'

The line of questioning then moved on to the computers at the centre of the case. It was pointed out that emails had been retrieved from a number of computers, three of which were in Ireland. Two of those had been located in the Downes and Howard office and the other at Ballybeg House. She was asked how many people had access to those three computers and she replied, 'I had, Robert, Niall and PJ and my lads would have access to anything in my house, but not in the office,' and looked over at her two sons Gary and David, who sat alongside her during most of the trial.

She said that a small number of other people would have had access to the office. Asked who these people were, Collins said, 'I think in interview that was put to me … Not everything was actually transcribed the way it was said. If my counsel put everything to the guards that I asked them to, we'd be here 'til Christmas and people want to get away.' Gesturing at the jury, Collins continued, 'I think the jury might be given the chance to see the tapes and see what's accurate and what's not accurate.'

Telling the court that she didn't spend a lot of time in the country, Collins said that the laptop was missing from Ballybeg House at one stage. 'When I came home from holidays in August [2006] it wasn't there.'

She then challenged Ms Ní Raifeartaigh to find reference to this in the Book of Evidence. This was after counsel had said to her, 'You didn't tell the guards.'

Collins was insistent, in her response. 'I certainly did. It's in the Book of Evidence. You find it and look for it.'

This didn't perturb counsel, who continued to fire questions at the witness. She put it to Collins that if Maria Marconi had been in Ireland in June, she couldn't have sent the emails in August, as she wasn't in the country at that stage.

Collins replied, 'For all I know, that woman I met might live in Ireland.' Asked did she accept it couldn't have been done in America, she replied, 'I've no idea. She could very well live in Ireland and I doubt her name was Maria Marconi.' Collins said she spent very little time in Ireland in August 2006 and added, 'I think the position I find myself in is ludicrous.'

Ms Ní Raifeartaigh put it to Collins that the level of detail contained in the emails was interesting.

Collins replied, 'I've often thought that.'

Counsel then brought to her attention that no trace of the assignments she had been doing for Maria Marconi had been found on the computers.

'So I'm told,' was Collins's simple response. Beaming from the witness box, she added, 'I stopped writing assignments in May 2006. We were travelling in a boat after that. I'm afraid I'm not like John Keating. I don't keep my records in a book unfortunately.'

At this stage, Collins had been in the witness box for over half an hour and she appeared relaxed and comfortable. As Úna Ní Raifeartaigh probed her about the content of the various emails at the centre of the case, Collins fixed the white top she was wearing inside her pin-striped black suit and continued to smile. Then came the suggestion the tense courtroom had been waiting for, from Ms Ní Raifeartaigh. 'You are 'lyingeyes'.'

The immediate response was a flat denial. 'I'm not. I suppose you can say that. It's your job to bring in a guilty verdict. I'm not 'lyingeyes', said Collins.

Counsel quickly put it to her that she hadn't a 'shred' of evidence to prove this and Collins was equally swift with her response. 'I thought the guards would find something … I wrote to the DPP and asked somebody to investigate the theft of my life, but they chose not to do that.'

Counsel said Collins couldn't accuse the gardaí of being lazy as they had engaged in an exhaustive investigation. Again, this yielded a swift response from the witness. 'I don't know if they are exhausted. There were a lot of holidays.'

Collins told counsel she did not believe 'for a moment that anyone ever intended to kill three people'.

Ms Ní Raifeartaigh continued with the quick pace of questioning, saying the presence of the ricin would contradict this.

Collins replied, 'I don't know anything about that, but I can certainly say I didn't intend to have three people killed.'

Counsel put it to her that there was a lot of detail in the emails that only a few people would know.

Collins then asked a question, 'Who do you think sent them?' Counsel replied, 'You, Ms Collins, you.' She said there was consistency between the emails and other proven facts, including that when Essam Eid had arrived at Robert Howard's house, he had photographs, while an email had referred to sending photographs of the three intended victims. She also pointed out that one email stated, 'I'm the devil in the red dress.'

Collins replied, 'I'm just amazed that somebody would identify themselves like that to a would-be assassin. Would anybody be that stupid? I think if somebody would set out to do something like that, they would try to cover their tracks.'

Counsel pointed out that emails found by Detective Garda Peter Keenan on a laptop had been deleted.

Collins replied, 'You are saying by deleting them that they wouldn't be found?'

Ms Ní Raifeartaigh agreed.

Collins asked another question, 'Why go to the bother of getting someone to break into the office?'

The questions were being thrown at a fast pace and Collins was feeling thirsty. She confidently leaned forward and poured herself a glass of water and then prepared herself to answer the flow of questions that continued to be thrown at her.

Counsel put it to her that one of the emails had suggested throwing a computer into the sea, when in fact it was thrown in bushes behind the Two Mile Inn hotel. 'So I believe,' was the reply.

Ms Ní Raifeartaigh asked her, 'You don't believe?'

Collins replied, 'I said, so I believe.'

She was asked if she was aware that deleted emails could be retrieved and she told the court that she was. 'I think people know these days that everything is retrievable,' she said.

She said she had done a computer studies course at the National Institute for Higher Education [now the University of Limerick] after she had completed her second-level education. 'We sent emails back and forth. I would have known that. I know IT has moved on since, but I would have been aware of that. I was 17 at the time. Máire my sister was wrong about my age,' she said. [Collins's sister Suzette, who had given her name in Irish, told the court earlier that day that Collins had left school at 18 or 19.]

Collins's interest in books briefly took centre stage and she laughed as she told Ms Ní Raifeartaigh, 'I haven't read a book in ages, except the Book of Evidence.' She said she enjoys reading thrillers, such as Dan Brown's *Da Vinci Code.*

Collins said she was not familiar with the term 'net analysis' when it was put to her and it was explained that it was the reconstruction of the use of a computer, second by second. 'I am not aware of it,' she said.

She told the trial she was very shocked that her own email address was being accessed, as she wasn't using it herself. She said her password was saved on all the computers she used.

Counsel then specifically referred to emails sent from the Advent computer in the Downes and Howard office on 2 August 2006. She said there had been searches for 'hitman' at 1.14 p.m., 1.49 p.m. and 3.46 p.m. She said that shortly after the search at 1.14 p.m., the email sharoncollins@eircom.net was accessed.

'I was shocked by that,' said Collins.

Asked, 'Who was it?'

She replied, 'I wasn't there so I don't know.'

She was then asked to tell the court who had a reason to set her up. 'Who has a motive for setting you up? You might as well say it,' said counsel.

Collins replied, 'I certainly wasn't in the office. I was only in the office at 2.45 p.m. as a call was made to my mother.'

Ms Ní Raifeartaigh pressed her, 'You've been hinting. Who has a motive to set you up?'

This question was met with a pause. Silence in the courtroom.

Then, some seconds later. 'I have been brought down to the garda station. I've been questioned at length. I've been charged with crimes I certainly didn't commit and never would commit. I've been put into prison. You couldn't imagine the effect it's having on my life. I'm not going to accuse anybody of anything when I don't know,' she said. She was asked could it have been PJ Howard and replied, 'No.'

Then counsel put it to her, 'Who's left? Are you suggesting it was one of the Howards?'

Collins replied, 'Well the guards said to me only a limited number of people have access to the office.'

Ms Ní Raifeartaigh asked her why the Howards would set her up.

Collins suggested, 'You'd have to ask them that.'

Counsel asked her could they have wanted to make money out of her, adding, 'You don't have money.'

Collins said, 'No.'

Ms Ní Raifeartaigh said the Howards were 'sitting on a big pile of money' and Collins accepted this. Counsel then asked her would it have been possible that the Howards wanted to get her out of the way and Collins accepted that this was possible. Collins said that PJ Howard had said in sworn evidence, 'he didn't think I did it'.

'You are with him for eight years,' said Ms Ní Raifeartaigh.

Collins replied, 'Ten years now.'

Asked if PJ Howard had been humiliated, she replied, 'I think if I heard somebody was planning to kill my two sons, I'd get over the humiliation. I know if I was shown the amount of evidence PJ was shown about someone trying to kill his two sons, I wouldn't let pride get in my way.'

Asked if she had discussed the evidence with PJ, she replied, 'Not really. I know the guards shared a lot of the evidence with him.'

Then counsel put it to her that PJ had not appeared in the courtroom since his evidence had concluded on the ninth day of the trial.

'Had he a choice?' asked Collins, 'after the humiliation he's been put through.' Asked to explain what she meant, she said she was referring to the letter she had written to the *Gerry Ryan Show* (in which she complained about PJ) being read out. The sensational letter had been mentioned and Ms Ní Raifeartaigh was not going to veer away from it, asking, 'PJ is also a man of secrets?'

Collins said, 'Yes.'

Counsel said, 'You let the secret out of the bag.'

Collins denied this, saying the letter she had written to the *Gerry Ryan Show* was intended to be read anonymously on air. She did not dispute that she had composed the letter but said she did not realise it had been sent via email. 'It was an anonymous and private matter,' she said.

Asked were the contents of the letter true, she replied, 'I think you know a lot of it was missing.'

Counsel continued to focus on the letter, asking were the allegations relating to PJ's sexual preferences true.

'It certainly was a topic that PJ and I had discussed,' she replied.

Asked again, 'Was it true?'

She said, 'Some of it was.'

Asked to elaborate on this, she replied, 'Various bits, but a lot of that letter wasn't true and doesn't give the full picture. I feel it shouldn't have been used in here when it was not [all] available.'

She was asked if the issue of sex with strangers had been discussed between PJ and herself and replied, 'That was discussed, partly in a fictional sense. I don't think I need to explain.'

Counsel then asked, 'That's a motive to kill three people?'

Collins replied, 'It's absolutely not a motive to kill three people.'

Collins said that PJ Howard had been 'harmed in here. I think he very much wanted me to go into the box to give evidence.' She was asked if PJ used transvestites and replied, 'Yes.'

Then she was asked if he had wanted her to work as a prostitute and she said, 'It was mentioned. As I said before, I most certainly didn't like it. After that, it was no longer an issue. It wasn't mentioned to me again. I'd imagine there are very few couples out there who don't have problems.'

There was no getting away from the email to the *Gerry Ryan Show* and it was put to Collins that she had described her situation as 'unbearable' in the letter.

'No it wasn't,' she told the court.

She was asked what the 'move' was that frightened her, as mentioned in the email to the *Gerry Ryan Show*.

'The move was if I'd leave and start all over again,' she said.

Counsel said to her that she and PJ were not married and she could have walked away.

Collins replied, 'I could have. However, I had already been through a break-up. It was my home. I wasn't anxious to leave. That was the move that frightened me so much and if the rest of the email was there, it went into that … PJ always told me if the relationship broke up, he would look after me. If I said to PJ, it's run its course, he would look after me extremely well. I'm giving you my word on that.'

Asked if he had verbally abused her, she laughed and said, 'Yes and I might have given a bit myself.'

It was put to Collins that writing to a radio station, making suggestions about 'black moods', was a 'bit extreme'.

Collins said, 'It can be known to happen.' She agreed that PJ Howard sometimes threw tantrums and used appalling language.

As questions on the allegations contained in the email to the *Gerry Ryan Show* continued to be thrown at her, Collins eventually had had enough and wasn't afraid to let the court know this. 'To be quite honest with you, I don't want to discuss this at all. I don't see how this relates to murder,' she stated. It was put to her that hatred could be a possible motive, to which she replied, 'I don't hate PJ. That kind of thing is a motive to leave somebody, not to kill somebody. I most certainly did not hate PJ. I think sometimes a person might hate or dislike a quality or an action. You could love somebody but not necessarily like everything they did.'

Counsel said, 'A package? I'd suggest to you the package is his money.'

Collins replied, 'Oh, God, no.'

With the questions relating to the email to the *Gerry Ryan Show* finally out of the way, Ms Ní Raifeartaigh then moved back to emails sent by 'lyingeyes'. She put it to the witness that an email sent on 16 August 2006 stated, 'I want to inherit.'

'The Prosecution case is the motive is inheritance,' said counsel.

Collins replied, 'I could have had a home and an income if I left PJ. You didn't ask him that when he was in here. He most certainly would have provided for me with a home and with an income without my risk of something like this happening.'

Asked about plans they had to get married, Collins said she drew up a document, which stated that they were not married. 'We both agreed on that. Of course I'd have loved to get married. Of course any woman would if they were living with someone for that number of years,' she said. She said the two of them planned the reception in Spanish Point together and PJ paid for it. 'It wasn't something I went off and did myself.' The reception was attended by 40 people and apart from PJ and herself, the only other person who knew they were not married was her sister Catherine.

The court, which generally sat up to 4 p.m. daily, sat until 4.33 p.m. on this particular day, while Collins was being cross-examined. She confidently stepped down from the witness box after the quizzing and went over to her two sons.

As the day's hearing came to a close, an elderly lady sitting behind me in the body of courtroom number 2 whispered to the man beside her, 'How does she keep going?' This was an indication of the cool, confident attitude that had been displayed by Collins throughout the afternoon as the tough questions appeared to run off her with little or no effect.

While most of the questioning of Collins was out of the way, there was still more to come and Ms Ní Raifeartaigh's cross-examination resumed the following morning, 2 July. While some of the allegations and suggestions made in the course of the trial were hard-hitting, one of the most dramatic aspects of the 32 days was Collins's overnight transformation. The cheerful, smiling Collins that left the witness box on the evening of 1 July was suddenly replaced by a quieter, somber and teary Collins the following morning. Gone was the brashness; gone was the confidence; replaced only by tears and sadness.

Just after 11.15 a.m. on 2 July, a pale-faced Collins resumed her place in the witness box and Ms Ní Raifeartaigh again began to fire questions at her. This time she focused on net analysis. Collins was asked why anyone else would access her email and she said she did not know. Counsel said that various searches were carried out on the Advent computer at the Downes and Howard office on 2 August 2006, for such things as astrology, various travel companies, mortgages, inheritance rights, domestic violence and women's aid. This was the same day that searches were carried out for a hitman. The lyingeyes98@yahoo.ie and the sharon collins@eircom.net email accounts were also accessed that day.

Collins said, 'I never experienced any type of domestic violence of any description … I didn't go into 'lyingeyes'. I didn't know anything about 'lyingeyes' until the guards told me.'

Counsel said that music videos were also accessed that evening, at 7.08 p.m.

'Relaxing after a day's work, looking for inheritance rights and contract killers.'

Collins said that she never accessed music videos.

Counsel put it to her that a search had also been carried out for weight loss tips. Collins told her she had taken Reductil, for weight loss in May and June 2006, but said it wasn't a pleasant experience, 'I wouldn't recommend it.' It was put to her that the search was carried out in August 2006 and she said that the only time she bought Reductil was in May.

Counsel noted that the user had gone into Tesco diets, and expressed the view that it was 'an odd place to go if a mystery man was setting you up for a conspiracy to murder'.

Collins replied, 'I just don't know. I have no idea.'

She was then asked about money she was alleged to have sent to Essam Eid. She replied, 'It wasn't sent to Mr Eid. It was sent to stop the blackmail.' Details of various emails sent by 'lyingeyes' were put to Collins and she repeatedly denied all knowledge of the email account. 'I can't comment. I didn't do that so I don't know,' was one response, followed by, 'I wasn't on 'lyingeyes', to 'It's dreadful, but certainly not written by me.'

Ms Ní Raifeartaigh said one of the emails had suggested that 'my husband might feel suicidal and jump off the building' in Spain, after hearing that his sons had been involved in an accident and asked her what her reaction to this was.

'My reaction is first of all I didn't write it. Anybody who knows PJ knows he wouldn't react like that. It's just crazy. When I read it first I was absolutely shocked.'

Counsel put it to her that her shock didn't show and Collins replied that she had read it several times.

'But you got over it,' said counsel.

'I'll never get over the shock of it,' said the witness.

Asked if she was suggesting it was Robert or Niall Howard who had written the emails, she said, 'I'm not suggesting anything. I didn't do this. I didn't set up 'lyingeyes'and I did not write these emails.'

Asked if she wanted to get rid of PJ Howard for the money, she said, 'I never felt like that and I didn't write that. It doesn't express the way I felt.'

Counsel said that the emailer had referred to her husband's 'miserable face' and said this was callous.

'I can only say I didn't write that,' said Collins.

Ms Ní Raifeartaigh replied, 'It's a fact. You seem reluctant to comment on the facts that were proven.'

It was put to her that there was an 'echo' in the language used in the 'lyingeyes' emails and the email to the *Gerry Ryan Show*. Collins said, 'There is and there's an echo in the language used to Marconi, but I didn't write this.'

It was then put to her that in one email, 'lyingeyes' had written to 'hitman' that she was 'still caught here with my sister and her husband'.

It was pointed out that Collins's two sisters Suzette and Catherine had told the court the previous day that they had not visited her in August 2006. It was also put to her that the two sisters had used their names in Irish, when swearing the oath in court. Collins explained that Suzette spends a lot of time in the Gaeltacht, while Catherine is a teacher. Asked if Catherine used her Irish name, she said she did not know.

'I'm suggesting they were trying to put distance between you, by using Irish names,' said Ms Ní Raifeartaigh.

Collins replied, 'I would say they are very embarrassed by the whole affair.'

Collins was also keen to tell the court that she had enjoyed a great relationship with Robert and Niall Howard. 'It's not coming across here. I had a really, really good relationship with PJ's boys. They were like sons to me. I tried to be like a mother to them.' She said she did everything she could for Niall, after the death of his mother in 2003.

The probing then moved on to the Iridium laptop computer that had been located at PJ and Sharon's home, Ballybeg House. Counsel referred to net analysis relating to 15 and 16 August 2006.

'The Iridium wasn't in the house,' said Collins. However, it was pointed out to her that the dial-up connections matched exactly, in that the usage had stopped at midnight on 15 August and recommenced at 8 a.m. the following morning.

Collins replied, 'We couldn't find it. We searched and we couldn't find it.'

Ms Ní Raifeartaigh proceeded. She said that there had been contact between 'lyingeyes' and 'hitman' at 8.19 p.m. At 8.26 p.m., the user accessed FedEx, with a tracking number. It was put to Collins that only she had the tracking number.

'You said you only gave the number to Garda Fahy,' said counsel.

Collins replied, 'I gave the tracking number to the blackmailer.'

Asked was anybody else at Ballybeg House that night, Collins said, 'I don't even know if I was there.'

At that stage, Ms Ní Raifeartaigh said that was ludicrous and accused her of insulting the jury's intelligence. 'You are telling lies,' she said.

'I am not telling lies,' replied Collins.

Counsel continued, by pointing out that the computer activity on the Iridium laptop at Ballybeg House resumed at 8 a.m. or 8.10 a.m. the following morning, 16 August 2006, 'and goes into 'lyingeyes'. Did you notice a blackmailer walking around your house that morning?'

Collins replied, 'I didn't set up 'lyingeyes'. I know nothing about it.'

Counsel quickly responded, 'It's a mantra and you are sticking to it. It is getting very thin, in the face of the evidence ... Was there an invisible blackmailer walking around Ballybeg House?'

Collins replied, 'I can tell you the Iridium wasn't in Ballybeg House.'

Asked about phone calls to Essam Eid, Collins said, 'I can't deny I made phone calls, I did, but I was talking to a woman. I didn't know anything about Essam Eid.'

Counsel then referred to 16 August 2006, the morning John Keating claimed he had been driving around Ennis with Sharon Collins. Ms Ní Raifeartaigh said the 'lyingeyes' email account was accessed at 12.23 p.m. that day, on the Advent computer at the Downes and Howard office, 'and straightaway the user carries out a search for FedEx and puts in the tracking number that you are the only person in Ireland that knows'.

Collins replied, 'All I know is I gave the number to a person on the phone. I definitely wasn't there that morning.'

Counsel then pointed out that Collins went to Spain on 16 August and said, 'It stops. The mystery person stops, the trail, but we know there was further contact from Spain to Essam Eid's phone.'

Collins said she never spoke to Essam Eid, but she did speak to a woman. Asked about the ricin, Collins said she knew nothing about it. Ms Ní Raifeartaigh then put it to her, 'The hard facts of internet evidence are staring you in the face. Yet, you say, "I know nothing." You seem to be riding a number of horses. First you said Maria Marconi, setting you up—'

Collins quickly said, 'I just don't know what happened. I wish I did … I can only comment on what happened to me. What happened to me was a dreadful, frightening thing. It has destroyed my life and my children's lives. I certainly didn't do any of this.'

It was put to her that logically it must have been either Robert or Niall Howard who had sent the emails, given the limited access to the computers used. Collins said she couldn't say that and was 'mad about those boys. I can only say what happened to me. I've said it so many times.'

It was suggested that she had insinuated it could be Robert or Niall in her interviews with gardaí. She replied, 'I'm sitting down here accused of conspiring to murder people I had a relationship with and I cared about, that I didn't do. I didn't set up 'lyingeyes' and I never saw those emails until the guards showed them to me.'

At this stage, the glow that had shone from Collins's face during much of the trial had well and truly disappeared. The pressure had got to her and she started to cry. The smiles from the previous day had faded and the misery clearly emerged. Her spell in the witness box was coming to a sad and sorry end and she was not enjoying it. She accepted that she had done wrong things, but fought back the tears to defend herself.

'The Marconi experience was the experience I had. I did stupid things. I did foolish things. I shouldn't have written the letter about PJ, but I certainly did not intend to kill anybody.'

At that stage, Mr Justice Roderick Murphy could see that Collins was struggling and asked her if she would like a break.

She nodded sadly that she would continue without a break and was given a tissue from the stenographer who sat close by. The final phase of her cross-examination proceeded and Ms Ní Raifeartaigh accused Collins of only telling the truth when she was forced to do so. It was also put to her that her story was 'growing legs to meet the evidence coming in', in reference to her interviews with gardaí during the investigation.

Counsel also accused of Collins of being 'emotional and manipulative' in her letters to the Director of Public Prosecutions, suggesting that her mother or one of her sons may die, if charges were brought against her. Collins said there was 'a lot of emotion but not manipulation'.

'I had been hauled out of my home, all kinds of allegations thrown at me. My family were in bits. I was absolutely shattered. I was trying to explain the damage this was doing to me,' she said.

Counsel quickly replied, 'You decided in the arrogance we've come to expect of you, to write [to the DPP], against the advice of your solicitor. You got in here to try and do what you always do, and you sit there, trying to manipulate the jury, smiling at the jury.'

Collins said, 'I'm not smiling at the jury.'

Counsel replied, 'You were yesterday.'

Collins said, 'I'm extremely nervous. When I'm nervous sometimes I smile. I'm here to tell the truth. I've always, always told the truth. I'm not here to mislead anybody,' she replied, in response to the final question from the Prosecution.

Collins's senior counsel Paul O'Higgins briefly re-examined her, before she left the witness box at 12.42 p.m., that day. He asked her to clarify if her sister and husband had stayed with her at Ballybeg House in 2006.

'No, definitely not. One of my sisters stayed at the house with her husband once, in 1999, and my other sister has never stayed at the house,' she said.

Collins then stepped down from the witness box and quietly made her way over to her seat, between her two sons. Her eldest son Gary put his arm around her petite frame and she fell into his arms, weeping uncontrollably. The two whispered and both Gary and David comforted their distraught mother.

This change in mood was most interesting and Collins never regained her composure for the remainder of the trial. Her pale face never regained its colour or glowing smile.

06 | PLEA FOR LENIENCY

S haron Collins did not see why she should be charged with offences of which, she claimed, she was entirely innocent and said she had been set up. She made her opinion on this very clear in three lengthy and detailed letters she had written to the Director of Public Prosecutions. The letters, written to James Hamilton on 13 March, 28 April and 25 May 2007, had suggested that she should not be charged with this 'appalling crime' and had claimed that if charges were brought, it would adversely affect her family and merely serve a 'media frenzy'. She had told Mr Hamilton, in the April letter, 'My life is very much in your hands.'

She had said she was going through a 'nightmare beyond belief' and had seriously considered suicide. She had claimed that her elderly mother Bernadette, her youngest son David and her partner PJ Howard would be most affected, if she was brought before the courts. Collins said that she was writing with the encouragement of PJ Howard, but against the 'very strong' advice of her solicitor.

She had said that her 'husband/partner' supported her and did not believe the allegations. She also said that PJ Howard had been shown a huge amount of 'so-called evidence' by the gardaí, but he still supported her and 'knows that I wouldn't do what the gardaí are suggesting.'

'He keeps telling me that we will sort it out, but I'm frightened that we won't. We are desperate to figure out who and why someone would want to set me up in this way. No-one would go to this trouble for nothing. I feel totally lost and can't understand why the gardaí won't investigate the theft and complete destruction of my life, to which, I have to say, they are contributing. I have so many questions as to what could have happened and as time goes on, so many theories too. But that is all they are and I have no way of knowing the truth. However, one truth I do know is that I didn't and wouldn't do what I was arrested for. I am an ordinary woman, living an ordinary life with which I was happy until this happened. I want my life back before it's too late,' she had written.

She had referred to herself as Robert and Niall Howard's 'surrogate' mother. She loved them both and had a fantastic relationship with the eldest son, Robert, in particular. She had said she was very worried about them and what they were feeling.

In the first of the typed letters, which was 21 pages in length, she had written about her own background and gave very detailed information on her own life.

She said she would like to tell the DPP, 'In my own words, what I do know and trust that you will consider it in conjunction with the evidence as submitted to you by the gardaí.'

'My solicitor tells me that it is a complete waste of time, but this is my life and that of my family and I must do what I feel is right. My solicitor's argument is that I will be giving away whatever my defence might be if charged, but I feel that the truth is the truth and I can only tell you what I know and I feel that now is the time as I would rather be dead than subject my family—both my immediate family and extended family—to the embarrassment of such a case. My life is in a shambles,' she had written.

'The problem is, the idea of being charged is so unbearable to me, I feel I must tell you what I know now. I can't just sit here and do nothing while our lives are torn to shreds,' she stated. 'My husband/partner has been fantastic and has been extremely supportive, but he has been told by the gardaí that I have paid money to have him and his sons murdered. He does not believe it. I love PJ Howard dearly. He looks after my every need. We have a great life together. He is fantastic to my two sons … I would depend my life on him. I need him,' she had written.

In the early part of the letter, she had referred to PJ Howard as her 'husband' but then went on to explain that he was not 'actually my husband'. She had explained how she had married Noel Collins at the age of 19 and they had two sons together, Gary and David. They had separated when she was 27 and later divorced. She had gained custody of the two boys and had stayed in the family home in Ennis with them.

She met PJ Howard in November 1998 and she and her two sons had moved into his home that Christmas, on foot of a suggestion from PJ. They effectively had remained on there, permanently.

'I didn't take the move lightly. A very short time after we met, PJ asked me if I thought we could make a life together and I had agreed to do so and so the decision was made to stay together. I loved him and still do, very much. He is extremely good to me and I have always been impressed with the way he took in two teenage boys and looked after them. If I am to be honest, though, I would have liked it if marriage was on the cards, however, he made it clear to me that it wasn't,' she had written.

She had said she was 'well settled' in his house by the time she had realised how definite PJ was about marriage, 'so there was nothing for it, but to accept it and make the most of what was a very good and close, loving relationship—not without its ups and downs, but certainly not worth throwing away.'

Collins explained how PJ's ex-wife Teresa had died suddenly from a brain haemorrhage in February 2003. Then, as time went on, she had realised it would now be possible for her to marry PJ. 'I know that sounds terrible, but it's true,' she had written, of her thoughts back in 2003. 'In time, PJ and I discussed the possibility. He wasn't too keen, but I told him that I'd always wanted to marry again and that he was the man for me and he agreed to think about it. He pointed out that he wanted his business to go to his boys and I could quite understand this. I would probably feel the same if I was in the position,' she had written.

She had said the two agreed that it would be vital to have a pre-nuptial agreement should they marry and, in January 2004, she thought her dream was about to come true: PJ had proposed to her! 'I was over the moon and so was he. However, this was short-lived, as his solicitor pointed out that a pre-nuptial agreement had no place in Irish law,' she said.

Collins had been disappointed and their plans had been put on hold. She said it had been suggested to PJ that they marry in the church only, as she had a Church annulment from her previous marriage. Both herself and PJ were happy to take this route and had booked a trip to Rome. 'It was really the church side of marriage that concerned me, if the truth be told,' she had written. However, PJ's solicitor had again advised him that even a Church marriage may leave him open to a claim on the assets he intended for his sons, should the relationship break up or should he die before her. She said that while PJ wanted to protect his business for his sons, he always looked after her extremely well.

As planned, the two had travelled to Italy in October 2005 and while they had not got married, they had said their vows to each other in a church in Sorrento, promising to stay together and to love one another. 'We resolved to tell family and friends that we had got married, which is what we did, to always refer to each other as husband and wife and never to tell anyone, except our solicitors, what we had actually done,' she had written.

'I was as happy with this arrangement as I could have been had we been legally married and he had nothing to fear with regard to his business. We had drawn up a few lines before we went away, stating that we would not be taking part in any actual ceremony with anyone presiding over it when we were in Italy and we both signed it. This was to be given to our solicitors,' she had written.

The couple had returned from Sorrento and had thrown a party for their families and friends in Spanish Point, Co. Clare. Everybody believed it was a wedding party, as they had not been told otherwise.

Collins continued writing and then moved on to the background to the allegations against her. She wrote how both herself and PJ could be quite 'abrasive' and certainly had had rows and disagreements in the past. She had said she had confided in someone that she had trusted, in relation to those disagreements, and she believed this had landed her in the trouble she was facing.

She had explained that she had come into contact with a woman she knew as Maria Marconi on the internet in December 2005. She said she casually registered with a website regarding working from home, through a pop-up on a computer. Almost immediately, she had began to receive several emails from other sources asking her to register and she had registered with some of them. She said that had appeared to open the floodgates to a lot of unwanted emails. However, one of these greatly interested her. It was an offer of assistance from a bestselling author to write a novel. She had filled out a form and had written a short piece about herself and had sent it back. This had been acknowledged and, some days later, she had received an email from Maria Marconi, who had told Collins she had been assigned as her mentor.

Marconi told Collins that she had written several bestsellers under a non-de-plume, but did not provide her with any more details about this. She said that Marconi had encouraged her to write again about herself and her life in detail. Collins said that while PJ had often encouraged her to write, she had decided not to tell him about Marconi at this stage and would wait until she had seen how she was getting on.

She said she found herself getting friendly with Marconi very quickly and found the writing very therapeutic. Collins said that her best friend had become distant from her and, apart from PJ, she hadn't had anyone to confide in. Marconi had become like a pen-pal and she had started to divulge personal information to her.

Around April 2006, Collins said that she and PJ had argued over personal matters relating to their relationship in a very heated exchange. She said she had emailed Marconi that day and said 'all sorts of derogatory things' about him, stating that she no longer loved PJ and that she, in fact, hated him. 'In my email, I attacked him on every possible level as a man. I really don't want to expand more and I don't see the need, suffice to say that the last thing I would want would be for him to ever see what I had written,' she had written to the DPP.

Collins said that Marconi was very sympathetic to her and the row with PJ soon blew over.

Collins said she put her writing plans on hold for a period of time in 2006 as she and PJ had been in Palma, Mallorca. Whilst in Spain, she said that Marconi had phoned her to tell her she would be in Ireland in June and suggested that they meet.

They met in Ennis on 16 and 17 June. She described Marconi as being 5′7″ in height, aged about 47, with straight, blonde, shoulder-length hair, brown eyes and sallow, clear skin. She allowed Marconi to use a computer at the Howard's office, Downes and Howard Ltd, Westgate Business Park, Ennis—where Collins worked as a part/time receptionist—and also a laptop at Ballybeg House, the home Collins had shared with PJ Howard. She also took Marconi on a drive around Ennis and to the scenic resorts of Lahinch, Kilkee and Quilty in Co. Clare.

The following month, July 2006, when Collins had been in Spain, Marconi had emailed her to say that her home had been broken into and her laptop had been stolen. Shortly after she received this email, she had received another email, telling her that for €100,000, her husband would be killed and she would be 'free and rich'.

'I was abhorred. There were a number of these. I emailed Maria and told her about these messages. I wondered how someone could know my details or that of my husband. There was more than just the offer to kill my husband, there was an offer to kill his sons too. Then there were threats to kill my sons, or PJ and his sons, if I did not pay. There were lots of these messages. I was very frightened by it,' she had written. She said that PJ was laid up after a bad fall on his boat and she didn't want to upset him by telling him about the emails.

Collins had returned home to Ennis, where she had received an email stating that she should send €20,000, to prevent an attachment being sent to PJ. She said that attachment was the letter she had sent to Marconi that April, criticising PJ. She said she had 'nearly died of shock' when she saw the attachment. She said the email had stated that when PJ would see it, he might pay the sender to kill her. Around that time, she said she had received a number of unidentified phone calls and each time she had answered, a male voice spoke.

She said she had gone on her annual pilgrimage to Lough Derg in Donegal on 8 or 9 August of that year, until 10 or 11 August. 'I would go and pray about it and I naively hoped it would all have stopped by the time I got back,' she said.

On her return, she checked her emails and one message stated that PJ would be contacted immediately if she didn't answer her cell phone. She said she had emailed back to say she didn't have any money to pay, but had then received several phone calls from a private number—from a male—asking if she had the money. She said it was vital to her that PJ did not see what she had written and after much distress, she had decided to send the money. She had withdrawn €13,000 from her AIB bank account and €2,000 from the Credit Union and sent it via FedEx to an address in Las Vegas that she had been sent. She said she was told to address it to T. Engle. She said she had packed the money into a box and put in a pair of electronic goggles and had written on the packet that the goggles had been left behind after a holiday in Ireland. She said when she had made the booking with FedEx, she had used the surname Howard, but she hadn't wanted to write her name or address on the accompanying documentation, so she had written a different Christian name. She received a tracking number for the package.

The following day, 16 August, she had gone to Spain. She said she was feeling a mixture of relief, distress and guilt. She hoped it was all over, but feared there may be further demands. She said that she had begun to receive more phone calls from a private number and had heard a similar voice as before. Around 19 September, Collins said she had received an email saying something like, 'You stupid, fucking bitch. Why don't you answer your calls? Did you think that €15,000 would get rid of me? You better think again and get more cash fast.'

She said that she didn't answer the message. She then got another one, telling her that her husband would be furnished with the material that she had written about him and he would be told that she had paid €15,000 to have him killed. She said she replied to this email, stating that she had told her husband about the original threats and had told him about the contents of her letter. She said that she had also made Marconi aware of what was happening. She did not receive any emails from 'blackmailers' after that.

She said that when the Downes and Howard office had been broken into in September 2006, she and PJ had been in Spain with friends. She initially didn't connect the break-in with the emails, but when Robert had been threatened the following day, 'alarm bells went off in my head'. She said that she went to an internet café in Spain the following day, to contact Marconi, but discovered that all of her emails—incoming and outgoing— along with her email address book had been deleted.

She said that her password for her eircom.net account was saved on the computer in the office and she assumed that her emails had been deleted during or after the burglary. She never heard from Maria Marconi after that.

Collins said she had told Marconi a lot of personal information and looked upon her as a friend. 'I know it really seems crazy now to divulge so much of your life to someone that you don't know, but at the time, I didn't see the harm. I was glad of someone to talk to. I liked it that no-one knew about her, I can't explain why. I know that seems childish now, but I felt she was a friend. I now realise that if I had mentioned her to PJ and if I had gone to the guards when the blackmail started, I wouldn't be in this position today,' she had written.

'I never told her about my 'marriage' arrangement with PJ. We had agreed not to mention that to anyone, with the exception of our solicitors. I always gave her the impression that we were married and she definitely believed that I had a lot to gain in the event of divorce or PJ's death. I did tell her that our marriage ceremony was out of the ordinary, but that it wasn't up for discussion,' she said.

Collins also referred to emails shown to her by gardaí that had been retrieved from Eid's computer at his Las Vegas home. The emails were addressed to Tony 'somebody' and were signed 'Sharon'.

'There were many things that were read out to me from these emails that sounded very familiar to me and that I believe were extracted from emails I wrote to Maria Marconi, however, they were not emails that I had written. It seemed that my emails had been edited and mixed in with other text in a way that makes it look like I had sent them to this 'Tony' fellow. Details that I gave her when doing 'assignments' and in conversational emails and telephone calls now sound like directions and instructions. Little details like what we were doing and where we were going are also worked in. I didn't take in a lot of what was read out to me during questioning. Much of the time, I just wondered if I had died and gone to hell. I could never have imagined being in this position. The only 'dodgy' thing I ever do is not always taxing my car, because we might be away for a portion of a month and I might 'chance' it until the next month,' she had written.

She said she could not remember what email address the gardaí had said the emails to the Las Vegas computer were sent from, but 'I most certainly did not set it up'.

In that first letter, Collins addressed seven points about various garda assertions in the case against her. These were:

1. WEBSITE FOR ASSASSINS:
The Gardaí believe that I contacted this Eid man through a website for hired assassins. I can't understand why anyone would do such a thing. Even if a person wanted to have someone murdered, how would you take a chance on a contact on the internet? Wouldn't it be daft to try to hire someone from a website—sure, you wouldn't know where or who they were. They could be your next-door-neighbours or connected with the police in any given country.

2. INHERITANCE RIGHTS:
The Gardaí maintain that I wanted PJ and his sons dead—all in the space of a couple of days, so that I could inherit everything that he has. But I have nothing to inherit in the

event of their deaths. If they all died, then PJ's brother and sister would inherit anything he has. I would be throwing myself on their mercy and they have their own families to look after. If I was legally married to PJ and he and his two sons were murdered, I'm quite sure I would be arrested within minutes of their deaths. The question would be asked 'Who is to gain here?' and I'd be hauled down to the station and charged immediately.

In addition, who in their right mind would want to have everyone in a family killed at one go? Wouldn't that raise numerous questions and suspicions? Another thing here is that I have been aware that my marital status gives me no protection if the relationship breaks down or, God forbid, if anything was to happen to PJ. Like most women, security is important to me and PJ has often mentioned that he wants to make provision for me in case anything were to happen to him, but that hasn't been done yet. I know that the law regarding co-habiting couples is under review and is expected to change at some stage in the future, which would give a dependant or co-habitee some rights, but at the moment, there is no protection for someone like me. Therefore, even if I hated PJ, which I don't, why would I want him dead at this stage? It doesn't make sense.

3. EMAIL ADDRESS:

The Gardaí say that I set up an alternative email address and emailed this Eid man from there, giving him all the details shown in emails that were retrieved by the FBI when searching his house. I can't imagine anyone giving a potential murderer personal details, like were read out to me. Mind you, I can't imagine contacting a person like that. Any personal details that I gave were to a woman calling herself Maria Marconi and I had come to think of her as a friend.

4. €15,000 PAYMENT:

The Gardaí maintain that the €15,000 was sent as a part-payment for murdering PJ and the boys. I've explained why I sent this money. I just did not want PJ to see what I had written as I thought it would have a detrimental effect on our relationship. I don't have many unusual transactions on my bank account. Rental income goes into it and mortgages, loans and bills are paid out of it. That is the bulk of what goes on in my account. Any big withdrawal would stand out a mile. I imagine if someone was plotting to kill someone, and would be a potential suspect, that they would not withdraw a large sum all at one go. They would surely withdraw it little by little, put it aside over a period of time and wait until they had enough.

5. KEYS AND ALARM CODE FOR OFFICE:

The Gardaí insist that I gave Eid the keys to the office and the code for the alarm and also PJ's credit card details to pay for the flights. For one thing, I would be able to kick that door in myself and I'm quite slight. It looks like a heavy door, but the locks on it are flimsy. Why, therefore, would I give someone keys if I wanted them to get in? I can't explain how they got the keys, the alarm code or PJ's credit card details. My son maintains that Maria Marconi could have handed the keys out to someone the second morning she was there and that they could have had copies cut and then given them back to her when she went down to her car again, but there's no way of knowing.

6. AMOUNT OF EVIDENCE STACKED AGAINST HER:

One of the detectives told me that in his 23 years of detective work he has never seen so much evidence stacked against someone. I keep thinking about this comment. I feel there are just too many paths leading to me. I know I did some stupid things, in trusting Maria Marconi or whoever she is, in not mentioning her to PJ, in divulging personal details of our lives to her, in giving in to blackmail demands, in not telling the gardaí and in sending €15,000 to the USA. I am aware how stupid that was and I will forever regret it all. But I am not a stupid person. If I was plotting such a dreadful crime, surely I would try to cover my tracks and not leave so many trails back to me. It all seems so far-fetched. PJ and my son both think it and so does PJ's son, Robert, even though he does blame me now for all this hassle. In addition, he is bound to have doubts now, having been told so much by the gardaí. I had a fantastic relationship with Robert. He confided everything in me and is like a cross between a son and a good friend to me. I love him. I also get on very well with PJ's other son, Niall, but if I was to be honest, Robert is my favourite. He an exceptional young man. But now I doubt that our relationship will ever be rebuilt again. Bad enough that they have lost a mother, now they've been told that their 'surrogate' mother wants them dead. It is beyond bearing.

7. PJ'S 'SUICIDE':

The police said that an email, supposedly from me to an assassin, said that PJ's death was to look like suicide after he heard that his sons had been killed. Anyone who knows PJ Howard would never believe that he would commit suicide. He is just not that type of man. If something happened to his sons while he was in Spain, he would be home on the next available flight, making arrangements and getting to the bottom of what happened. He is a very capable, astute businessman. I think I remember the gardaí mentioning during questioning that death by natural causes would also be a way for PJ to die. How could anyone believe that this would be possible in this day and age? I am quite sure that an autopsy would show that this was not so. It is all ludicrous.

She said she understood the gardaí had a job to do and that they believed they were on the 'right track'. However, she said she believed that 'someone out there has the capabilities to set me up in this way and it had to be done in the hope of financial gain. No-one would go to this trouble for nothing.'

Collins concluded her first letter by writing, 'If by writing to you in this way, I have over-stepped the boundaries—and I strongly suspect that I have—then please accept my apologies and realise that it is only because I am at the end of my tether and I am desperate to be heard and to see an end to this.'

Less than seven weeks later, on 28 April, 2007, Collins again put pen to paper and wrote her second letter to the DPP. This was much shorter, a seven-page letter, with an additional note, which she said she was faxing to the DPP's office 'for the sake of speed'.

She said she had felt 'compelled' to write the second letter, following on from an article in that day's *Daily Star* newspaper. The article stated that a 'rich wife' had hired someone to poison her husband and that traces of a poisonous substance had been found on personal items belonging to a foreign national. She said that she had flown in to Dublin from Spain the previous evening and PJ had driven up from Ennis to meet her:

> We were enjoying each other's company and trying to give each other some comfort about the dreadful situation we are in. We were hoping that the week might bring some good news and planning for him to join me in Spain next weekend, all going well. Then PJ got a telephone call regarding the article and he rang one of the investigating gardaí who confirmed that it was related to their investigation and that he was to meet with them this evening …
>
> PJ rang me after speaking to the gardaí and the situation looks extremely serious. He said that the gardaí are adamant that I am involved in hiring this man to kill him and his sons, Robert and Niall. Apparently, he had an extremely toxic substance and they told him that he had enough to kill thousands. It said in the *Daily Star* that it was a substance called ricin. I can only say to you, as true as God is my witness, I have never heard of such a thing before. I am abhorred by it. I explained to you in my previous letter how I was threatened and blackmailed and how I subsequently paid €15,000 to stop the threats, but the idea that this could in anyway finance someone who would travel with a substance like this, sickens me to the pit of my stomach.

She stated that she had believed the whole thing had happened
for one of two reasons:

> Firstly, I thought it was some kind of a scam, that I was fool
> enough to leave myself open to, and someone thought I was
> an easy target and had access to money, believing that I was
> actually married to PJ.
>
> Recently, I have been thinking that there's more to it than
> that and that someone thought they had had something to
> gain—or not lose—by setting me up in this way, by
> discrediting me in this way and, perhaps, had hired someone
> to frame me. This was a theory that only began to dawn on
> me in the past few weeks, as various things came to mind and
> I have very, very strong suspicions regarding it, but I can't be
> sure, and therefore will not accuse anyone, as I know I could
> be completely wrong. I know what it's like to be accused in the
> wrong and I wouldn't wish it on another soul.
>
> All along, I didn't think that anyone had any intention of
> killing anybody and I told myself it would all come to light,
> but now, it turns out this man, Eid, actually did have serious
> means of killing someone. Terrifying stuff, and, even more
> terrifying to me, that the gardaí believe that I employed him
> to use it on PJ and, worse still now, that I feel that maybe I
> could have prevented it, if I had gone to the gardaí as soon as
> the threats began. I read in the paper that he threw the
> substance away, but thankfully, no-one was affected by it. I'm
> finding it so difficult to get my head around this. Really, then,
> was it my fault for divulging details of our lives to Marconi or
> maybe for my stupid vanity, in thinking that I could actually
> write a novel, and was I the catalyst then that drew a
> dangerous person like that into the country? If I was, then I'll
> be forever sorry, but to be accused of hiring this person to kill
> three people whom I care for, my God, there is just no way.

Collins, writing from Spain, said she was worried about PJ's
health as he had chest pains and pain in his left arm and hand
over the previous few weeks:

His solicitor, Michael Houlihan, and his sons have been
putting him under enormous pressure to cut his ties with me.
His solicitor even told him that he would stop representing
him if he continued his relationship with me and Robert and
Niall have argued with him several times. He told me that he
never thought his sons would fall out with him until now. I
can't allow this to happen to him. He has been so, so good to
me and my boys for all these years. I have asked a friend if I
can stay with her for the time being when I go home, to try to
alleviate the stress for PJ and I have told him so. At the end of
the day, if I am charged in relation to any of this, he will need
his sons for support, as I don't think I would be able to stay
and look after him then anyway.

She said that herself and PJ loved each other deeply and were 'as
happy as Larry' together. They were never getting on as well,
'when all this happened'.

I'd do anything for PJ and this is breaking my heart. I'm
worried that he won't be well and I won't be there to take care
of him. Do you know that when PJ had his by-pass, I would
arrive at the hospital at 8 a.m. every morning and I wouldn't
leave until they kicked me out each night at midnight?. I
wouldn't leave his side … I can't begin to explain how much
it upsets me that someone would even think that I would
want to harm a hair on his head. Then I read in the paper
today that the poison that was found would bring about a
slow and agonising death, and the Gardaí are telling him that
I hired someone to give him this and I just can't tell you how
sickened I feel by that.

Referring to the garda investigation, she said that 'everything is
adding up and it's like joining the dots, but, the problem is, I
didn't hire anyone to kill anybody'.

Addressing the DPP in that second letter, she wrote:

You are the only person who can decide if our lives are to be destroyed or not. I know what I did—I was an ass for giving away information about myself and those around me and I was an even bigger one for allowing myself to be blackmailed and for paying money to a blackmailer. This is what I did and it was 100 per cent stupidity and I am guilty of that and am most certainly paying the price of that stupidity. Apart from that, I have lived my life to the best of my ability. I am family-orientated, maternal and, PJ tells me, quite domesticated. I am out-spoken, direct and can be a bit abrasive, but I am very soft behind it and feel very deeply for people. I also have very definite views on crime and, dare I say it, believe that the death penalty should have its place in certain circumstances—perhaps I should change my mind about that now given the present situation I find myself in.

She said that PJ and herself had often debated the execution of Saddam Hussein. PJ had thought it was wrong to execute him, while she had thought it was right, but that it could have been done more humanely.

She also said that in certain circumstances, she felt that abortion was acceptable and sometimes necessary, but mostly was very wrong and selfish. She also said that she believed in euthanasia when someone had no hope of recovery from illness and was in unbearable pain.

'With the exception of self-defence, the above are the only circumstances in which I believe it is acceptable to take another human being's life. I want to be 100 per cent clear about that. To me there are no excuses for it and I certainly wouldn't do it or want it to be done—to anybody.

'If I am charged, my relationship with PJ will be over—how could it possibly survive? As it is, I feel I must move out so that he is not compromised and so that his sons will stop arguing with him,' she added.

Collins said she feared for PJ if he was left to live alone he would end up eating junk food every day and this would probably put him into an early grave:

My mother is 73, still very active, but beginning to show her age, she is very attached to PJ—news like this would kill her. My sister Catherine and her husband are secondary school teachers in Waterford. They are good, decent people and I know that a scandal like this would cause them great distress. My other sister, Suzette is some kind of psychologist with the Department of Education and is married to the Managing Director of a large pharmaceutical company near us. Being associated with something like this would affect them very badly indeed. For myself, well, being charged would be a very severe punishment indeed for something I did not do. Not alone would I lose my relationship and my home, but I am also totally financially dependent on PJ and that would be gone too. Can you imagine how heart-breaking it is for me as a mother to listen to my 21-year-old son, David, crying on the phone as he feels so helpless? His life is falling apart now. He is making arrangements to move out of his home and it's killing him. He loves PJ like a father. He works in retail and was sent home from work today as he kept breaking down.

I can't imagine how badly the news will affect my older son, Gary. As I've said he is in Australia at the moment, and I don't want to worry him, but if I am charged or if it is in the papers, he would hear it immediately and I know he just wouldn't be able to cope with the news. He would be completely devastated. I am not exaggerating when I say to you that I am afraid that one or both of them would take their own lives, as you hear of young men doing that all the time these days.

… So, Mr Hamilton, if you were me, what would you do? I admit I have seriously considered suicide myself on the basis that it would save my family all the embarrassment and stigma of being associated with me if I were charged and it would stop the not knowing. I would have something to leave my boys and I have three rented properties that are mortgaged to the hilt but are covered by life assurance policies. I wouldn't have to face the prospect of a very high-profile trial where every aspect of our lives would be examined and reported in the papers and TV. That, too, would save PJ on many different levels and I would like to do that for him. As well as that, we all die sometime, so why not now for me? I've recently had a mammogram done that shows a small mass on one breast and the doctor wants me to undergo further examination—he says it's probably non-malignant—but what if it isn't, that could get me anyway? So, I've certainly thought why not take this option. This is all way too much for any one person to bear and I'm not sure I'm strong enough. The only problem here is, I didn't do this thing and if I take this option, I won't be able to defend myself and my good name and my family will have to live with the stigma of it anyway. The spiritual implications weigh heavily on me too, should I take this option.

She said that alternatively, if charged, she could 'fight' it:

I have very strong suspicions these days as to who could be behind this and I could point this out—it's a theory that makes a lot of sense to me, but I could be wrong. Anyway, hopefully I'd be found not guilty, but what kind of life would be left for everyone after that? I can't even bear to imagine what would happen if I was to be found guilty. This would destroy my family completely … I did not hire anyone to kill PJ, Robert and Niall. I did not hire anyone, full-stop.

She said she would give anything to be able to help gardaí find the truth and was extremely alarmed to hear that 'this man had a substance that could have killed people'.

Collins noted that she was in danger of sounding like she was protesting too much, but she was 'very much at breaking-point at this stage'.

'I have never experienced such depths of despair in my life. I am by no means a saint, but I am not a bad person. I am not a dangerous person,' she said.

Collins said that herself and PJ were a 'good team' who practically finish each other's sentences:

I remember noticing PJ when I was a little girl, perhaps nine or ten. He was a grown man. I didn't know him until we started going out together but the memory of seeing him where he worked stayed in my mind. Then when I saw him walking into my shop eight-and-a-half years ago, after seeing him out a few nights previously, I knew he was coming in for me. It was almost like a premonition. It felt like I had been expecting him, even though I wasn't, until he walked it. I know that sounds strange, but that's the way it was.

… I believe that charging me with this horrendous crime will only serve to feed a media frenzy and will probably not get to the bottom of what really happened and if it does, too much damage will have been done to innocent parties, namely, myself, PJ and my family. As it stands, miraculously, no-one has been injured, thank God, and any hurt that does exist is not physical and can be healed with time.

… Life is just too short for it to be wasted with this kind of thing and if I only knew what to do or say to help get to the bottom of it, I would, in a heartbeat … Lastly, Mr Hamilton, I want to ask you to please not have me charged in relation to this matter. Please let us get on with our lives. They are ordinary lives, but we were happy in them and could be happy again. I have told the truth about everything I know and I pray that you will see that. The lives and happiness of many people are in your hands.

This was Collins's conclusion to her second letter to the DPP.

Collins's third letter, written in Spain on 25 May 2007, was the shortest of the three and was six pages in length. In it, she had written that she felt her youngest son David was 'more of a casualty than anyone else in all this and my heart is broken for him'.

She said she did not feel she could go back to her home town Ennis, where news of the investigation had become known. She said that while her mother hadn't heard it, it was only a matter of time before she was made aware of it and it would kill her.

She said that in the past, there were times when she had felt like 'killing him (and I don't mean literally!!)—perhaps 'throttling' would be a better word—but those times had passed and we had reached a deeper understanding of each other and we had 'mellowed' too, which was really good for both of us'.

In that third letter, Collins said she had tried to imagine what she would or would not have done if she was in the position of someone trying to do what was alleged and said that a five-year-old child would have covered their tracks better. As she completed the letter, she wrote that she had put herself in a 'murderous' frame of mind and could definitely say the following:

* I would not use any computer that I usually use to set up an email address. I wasn't familiar with the term IP address, but I certainly would have known that it could be traced. I think anyone would. I'd have gone to a place that wouldn't be associated with me. I don't imagine it's too difficult to find a computer to use in an unrelated location.

* I would not have obviously withdrawn money from my bank account to send to someone like that. (I didn't have access to any additional money anyway, and I can't imagine doing something like that for the sum of money I sent.) Also, I wouldn't have mentioned anything about sending money to the gardaí after the office break-in.

* I can't imagine contacting someone on the internet for this purpose, but, for the sake of this exercise, if I did, I would not have given any personal information about myself to a dangerous person. In fact, I wouldn't identify myself at all. That would be lunacy. I'd stay anonymous.

* Then there is the question of wiping out an entire family, three people, no less. How could someone expect to get away with that? If I had inheritance rights, which I hadn't, I would have known that I would be the obvious suspect. If I was doing it just for the hell of it—well—why would I risk

everything for that? If I was unhappy with my relationship with PJ (still assuming the 'murderous' frame of mind) why not have just him killed? I would have thought that Robert would have looked after me if anything happened to PJ.

* There's the question of timing, why then? Why the rush? Why not wait until a dependent co-habitee had some inheritance rights? Or why not wait until PJ had something in place for me? My son David had just bought a house for investment purposes with PJ's help. PJ had guaranteed the mortgage and I was delighted for David. He had said he would do the same for my other son, Gary. Why would I want to prevent that from happening? PJ had also just helped me to buy an apartment in Limerick and had told me that he intended buying a commercial property for me, which would be mortgaged, but would be paid for out of his estate if anything happened to him so that I would have an income. If you wanted to kill someone, wouldn't you wait for that first so that you would have security?

* Then I most definitely would not have used my son's house for any purpose, i.e. leaving keys there. There are plenty places one could use instead.

* On top of that, I don't see why I'd want anyone to get into the office in the first place. Why do that?

07 | THE NAILBITING WAIT

'Lying eyes' made it clear to 'hitman' that it was imperative she wouldn't end up in jail. As she went about hiring a hitman on the internet, 'lyingeyes' wrote, in an email in August 2006, 'I've got children of my own and intend on being around for them. That's another reason why I want to be as careful as possible that I don't end up in jail.' But as the case drew to a close, it seemed Sharon Collins was facing this very real possibility.

The final outcome of the dramatic case came after lengthy closing speeches by the Prosecution and Defence legal teams, followed by the charge to the jury by Mr Justice Roderick Murphy. He had sat patiently throughout the trial, listening to compelling evidence, hours of legal argument and tense exchanges between the opposing counsel on several occasions.

The beginning of the final phase of the trial got underway on 3 July, when Ms Ní Raifeartaigh, BL for the Prosecution, and Michael Bowman, BL for Collins, delivered their closing speeches. David Sutton, SC for Eid, delivered his closing speech the following day, 4 July, while Mr Justice Murphy's charge to the jury also commenced that day and concluded on Monday, 7 July. The jury began its deliberations at 3.44 p.m. that day and returned its verdicts throughout the afternoon on Wednesday, 9 July, the last one coming at 5.40 p.m.

It was just after midday on 3 July when Ms Ní Raifeartaigh rose to her feet to present what the Prosecution believed was a convincing speech, summarising the main thrusts of its case. One hour and 43 minutes of talking later, she sat down, having made her final submissions to this dramatic trial. She began by reminding the jury that the trial had been 'very long, extraordinary and bizarre' with a 'mountain of evidence' and said it was her task to 'pull it all together'. 'Inside and outside the courtroom it may have sounded like the plot of a film or sometimes a cheap thriller. One can be reminded of the old saying 'Truth can be stranger than fiction,' she enthused. 'This is a tragedy. It may not be a tragedy about dead bodies. It is a ridiculous plot between two people whose lives should never have intersected. Ms Collins was pouring poison into those emails. This shameful plot has managed to destroy lives. That's what is tragic,' she said.

There was an incredible amount of greed, callousness, deceit, dishonesty, manipulation, arrogance, hatred and love degenerating itself and corrupting itself into hatred, she said. 'All that glitters is not gold. Treachery lies in honeyed words.' She said there were 'almost farcical' events, plots and sub-plots. 'Ms Collins said to me, "You are out to get a conviction." That's wrong. That's not how the system works. Perhaps she has been watching too many American programmes or read too many American thrillers … Hard facts you have to try this case on.'

She said the existence of so much evidence wiped out the possibility of reasonable doubt. 'There is a feeling at times there's a triviality to this case because no-one was killed,' she said, adding, 'Ricin was found in the prison cell of Mr Eid. That takes this out of any idea of fantasy. He travelled to Ireland with one of the most deadly poisons, to kill Robert, Niall and their father and then changed his mind. No thanks to Ms Collins this case did not proceed.'

She said Collins had sent 'vicious' emails where she had speculated about staying with PJ Howard's body in Spain. 'This is the level of callousness we are dealing with. She used PJ's credit card to fly the assassin over and he wouldn't know, because he'd be dead,' she said. The jury had heard that on 19 September 2006, two US Airways flights to Ireland were charged to PJ Howard's American Express card. Accommodation with Alpha International was also booked on the card, all without his knowledge.

Telling the jury the State's case was that 'Mr Eid is 'hitman' [Tony Luciano] and Ms Collins is 'lyingeyes' she said the deception appeared to have started in late 2005, when Collins obtained a proxy marriage certificate online, without PJ's knowledge. 'Sharon Collins wants to marry PJ Howard. PJ Howard doesn't want to marry Sharon Collins. They were not married,' she said.

She reminded the jury that Sharon Collins's passport was damaged by water and she had to get a new one. She did this in the name Howard. 'Did she have to get one in the name Howard?' she asked. She said that Collins went to the passport office in Cork 'with her con job of a marriage certificate and gets a passport, perhaps a dry run to see if the marriage cert. would work in future, maybe I'm wrong'.

She said that Sharon Collins's decision to call RTÉ 2FM presenter Gerry Ryan to give evidence was done to feed her ego as his evidence did not bear any relevance. Mr Ryan was called to give evidence regarding an email that Sharon Collins sent to him, complaining about PJ Howard. Mr Ryan told the court he hadn't personally seen the email.

Counsel said that August 2006 was a key month. Lyingeyes98@yahoo.ie was set up on 2 August at 1.54 p.m., when Sharon Collins was in Ireland. An email was then sent from that email address to Sharon Collins's email account, sharoncollins @eircom.net. On 8 August, various searches were carried out on the internet, in between visits to lyingeyes98@yahoo.ie.

'She accepts an awful lot of things searched would be things she was interested in, travel plans, dieting, Reductil … ' said counsel. She said there was a lot of email activity between 10 and 16 August and there was no more internet activity after 16 August. She said that 'disgusting' flirtation slipped in to some of the emails between the 'lyingeyes' and 'hitman'. She said there were also several telephone calls between Collins's mobile and Eid's mobile. 'Look at the records. She made the calls. How is she going to get out of that? They must be in cahoots together,' she said. She stressed the importance of the email and phone charts, which were included among the exhibits in the case.

'I invite you to draw the inference she was chatting to him about his second mission. The first mission had failed. Teresa [Engle] and Ashraf [Gharbeiah] called at the end of August. Mission One fails. Mission Two: Essam Eid to come himself in late September and do the job himself,' she told the jury. She said the hiring was done in a 'very cold, very calculated and very businesslike' manner and the cold detail of the methods discussed was 'nauseating' and 'callous'.

'There was a lot of haggling over the price of these three lives,' she said. She pointed out that Collins had claimed she was being set up, but to do this, someone would have to get into the psychology of a mother, as the person writing the emails had made reference to spending quality time with her sons.

'She cleaned out her AIB account. She parcelled it up and sent it to a Camden Cove Street address. She says it was in response to blackmail. The Prosecution says it was the down payment for the hit. These two conspirators sitting across the court are talking about the down payment. It all hangs together perfectly,' she said.

'Most importantly the Iridium [computer] in the home of Sharon Collins is being accessed at midnight and at 8 a.m. If this mysterious person is setting her up, they are doing it in her own house. She doesn't recall anyone being in her house. She didn't give it [the tracking number for the FedEx package] to anyone in her what you'd call Howard entourage. Yet we have her at 8.10 a.m. on 16 August going into 'lyingeyes' and immediately afterwards checks the tracking number. She's caught in what we'd call a smoking gun. 'Lyingeyes' is checking the tracking number,' she said.

'Her smoking gun unfortunately is made up of digits. She can talk and talk and talk but she cannot explain that. It is impossible to explain unless that is 'lyingeyes'. She has to be 'lyingeyes', unless we're going to get ridiculous and suggest she hopped out for a cup of coffee and a mystery person hopped in,' she said. Ms Ní Raifeartaigh said Collins was 'caught red-handed' by inputting the FedEx tracking number as she was the only person—apart from the 'blackmailer'—to have the tracking number. 'Ludicrous, bizarre and ridiculous in the extreme,' she said.

Referring to John Keating's evidence, she remarked how he could remember what he was doing almost two years earlier. Mr Keating had told the trial he had spent the morning of 16 August 2006, with Collins, at a time when emails were sent by 'lyingeyes'. 'He may not be trying to mislead you. Maybe he's trying to do the best for someone in a tight spot. He likes her. They are friends. She put a lot of work his way,' she said. Counsel said that an Irish solider Brian Buckley received emails and telephone calls saying: 'We have intended targets, one in Spain and two in the west of Ireland.' 'That's Mr Eid seeing if he can get a local outsourcing of his hit. It's absurd. We're dealing with fools here, but they are dangerous fools,' she said.

She recalled how Teresa Engle had told the court that she and Eid had made the dangerous poison ricin at their home in Las Vegas, from a recipe off the internet. They then flew to Ireland where they went into the Downes and Howard office in Ennis. According to Engle, Eid was 'quite furious' when he couldn't get in touch with Sharon Collins. 'Then he decided to go to Robert and sell the contract. That's the turning point, when things started to go wrong for her. If she had answered, these two boys wouldn't be here right now and this would be a murder trial, not a conspiracy to murder trial, but thankfully Mr Eid had a short fuse,' she said, pointing to Robert and Niall Howard who sat two rows directly behind her in the courtroom.

She said that when Eid called to Robert Howard's home, Robert had a good opportunity to see what he looked like, having spoken to him on the doorstep for 20 minutes. After that visit, Robert had rung his father PJ, who had been in Spain with Collins at the time. 'The plan is starting to unravel and now, for the first time, she tells PJ Howard about Maria Marconi. This is the start of her covering her tracks,' said Ms Ní Raifeartaigh. She said that while Collins had uttered 'dark hints' and 'dark mutterings', she wouldn't even 'come out and accuse the obvious people' of setting her up.

As she continued with her closing speech, she recalled how Essam Eid was arrested across from the Queen's Hotel in Ennis on 27 September 2006 and later picked out by Robert and Niall Howard in an identification parade. She warned the jury on the evidence relating to the parade, 'identification evidence is fraile. People make mistakes. You are going to have to treat identification evidence with care and caution but you are entitled to use it as long as it is beyond reasonable doubt,' she warned.

Counsel then spoke about the discovery of the ricin in Essam Eid's cell in Limerick prison in April 2007. 'The defence will say there was no evidence how it got in there. Isn't it extraordinary we have reference to ricin in an email, Ms Engle describes how it was made and then it was found in Essam Eid's prison cell. It's no coincidence. Ricin is one of the most dangerous substances known. The Prosecution case is squarely, the scientific evidence is that this was ricin,' she said.

Ms Ní Raifeartaigh said the summary of the case against Eid was more brief than in the case against Collins. 'This is much simpler. It's overwhelming, open and shut,' she said. The main evidence against him was Teresa Engle's evidence, the identification parade, the items found in his hotel room and the forensic findings relating to the Toshiba laptop computer that had been taken from the Howards' family business and later returned to Robert Howard. She said the evidence presented during the trial pointed to Essam Eid as Tony Luciano who in turn was 'hitman'.

'It proves Essam Eid's intention to kill and not with a view to coming to Ireland to extort. If this was a shakedown, he would have come to Ireland without any ricin. He went to the bother of manufacturing the ricin. There was a very clear plan going on. There's an intention to kill coming out of those emails. If there was no intent to kill, why would he contact Brian Buckley?'

Ms Ní Raifeartaigh then told the jury there were 14 points which proved that Sharon Collins was 'lyingeyes'.

1. The person who sent the emails from the 'lyingeyes' account must have had access to all three computers used—the Advent computer at the Downes and Howard family business, the Iridium laptop which was located at PJ Howard and Sharon Collins's home [Ballybeg House] and the Toshiba laptop stolen from the Downes and Howard office.

2. Because of the times of usage of the three computers.

3. The content of the emails: sent by someone calling herself 'Sharon'.

4. The knowledge shown in the emails. According to the Prosecution, the sender had in-depth knowledge of the personal lives and movements of the Howards.

5. The language of the emails was similar to the letters Sharon Collins wrote to the DPP and her letter to the *Gerry Ryan Show*, for example the use of the words 'unbearable' and 'vulnerable'.

6. The consistency between the emails and the plan being carried out, for example the ricin, getting rid of the computers and references to keys and photographs.

7. The general user activity on the computer. Searches for weight loss, inheritance rights and kitchens were interwoven with searches for hitmen and assassins.

8. Because of the times of the user activity.

9. The consistency between Sharon Collins's movements and her emails.

10. The consistency between email activity and phone calls, particularly on 15 and 16 August, when the deal was being closed on the 'hit'.

11. The fact that there has been no sign of Maria Marconi on the computers indicated that Sharon Collins was 'lyingeyes'.

12. Sharon Collins's mother's maiden name, Cronin, was used, particularly on the application form on the 'hitman' website.

13. The fact that she made certain admissions in relation to the FedEx tracking number, for the €15,000 package she sent to Las Vegas, was the 'smoking gun', according to the Prosecution.

14. The user went in and out of the sharoncollins@eircom.net and lyingeyes98@yahoo.ie email accounts.

She urged the jury to take Collins's stories and examine them to see if they stood up. 'There are a couple of different ones going on at the same time … Maria Marconi is a complete figment of Sharon Collins's imagination,' she said.

In summing up her lengthy speech, Ms Ní Raifeartaigh told a tense courtroom that PJ Howard's affection, loyalty and trust yielded nothing more than deception, betrayal and public humiliation in response from Collins. Given the widespread media coverage on the RTÉ television news every night during the trial she asked, 'Can he ever go back to Ennis?' She said that Robert and Niall Howard were just starting out their lives. 'There lives were to be snuffed out because they just got in the way of Ms Collins's greed. Last of all and equally tragic, Ms Collins's two sons, sitting there day after day looking crushed, angry that these things be said about their mother. She has betrayed her own sons, made them unwitting allies in her own deceit. There's tragedy in all of this,' she said.

She concluded her speech with two lines from the Eagles' song 'Lyin' Eyes': 'You can't hide your lyin' eyes, and your smile is a thin disguise' and then quoted from Shakespeare, 'A man may smile and smile and be a villain.'

Shortly after Ms Ní Raifeartaigh sat down, having completed her closing speech, Collins's barrister Michael Bowman BL rose to his feet to deliver his speech. He said that his client maintained her innocent plea 'from beginning to end'. Mr Bowman said that on 2 October 2006, Sharon Collins first provided a statement to gardaí. 'She answered the questions. She pleaded not guilty [when she was later charged] and stood firm with that plea. Bear that in mind. I'd ask you to consider she took the witness box. She is not blind, not deaf, not dumb, she saw witness after witness taking the stand. She knew what was coming,' he said.

He noted that the jury had shown tremendous patience throughout the case and pointed out that the decisions on the charges should not be taken 'lightly or flippantly'.

He referred to phone records mentioned during the trial and pointed out that two phone calls had been made from Ballybeg

House to a number in California on the evening of 14 July 2006, when Sharon Collins was out of the country. 'Nobody took the time to pay any regard to parts of Ms Collins's story. No-one took the time to go through every phone call,' he said.

He said that phone calls were made from Ballybeg House to four phone numbers—PJ Howard's mobile number, Sharon Collins's Spanish mobile number, Gary Collins's mobile number and David Collins's mobile number—on 13 September 2006, adding 'all made at times Ms Collins and her entire family are in Spain. Clearly somebody has access to the house'.

He also remarked how an incoming us call—from Essam Eid's number—was made to the Howards' family business in Ennis on 23 August 2006, which lasted seven minutes. 'If there was an explanation consistent with the Prosecution it would have been introduced,' he said.

He then referred to the email evidence that had been introduced. He said that according to gardaí, the 'lyingeyes' email account was set up on 2 August 2006, at the office of the Howards' family business. 'To be without doubt, we must have Sharon Collins sitting in the office at that time, that day,' he said. However, he pointed out that she received a phone call from the office to her mobile phone at 10.50 a.m. that morning. 'The inference is Sharon Collins is not in the office at that stage,' he said. He said that Sharon Collins's mother phoned her on her mobile at 12.35 p.m. 'If the Prosecution is capable of analysis of cell site, why not retrieve information to tell us where she was? That hasn't been done. That's a critical part of the case. That's absent from the case,' he said.

Mr Bowman pointed out that the contents of an email sent from ennispeople06@yahoo.com to hire_hitman@yahoo.com on 17 August 2006 were identical to those in an email from lyingeyes98@yahoo.ie to hire_hitman@yahoo.com, later on the same date.

'It would appear somebody is sending a document from an address 'ennispeople' to 'hitman', specifically, with personal information on PJ and his sons, in the morning. The exact same document is sent from 'lyingeyes'. It would appear that information is within the knowledge of someone who is working nine hours ahead in the US,' said Mr Bowman.

He said that Ms Ní Raifeartaigh had used colourful language to describe Ms Collins, adding, 'but PJ Howard knows Sharon Collins for far longer than that. That is at variance to PJ's description of her.'

He said that the investigation was 'flawed'. 'Like a dog with a bone they [gardaí] picked up the idea and ran with it. Maybe we were delighted to be going back and forth to the US, working with the FBI. Nobody considered the alternative. Moloney [Detective Sergeant Michael Moloney] and Fahy [Detective Garda Jarlath Fahy] were the heavyweights brought in to crack this case and I don't mean that in any disparaging way,' he said.

He said that gardaí declined the opportunity to make a liar out of Sharon Collins in relation to the Maria Marconi story, particularly in relation to the tour of Clare that Collins claimed they had taken. 'I thought we were going to get cell site analysis. She told them chapter and verse … Prove it wrong … but that hasn't been done … Nobody took the time to go through the phone records with a ruler and a highlighter,' he said.

Mr Bowman stressed that PJ Howard had written to the Director of Public Prosecutions, on 23 March 2007, expressing concern about what was going on. In that letter, Mr Howard explained that he had known Collins for over eight years and had never known her to harm anyone. Mr Howard stated that she had helped him through his by-pass operation in 2000. 'I firmly believe Sharon should not be prosecuted. This was a scam by Essam Eid, Teresa Engle and Maria Marconi to extract money from Sharon,' PJ Howard had written in the letter.

The ricin element was also mentioned in Mr Bowman's closing speech. He pointed out that when Limerick prison was searched for ricin, everybody was 'dressed to the nines in spacesuits'. Yet, when the army officer, retired Commandant PJ Butler was handed the contact lens case, he was only wearing 'rubber gloves and no mask. You and I wear Marigold gloves washing the dishes. This is third most dangerous substance known to mankind! …'

He said that FBI agent Ingrid Sotelo went to Eid's house in Las

Vegas, where she took photographs of acetone drums, but didn't consider taking photographs of what was believed to be ricin. 'Agent Sotelo did absolutely nothing,' he commented. He said the ricin had taken on an importance in the case, to which it was not entitled.

He told the jury that the evidence from John Keating was crucial in the overall case and his heart went out to him. He said that Mr Keating had made a passing reference to something and a cell site analysis had been carried out by gardaí, as a result. Mr Keating, he said, was a 'microcosym' or a 'snapshot' of the case as a whole. He said that while he was a prosecution witness, when he said something that could be advantageous to the defence, 'no expense was spared to tear the man asunder, but he was resilient'.

'John Keating is a man who you can believe, a man who you can trust. It puts a question mark over the integrity of all the other evidence. If John Keating is an honest man, and I believe he is, he has been treated appallingly,' he said.

He said that after giving evidence to the trial on 5 June, Mr Keating was taken aside and questioned for over three hours by gardaí. 'He was asked to make a statement. He was questioned and questioned about this. He got a good dose of garda company,' he said. He said that Mr Keating's records were taken by gardaí, who sought to prove him a liar.

'The Prosecution case, while it appears comprehensive, it's not so. You cannot be sure Ms Collins did anything alleged by the Prosecution. She says she has been put through hell and back. Her family has been torn asunder. She's been pilloried in the community, ridiculed in the media. There's a momentum in this case almost free-wheeling to a conviction, which you cannot allow to happen. Put the breaks on,' he urged the jury.

'If she's guilty, as the day is long and she stood up and humiliated herself and her two sons, PJ Howard and his two sons, why on earth would she not plead guilty? You have to look long and hard at the facts,' he said. He urged the jury not to 'slavishly' accept the computer evidence, adding, 'I am asking you to look at the inconsistencies found in the Prosecution case. Nobody paid any attention to Sharon Collins's story.'

Sharon Collins, leaving the Four Courts, on the first day of the trial, Wednesday, 21 May 2008. (*Courtpix*)

The three targets of the murder plot Niall Howard (*left*), Robert Howard (*right*) and their father PJ Howard (*background*) arrive at the Four Courts on the first day of the trial, Wednesday, 21 May 2008. (*Courtpix*)

Chief Prosecution witness Teresa Engle, who told the trial that she had manufactured the deadly poison ricin with her husband Essam Eid at their Las Vegas home, before bringing it to Ireland in a contact lens case. (*Stephen Collins/Collins*)

Multimillionaire businessman PJ Howard, leaving the Four Courts, after giving evidence in the trial. Mr Howard told the court the allegations against Collins did not make sense. He kissed her fondly in open court, after he had stepped down from the witness box. (*Courtpix*)

Ballybeg House; PJ Howard's plush home, located on Kildysart Road, on the outskirts of Ennis. Sharon Collins moved into the house in December 1998 and it became her home for over eight years. (*Press 22*)

Sharon Collins arrives at the Four Courts, with her sons Gary (*left*) and David (*right*) on the second last day of the trial, Tuesday, 8 July 2008. (*Courtpix*)

Sharon Collins, leaving the Four Courts with her solicitor Eugene O'Kelly, on the second last day of the trial, Tuesday, 8 July 2008. (*Courtpix*)

A smiling Essam Eid, leaving court after the second day of deliberations, Tuesday, 8 July 2008. (*Courtpix*)

Sharon Collins's two sons Gary (*left*) and David (*right*) with their father Noel Collins (Sharon Collins's former husband) awaiting the jury's verdicts. They are pictured outside the Four Courts building, on Tuesday, 8 July 2008. (*Courtpix*)

Detective Sergeant Michael Moloney, who was one of the chief investigators in the case. He is based at Ennis Garda Station, Co. Clare. (*Courtpix*)

Sharon Collins is escorted to a prison van to be brought to the women's section of Mountjoy prison, after being found guilty of soliciting and conspiracy to murder her partner PJ Howard and his two sons Robert and Niall, on Wednesday, 9 July 2008. (*Courtpix*)

Sharon Collins's solicitor Eugene O'Kelly appeals for privacy for his client's two sons Gary and David in the immediate aftermath of the conclusion of the trial, Wednesday, 9 July 2008. The boys' father Noel Collins is in the background. (*Courtpix*)

Mr Justice Roderick Murphy, who presided over the trial of Sharon Collins and Essam Eid, at the Central Criminal Court, from 21 May to 9 July 2008. (*Courtpix*)

Army Private Brian Buckley, leaving court on Friday, 13 June, after giving evidence at the trial of Sharon Collins and Essam Eid. (*Courtpix*)

Mr Bowman's 99-minute speech brought to an end an emotional day. It was just before 5.30 p.m. on that Thursday when the day's proceedings were brought to a close and as the case was nearing a conclusion, courtroom number 2 was filled with tension and anticipation. As two jurors had made it known to the court that they were going on holidays during the following week, the end was in sight and the possibility of sitting on Saturday, 5 July, was mooted, but four or five jurors had difficulty with this due to prior commitments and it did not materialise.

The court sat 30 minutes early, at around 10.30 a.m., on Friday, 4 July, to hear David Sutton SC make his closing speech on behalf of Essam Eid. Mr Sutton raised his strong voice a number of times during his 57-minute speech. He began by referring to the charges that the jury had to decide on and then spoke about the identification of Eid in an identification parade. 'Robert Howard answered the door to a man, a man he never saw before. He had a conversation with him. A request was made for money, indicating there was a contract on his life and his brother's life and his father's life. That is the arrival at what the Prosecution says is Mr Eid. Niall Howard was looking out the side door. The Prosecution has to establish that this was Mr Eid. To do so, they have to rely on the witnesses that were there. Mr Howard simply mis-described that person. This is the opening shot in their [the State's] case against Mr Eid. One of the most basic building blocks of a criminal trial is identification and that's where the case against Mr Eid starts and where it might end,' he said.

Mr Sutton said the Prosecution had claimed there was nobody else apart from Sharon Collins who could have sent the 'lyingeyes' emails, but 'The State has never said there was anybody other than Tony Luciano who sent those messages'. He said, 'No-one was there to murder anybody. They were there to do a shakedown, nothing else, and in Ms Engle's case, the same went on in California.' Noting that no charge of conspiracy to murder was brought in the US, he said, 'Maybe the FBI take a more hard-nosed approach and they don't get carried away.'

Mr Sutton said the ricin evidence was 'dramatic' and the tip-off in relation to it 'I assume came from Teresa Engle'. 'Mr Eid denies ricin. How did the contact lens case get there? It's the prison. They check things coming in and out of the prison. There is no evidence of any amount of ricin that could kill anybody and if there was I'm sure we'd hear all about that. They [the State] know in their heart of hearts that what was going on here was a shakedown. What was going on here was soliciting, not a conspiracy. They know that the conspiracy to murder charge is a bridge too far. Simple as that and nothing Teresa Engle would say could change that. She says the intention was murder. She hasn't a notion as to how this murder was to happen,' said Mr Sutton.

He said the jury had to be satisfied that Eid was there at all and that he was Tony Luciano, which he was disputing. 'I say that evidence is not there and it cannot be welded together by self-serving perjury … I say it was a fraud operation from start to finish. It wasn't dial M for murder. It was dial M for money,' he said. He said that senior counsel for the Prosecution, Tom O'Connell presented a 'long and enthusiastic' opening speech, but the evidence in the case was 'inconsistent'.

And that was it. It was 11.44 a.m. on Friday, 4 July 2008 and all of the closing speeches had been heard. The task was now left to the trial judge, Mr Justice Murphy, to sum up the evidence and charge the jury. This got underway immediately and continued throughout the day, finishing after 4.30 p.m. He resumed the lengthy process on Monday morning, 7 July and given the huge amount of evidence, it was no surprise that it took more than six hours for him to complete the charge.

He spent most of this time recapping the evidence that had been presented during the case. In the early part of his speech, the forewoman of the jury requested that his words be more audible—the judge's quiet tone contrasted sharply with the speaker immediately before him, Mr Sutton. The judge quickly addressed the matter, before advising the jury of eight men and four women to concentrate on the 'technical' and 'complex' evidence in the case. The issue of identification had been raised several times during the trial and the judge said it was important for the jury to consider identification through all of the evidence that had been offered during the case.

'Evidence against one is not evidence against the other. It's a matter of fact, not of emotion. You've got to set aside your feelings in relation to your views on alleged actions by any of the parties. Consider the evidence as coldly, as dispassionately and objectively as you can. Leave aside all your prejudices and deal with the facts,' he urged the jury.

On the previous Friday, prior to the deliberations resuming, the jury had raised a query on the conspiracy to murder charges and immediately prior to sending the jury out on Monday afternoon, the judge said he wished to clarify this matter.

'The matter is simple at one level and a little bit more complex when you get down to it. It takes at least two to conspire. One would have thought it followed logic. If there is a failure to prove against one, automatically there is a failure to prove against the other. Be careful in some cases that there is some evidence against one and not evidence against the other. I don't want to complicate the matter a little bit more than is necessary,' said the judge.

He told the jury that where there is a doubt, the benefit of that doubt must be given to the accused.

As the judge concluded his charge to the jury, a pale-faced Sharon Collins wrapped her arm tightly around her youngest son David. The end was near and the trauma was clearly visible on her face. It was 3.44 p.m. when the jury finally retired from the courtroom to begin its deliberations—deliberations that were to take 11 hours, over three days, before the curtain was drawn on the trial.

For Sharon Collins, her two sons, her former husband Noel Collins and his wife Fiona, the tension was palpable, while Essam Eid showed no sign of the strain that was in evidence on his co-accused's face. It became a case of standing room only in the courtroom as gardaí and legal personnel involved in the case, interested onlookers and an increasing posse of journalists packed closely together in the near suffocating conditions. But the judge's task had not been completed as barristers for both Collins and Eid were quickly on their feet, immediately after the jury left the courtroom to begin deliberating.

First up was Paul O'Higgins, sc for Collins, who said he had a
number of requisitions to make. He said it was his case that the
court had not adequately charged the jury and he had several
points to make in relation to this. He said the warning in relation
to accomplices—which had been given to the jury by the judge—
was insufficiently strong, particularly in relation to Teresa Engle,
who still faced sentence in the us. 'She has an unusually strong
vested interest as an accomplice and the jury should be warned
about that. It is dangerous to convict on the uncorroborated
evidence of an accomplice,' said Mr O'Higgins.

He also said the difference between the standards of proof in
civil and criminal cases should have been made clear to the jury.
Among the other points he had raised was the issue of how the
court dealt with conspiracy, in the judge's charge. 'It doesn't deal
with the fact the jury should be told it is all or nothing,' he said.

He also raised the soliciting charges and the way that issue had
been presented to the jury. 'If the jury entertained a reasonable
doubt, for example, that Sharon Collins had talked to Essam Eid
but didn't realise it, had talked to a phone number, if the jury felt
there was a reasonable doubt it was Teresa Engle or Ashraf
Gharbeiah or a combination of either of them, is that reasonable
for the jury? I [Sharon Collins] can't in those circumstances be
convicted of soliciting Essam Eid and the jury hasn't been told
that at all. It's absolutely critical the jury understand that to be so,'
said Mr O'Higgins.

Michael Collins, BL for Eid, then raised a number of issues on
behalf of his client. He said that his client had exercised his right
to silence, by not giving evidence in the trial and it was important
to point out to the jury that he was not obliged to give evidence.
He also made reference to the evidence given to the trial by Teresa
Engle. 'There was no evidence to suggest Teresa Engle was
pressurised, but she has a vested interest. The bones of her
evidence have a bearing on her sentence in the us. She told bare-
faced lies. The court has to specifically give an accomplice
warning to the jury,' said Mr Collins.

After the defence had made their requisitions, the jury requested the exhibits in the case and also sought a cigarette break. This was almost an hour-and-a-half after it had began deliberating. After returning from their break, at 5.40 p.m., Mr Justice Murphy said he would not leave the jurors deliberating too late that evening. He said he would like to give them a little more opportunity to deliberate and asked were there any questions. There were no questions and the jury resumed its deliberations at that stage.

Senior counsel for the Prosecution Tom O'Connell then replied to the defence requisitions. He started by remarking, 'I've never heard of defence requisitions that have gone on for nearly two hours and I've been nearly 35 years at the bar.' He then referred to comments made in relation to Teresa Engle and pointed out that the sentencing court in the us was not bound by any agreement entered into by Teresa Engle and the FBI and the jury had been told that.

At 6.58 p.m., the jury was recalled and was sent to a hotel for the night. Mr Justice Murphy told them he would recharge them in the morning on matters. 'Relax this evening. Don't bother deliberating. Relax and have a drink as well. You are entitled to that at this stage,' the judge told the weary looking jury, before they left the courtroom at 7.05 p.m.

The courtroom emptied and the tension subsided for the evening, but for the two defendants, the waiting continued, even when the last individual had left the Four Courts that night.

The huge sense of anticipation was in evidence again the following morning, Tuesday, 8 July, as verdicts were expected to emerge at some stage during that day. Sharon Collins's weary, gaunt face was dotted with tears from time to time throughout the day, but Essam Eid's chirpy attitude continued to prevail. The media presence had expanded to more than 20 personnel as newspapers, television and radio stations had increased their resources for the closing stages. This was no major surprise as it has become the norm in high-profile sensational trials in recent years.

At 10.22 a.m., Mr Justice Murphy addressed the jury on a

number of issues that had been raised by counsel for the accused the previous evening. He firstly made reference to the difference between civil proof and proof in criminal cases. 'In the vast majority of cases we are dealing with in the Four Courts, we are dealing with civil cases, where proof is on the balance of probabilities. From the point of view of criminal cases, you are required a much greater standard of proof, that is beyond reasonable doubt. The jury must be satisfied beyond reasonable doubt of the guilt of the accused. The accused is entitled to the benefit of the doubt,' he said.

He also made reference to the solicitation and conspiracy to murder charges. 'You have to distinguish between agreement between both accused and the solicitation as well between those two parties,' he said. He also spoke about corroboration, telling the jury it should 'exercise special care when an accomplice has been granted immunity from prosecution'.

At that stage, the forewoman of the jury sought a number of exhibits. She requested the taped interviews of Sharon Collins at Ennis Garda Station, photographs of the interior of Essam Eid's home in Las Vegas, PJ Howard's letter to the DPP (written in March 2007, suggesting that Ms Collins should not be charged), the ricin test results and the Advent computer which had been taken from the Howards' family business and later found at the rear of the Two Mile Inn hotel in Limerick. The jury was sent to the jury room while these requests were discussed by the judge and the legal teams. At 11 a.m., Mr Justice Murphy recalled the jury and told them there was no difficulty with regard to the tapes and a monitor would be set up in the jury room for them to view them. However, he said the photographs weren't introduced in evidence and therefore had no status. He said that PJ Howard's letter to the DPP hadn't been brought into evidence either. 'There has been reference to that, just the one line, but that wasn't put in evidence either. That isn't a matter that should trouble you, other than the one line,' he said. He said the ricin test results and the Advent computer would be supplied to the jury.

The deliberations resumed and apart from a number of breaks, continued throughout the day. At 4.10 p.m., the judge told the jury, 'Take your time. If you need another day, so be it.' At that stage, the forewoman asked for Essam Eid's wife Lisa's 'PayPal', the account on which the castor beans—allegedly used in the manufacture of the ricin poison in Las Vegas—was purchased, via the internet. The jury was told by the judge that no documentation in relation to this had been introduced during the trial. Mr Justice Murphy said that this had been referred to by us Agent Ingrid Sotelo during her evidence, adding 'that's all we have. That's all we do know.'

The forewoman of the jury then said the 'PayPal' date was sought. The judge pointed out that there had not been evidence of a date and he read Agent Sotelo's evidence in relation to the 'PayPal'.

As the day wore on, speculation mounted about the outcome of the case. Was the jury undecided on all charges or were there issues in relation to some of them? Or simply, was this a thorough jury prepared to sift through every shred of evidence? They had deliberated for over five hours at that stage, after being been recharged earlier that morning.

At 7.05 p.m., Mr Justice Murphy recalled the jury and sent them to a hotel for the second night. With two jurors due to go on holidays on Thursday, it was virtually certain that the case would come to a close the following day, Wednesday, 9 July.

Sharon Collins arrived in court that morning in a black pin-striped suit, similar to one she had worn throughout the trial. She donned a round-necked low cut white top and a silver chain with a cross. The anxiousness that had crept in on her face as the trial wore on was very apparent on this particular morning. The tension that had built up over the previous 31 days of the trial had clearly taken its toll.

The jury resumed deliberating at 10.10 a.m. that morning and was sent to lunch at 1 p.m. The judge indicated that he would give them the option of a majority decision at 2.15 p.m. And it was at this stage that the fireworks began to emerge. At 2.19 p.m., the jury was asked had verdicts been reached on any counts, on

which all 12 members had agreed. The forewoman replied, 'Yes.'
They all trudged back into the jury room to fill out the issue
paper and after an extremely anxious six minutes, at 2.22 p.m.,
they returned and the verdicts were read out:

Count Number Four: Sharon Collins Guilty.
Count Number Five: Sharon Collins Guilty.
Count Number Six: Sharon Collins Guilty.
Count Number Seven: Essam Eid Guilty.
Count Number Eight: Essam Eid Not Guilty.
Count Number Nine: Essam Eid Guilty.
Count Number Ten: Essam Eid Guilty.

One thing was clear: it was immediately apparent that counts
numbers four, five and six referred to the charges of soliciting.
Sharon Collins had been found guilty of soliciting Essam Eid to
murder PJ, Robert and Niall Howard, within the jurisdiction of
the Central Criminal Court, on 15 August 2006, while Essam Eid
had been found guilty of demanding €100,000 from Robert
Howard, to cancel a contract on his life and the lives of his father
PJ and brother Niall, at Ballaghboy, Doora, Ennis, on 26
September 2006.

The jury had not decided on the conspiracy to murder charges
against both accused.

As those involved in the case fumbled with pages to clarify exactly
what Eid had been found guilty of, all eyes were on Collins. What
would her reaction be? But there was no instant explosion of
emotion. She looked straight ahead of her and held the serious
expression she had maintained throughout the day. It was her
two doting sons Gary and David who showed instant emotion
and broke down within minutes of the verdicts emerging. Her
eldest son Gary just bowed his head down and held it in his
hands, rooted to his seat. It was the mother who was consoling
her sons as an emotional, tearful David rose to his feet and
hugged her.

As the jury was sent away to continue deliberating on the

remaining three charges, Collins's former husband Noel and his wife Fiona quickly made their way over to console the woman who had just been convicted of three charges. As the gravity of events hit her moments later, Collins began to cry, quietly, but the fact that three of the charges were still being considered meant that any grand finale was put on hold, temporarily.

Seated yards to Collins's left was Essam Eid who sat back and smiled as the verdicts were relayed to the court. As he spoke to his solicitor John Casey, it became clear that the charge on which he had been acquitted was the burglary allegation, at the Howards' family business, Downes and Howard Ltd, Unit 7A, Westgate Business Park, Kilrush Road, Ennis, on 25 September 2006. Along with the extortion charge, Eid had also been found guilty of two counts of handling stolen property.

At 3.05 p.m. the waiting was over for Sharon Collins as the jury announced it had reached a decision on one defendant, in relation to the conspiracy to murder charges:

Count Number One: Sharon Collins Guilty.
Count Number Two: Sharon Collins Guilty.
Count Number Three: Sharon Collins Guilty.

Sharon Collins turned white, matching the top she was wearing.

Over the previous 32 days, the court had seen a smiling Sharon, a tearful Sharon, a pale Sharon, a pretty Sharon, an emotional Sharon, a sad Sharon, a confident Sharon and a Sharon who clearly doted on her two boys. And now this. Convicted on all six charges she had faced and a stint behind bars inevitable. David Collins put his arm around her and left it there for several minutes as the realisation of what had just unfolded began to set in. Gary, as he had done less than an hour earlier, again buried his head in his hands.

The emotion took its toll too on the jurors as three of the four female jurors burst into tears. The tension that had built up over the previous eight weeks began to evaporate. But the jury's job was not yet out of the way. They still had to decide if Essam Eid was guilty on the three conspiracy to murder charges and was sent back to the jury room to continue deliberating.

Tom O'Connell rose to his feet to suggest that Collins be remanded in custody. 'Now that Ms Collins is a convicted person she should be remanded in custody,' he said.

Paul O'Higgins then asked for the court to certify for psychological reports for her. He said there would be no danger of his client not turning up for her sentencing hearing.

However, Mr O'Connell was adamant, 'Her status has now changed. She is a convicted person. She has been convicted of very serious crimes. My application is to have her remanded in custody,' he said.

Mr Justice Murphy noted that the application was for Collins's status to 'remain as is, on bail' but refused this. 'There is no necessity for someone to be on bail for psychological reports. It does seem to me that the status of the first named defendant has changed by virtue of the jury's decision this afternoon. Therefore I refuse your application. I certify for a psychological report.'

Mr O'Higgins sought the sentencing to be adjourned until a date the following term. Collins remained without emotion as she sat still between her two sons in the stuffy courtroom as the jury was given the option of returning a majority decision—10:2 or 11:1—on the three remaining charges, at 4.25 p.m.

At 5.16 p.m., Eid's barrister Michael Collins BL argued that the jury should be told it was entitled to disagree on the remaining charges against his client. 'The forewoman already indicated they are not able to reach a verdict, majority or unanimous. I'd be very concerned undue pressure is being brought to bear on the jury. They should be entitled to disagree,' he said. However Mr O'Connell said one should not underestimate the intelligence of the jury. 'The jury should know it can disagree,' he said. At 5.30 p.m., Mr Justice Murphy enquired of the jury had at least 10 of its members agreed on any count and was told, 'No.' He then told them they were entitled to disagree.

Then, at 5.40 p.m., with the amount of time spent deliberating fast reaching 11 hours, verdicts of disagreement were recorded in relation to the three conspiracy to murder charges Essam Eid had been accused of.

Sharon Collins sat arm-in-arm with her two sons and Essam Eid continued to portray a relaxed composure as the judge thanked the jury for its patience and diligence throughout the case. 'The court appreciates the role you have played and the way you have played that role. You've been involved in a complex case, because of the complexities of new technology, phones, emails, text messages, also in relation to scientific evidence it has been complex,' he said and excused all 12 jurors from jury service for 20 years.

Eid's barrister David Sutton SC then asked for free legal aid to cover medical reports for his client and this was granted. Mr Justice Murphy said that the matter of disagreement on the three charges was a matter for the DPP. He remanded both accused in custody until 8 October when the sentence date would be mentioned. Mr O'Higgins then asked for Collins to be remanded to Mountjoy women's prison, rather than Limerick prison. He said this was to ensure she was near her two sons who live in Dublin and also to facilitate the preparation of psychological reports. The judge said that was a matter for the State, but the court would be happy to make such a recommendation.

Finally, the drama was over and the nailbiting wait had come to an end. The trial, which at times looked like it would run into the summer recess, had come to a conclusion. The packed courtroom slowly emptied out. The members of the public who had attended daily—they had grown substantially in number as the trial had gone on—had enjoyed what they saw. They came equipped every day. One woman had arrived with her flask of tea, while a man flicked through the pages of *The People versus Catherine Nevin*—a book written by Liz Walsh on the Catherine Nevin trial.

Like Collins, Nevin was another woman convicted of soliciting to kill. (Nevin was jailed for seven years in 2000 for hiring three men to murder her husband Tom in 1989 and 1990. Nevin was also jailed for life for murdering her husband at Jack White's Inn,

Co. Wicklow, in 1996. Nevin was only the second person in Ireland to be convicted of soliciting to murder. Gort man Patrick Gillane was jailed for eight years in December 1997 for soliciting two men to murder his wife Philomena in 1994. The body of Philomena, who was pregnant, was found in the boot of a car at the railway station in Athlone on 18 May 1994, a week after she was reported missing. Nobody has ever been convicted of her murder.)

Collins said her tearful goodbyes to her sons and her ex-husband, while a relaxed Eid chatted to prison officers. The two were led away to prison vans, which quickly transported them away from the Four Courts. The ink had barely been dry on the issue paper on which the verdicts were written when PR consultant Caimin Jones issued a statement on behalf of the Howards. It was a short statement, in which privacy was sought. 'We are relieved that this long trial has come to a conclusion and we would like to express our appreciation to the members of the jury for their patience and attention. It is also appropriate to record our gratitude to the many people who have assisted us during this difficult period. We now look forward to getting on with our lives and we request the privacy that's necessary to assist us in this respect. It is not our intention to make any further statement.'

While Eid's solicitor John Casey declined to comment, saying it was inappropriate to say anything until after the sentencing, Collins's solicitor Eugene O'Kelly chose to make a statement outside the precincts of the Four Courts. Standing alongside a visibly upset pair of brothers—Gary and David Collins—and Sharon Collins's ex-husband Noel Collins, Mr O'Kelly appealed for privacy. 'Sharon Collins has maintained her innocence in this trial. The jury has found her guilty. The judge has adjourned sentencing for the preparation of reports. Accordingly, in relation to the verdict, it's inappropriate to comment any further at this stage. I would like to say that the two persons that are most affected, other than Sharon, as a result of this verdict, are her two sons. These are two fine young men that have displayed loyalty, devotion and love for their mother. They have stood by her in this trial and their lives have now been shattered as a result of the outcome. I would ask that they would be afforded respect and privacy so that they can adjust to the changed circumstances. These circumstances are entirely not of their making and they now have to move on and I would ask that you would afford them the privacy and space so that they can do this with dignity,' he said.

And with that, the solicitor and the three grieving men walked back into the grounds of the Four Courts, without the woman who had confidently walked in those very gates every morning for 32 days. As Sharon Collins was driven away in a prison van, her two devastated sons began to contemplate life without their mother, to whom they were extremely attached.

08 | REVEALED: THE
WEB OF DECEIT

Given the nature of the case, the emails were crucial in identifying what exactly had happened and how lyingeyes98@yahoo.ie had crossed paths with hire_hitman@yahoo.com. Several computers, notably three in Ireland and two in the US, were analysed as part of the investigation and this was crucial in cracking the case.

From the moment prosecutor Tom O'Connell began to deliver his sensational opening speech in the trial on 22 May 2008, the case was always going to be centered on email evidence. Yet, nobody could have prepared for the cold, callous and specific nature of the emails in which Sharon Collins addressed the issue of killing her partner and his two sons.

According to information given to the FBI by 'yahoo', the email address hire_hitman@yahoo.com was set up by a man calling himself Tony Luciano on 3 June 2006, at 5.23.47 a.m. GMT. It was the Prosecution case that lyingeyes98@yahoo.ie was set up on 2 August 2006 by Sharon Collins, on an Advent computer at the Howards' family business, Downes and Howard Ltd, Ennis, where Collins was a part-time receptionist.

Throughout the trial, the jury heard extracts from the various emails and a chart of the email traffic was given to the jury as an exhibit during its deliberations. A representative of 'yahoo' did not give evidence during the trial and this resulted in about ten per cent of the emails not going to the jury.

Gardaí believe that the recovery of the email evidence, allied to phone records showing over 70 phone calls between phones related to Collins and Eid, was significant in ensuring a breakthrough in the case.

The following emails between lyingeyes98@yahoo.ie and hire_hitman@yahoo.com were at the centre of the case and were retrieved from computers in Ireland and America.

Date: Tuesday, 8 August 2006. 3.44 p.m.
From: lyingeyes98@yahoo.ie
To: hire_hitman@yahoo.com
Retrieved from a printout in a folder beside a computer at Essam Eid's home in Las Vegas.

Email contents:

Name: S. Cronin
Phone: 00 353 86 xxxxxxx
Contact time: within the next 15 hours
Comments: 2 male marks in Ireland. Asap. Usually together. Mu like accident. Then possibly a third within 24 hours. Prefera like suicide. Would appreciate a call by return.

Date: Not listed
From: hire_hitman@yahoo.com
Retrieved from the Iridium laptop at Ballybeg House

Email contents:

I got your email. We will call you within 30 mints … can you e-mail us back with more info before we call

Date: Not listed

From: lyingeyes98@yahoo.ie

Retrieved from the Iridium laptop at Ballybeg House

Email contents:

Hi.

We were just talking. As you can imagine, I am extremely nervous about sending this message and even talking on the phone.

There are actually three, but two of them would probably be together and the third would not be in Ireland he would be in Spain.

I don't want to give you the names of the people involved just yet, but, I will give you the location and, tell you what I want—ideally.

The first two, live in Ireland, as I said. The town they live in is Ennis, Co. Clare in the west of the country. They are brothers, one aged 27 (big guy) and 23 (not so big). They share a house, at present, but there are two others living in the house as well.

They work in the same place and spend a lot of time together. I do not want it to look like a hit. This is important. I want it to look like an accident—perhaps travelling in a car together or in a boat (they do a lot of boating) off the west coast. Or maybe you have some ideas of your own.

The third is an older man—aged 57 and not very fit or strong. He would probably be in mainland Spain, if not in Ireland. His location would depend on when the job could be done. Again, it is imperative that it does not look like a hit. I would prefer suicide—or is it possible for it to look like natural causes? He's got a lot of health problems.

What I need to know is:

How soon could the above be done? Days, weeks, months? If the first job is done in Ireland, is it possible for the second job to be done within 12—24 hours in Spain if that's where he is?

How much would it cost and how much of a deposit would be needded up front? I ask this because, I would have no problem getting my hands on the money immediately afterwards, but it certainly would be very tricky beforehand.

Can it be done in the manner I've stated—without causing suspicion?

Most importantly, if a deposit must be paid—how do I know that you would not disappear with the money and not do the job? After all, who could I complain to?

Where are you located?—Just curious about that.

It might be easier to email back for now. I'm not comfortable talking about it on the phone—even though this phone is unregistered and not used for anything else. I may get a chance to email you again within the next hour, but I will be tied up tomorrow for approx 3 days.

Date: Tuesday, 8 August 2006. 3.13 p.m.
From: hire_hitman@yahoo.com
To: lyingeyes98@yahoo.ie
Retrieved from the Iridium laptop at Ballybeg House

Email contents:

I got your email and I agree with you about the phone and everytime you e-mail me deleted it … i will email you tonight and give you an answer … We have people all over the world in irland and spain too. Just take a day tile contact them … if not I have people from uk too … so, now that's my problem not you … i will contact you asap … let you know all info … But the most we have to trust eash other … If these people related to you try don't contact them and go away from them …

Date: Tuesday, 8 August 2006. 11.11 p.m.
From: hire_hitman@yahoo.com
To: lyingeyes98@yahoo.ie
Retrieved from the Iridium laptop at Ballybeg House

Email contents:

Hello, well: we discues about your situation and we assume that these people is your 2 stepson and your husband … maybe we are right and maybe we are wrong … its important tho know that to protect you and protect ourself too … for your safty if that so … we can do 2 male first and after cool off we will do the third one … If that right tell us who the most beneficial to you we can do it first …

Now for all your question that you ask us earlier…our price per person is $50000 USD … but cause 3 bird in one stone it will be $90,000 USD … before we start we have to have a deposit of $45,000 USD … you have a choice of fedex money order or cashier check or you can transfer the money to our bank …

If we agree we can finish or job Sat Aug 19. Either one of them the 2 guse or the third person … When we get the money we will process and our experience do what the best for both party … You get your money back if we are failed or we didn't do the job … But if you cancelled your deposit is non refund … I guess we answer all your questions … just tell us more info about our target
Thanks
Tony Luciano

Date: Not listed
From: hire_hitman@yahoo.com
To: lyingeyes98@yahoo.ie
Retrieved from Iridium laptop at Ballybeg House

Email contents:

Let me know if you got our msg … if you agree or not

Date: Not listed
From: lyingeyes98@yahoo.ie
To: hire_hitman@yahoo.com
Retrieved from Iridium laptop at Ballybeg House

Email contents:

Hi Tony,

Yes I got the message, but only just now—ive been away and had no access to the internet. Obviously, at this stage, I realise you probably would nt be able to get the job done by 18th August.

Anyway, you are right about my relationship to the men in question. I know it must seem terrible of me, but my backs to the wall and I don't have much choice. I would prefer it if it was just my husband, but because of the way he has arranged his affairs, it would be way too complicated if his sons were still around and I'd still be in much the same situation as I am now.

Regarding payment. The price you quoted seems very fair, and I would gladly pay it, but I will have to give some thought on how to come up with the deposit. I could put my hand on it, in cash immediately, but the two sons would see it gone and would know it was me and that would cause too many problems for me. I'll have to try to borrow it and that will take a little time. Im not even sure that I will get it—I don't have any assets of my own to borrow against, but I'll certainly give it a go.

Now, you said in your message that you'd leave a cooling off period between the first two and my husband. How long are you thinking of? I'll tell you the way I was thinking. My husband is in spain and lives on the top floor of a tall building while he's there. If he were to hear that his sons had a fatal accident—he might suddenly feel suicidal and just jump off the building. Is that too far fetched do you think? Otherwise, he would find out about the missing money (if I try using that) and if I borrow it from the local bank (the only place id have a chance of getting it) he'd hear that too and put two and two together. Its very parochial here. My husband is very friendly with the bank manager and they talk a lot. Another thing, ill have to look into is the cashiers cheque or bank draft. There's a record kept here of anything over a certain amount—Im not sure if its 5K or 10K, but I assume I could send few drafts. Id be worried that if the cops got suspicious, though, and looked into it, I wouldn't have answers. Do you know if cash can be parcelled up and Fed Ex safely?

I have to go to Spain next week—my husband is putting me under pressure to join him and I must try to keep him happy for now, while I figure things out.

You quoted in USD, so I assume the money goes to the US and then the guy or guys doing the job get their cut from there. I'm saying this, just in case it would be possible to give you the location of cash to be picked up after each job is done. Is there any chance of that, do you think? It would be very uncomplicated for me in that situation. I could go ahead with it straight away.

The other thing I need to know is, if its possible for it to look like an accident and not a hit?

I look forward to hearing from you.

S.

Date: Friday, 11 August 2006. 12.12 p.m.

From: hire_hitman@yahoo.com

To: lyingeyes98@yahoo.ie

Retrieved from the Iridium laptop at Ballybeg House and a printout in a folder beside a computer at Essam Eid's home in Las Vegas.

Email contents:

We have already reservation at hotel called greenhills at ennis rd limsrick, the 18 aug but we will do it the 19 ... we deside to send 2 woman and a man to do that job and I will do third one myself in spain … we will poison the two guys we will used the 2 woman to get close to them … about the money you cant send cash but you can got to any other bank not your and make cashier check and send it

And we have to have deposit before I give my order to my people to do the job … Im here in US but my people the man from German and one woman from Ireland and other woman Romania … if you have any question e-mail me or I can call you if you want … thanks
Tony Luciano

Date: Not listed
From: lyingeyes98@yahoo.ie
To: hire_hitman@yahoo.com
Retrieved from the Iridium laptop at Ballybeg House

Email contents:

Thanks for getting back to me so fast. Wow. Im a bit scared, to be honest.

The two guys here usually go to a place called Kilkee on the West coast of clare, each weekend. They've got a holiday home there. They usually have friends with them and they younger one usually has his girlfriend with him. The older guy (27) broke up with this girlfriend a couple of months ago and might be open to being chatted up etc. I think he has been dating lately, but I don't know yet if be might . bring that girl with him. I can find out, but it will be Monday before I will see him—it would be two suspicious for me to ring him over the weekend to ask.

They drink in a bar called the Greyhound Bar on the main street in Kilkee. It s easy to find. What do you plan— putting poison in their drinks? I have to ask you what poison it would be—autopsies would be done and I need to know what they would be concluded from the autopsies. I think it might be easier for your people to stay in a hotel in Kilkee and get talking to them in the bar, but then you know your business—I don't.

I would be in Spain with my husband when the above job would be done, if its arranged for next weekend or even after that. What would you do about him? Especially with me around. You say you will take care of him yourself. You'd be coming a long way from the US to Spain. I could get the keys of his apartment to you and arrange a time to be out, I would be a suspect, if anything looks suspicious, especially when I would be the one to inherit. Many people think i,m with him for his money anyway— he's a bit older than me etc. and that would also look suspicious.

Please realise that I may not be ready to go ahead as soon as next week. Im leaving here to go to Spain on Wednesday and it will take a lot longer than that for me to arrange a loan. I wont be back in Ireland until some time in September—it may be towards the end of the month before im back.

You see, as I said I could use cash that I have her and buy a cashiers cheque, or a number of them, with it, but the sons might notice the money gone after I leave on Wednesday and ring my husband and tell him. And he would know that I took it … And then what? This is my problem and I will have to work it out. But as I say, It might not be as soon as I hoped—id really like to see an end to all this soon, though.

I cant talk on the phone right now and I will be away from the computer for the next few hours. You could always send a text to my mobile phone, but it would be better for now to send an email.

I appreciate all your help and we will definitely do business. Ive no conscience about my husband, he's a real asshole and makes my life hell, but I do feel bad about the others, however, I thought about it long and hard and I realise that it is necessary or there is no advantage to getting rid of my husband other than not having to look

at his miserable face again. But I must be sure that I will
be ok financially ect.

S.

Date: Friday, 11 August 2006. 6.30 p.m.
From: hire_hitman@yahoo.com
To: lyingeyes98@yahoo.ie
Retrieved from the Iridium laptop at Ballybeg House

Email contents:

I think you will never worry about any think we will take
care of them and no one point to you … that's guarantee
… This is our business … but sorry we have to have the
deposit before we proceed … that will be before wed aug
16 … and why you worry bout that they don't have the
time or days to check about the money cause they will be
gone … we are planning aug 18 or 19 … and your husband
aug 20 … we can arrange to meet you and get the key or
we have our ways in without keys … And we have to have
pic of the two guys and your husband too … if you don't
have it we will figour out that …

Thanks

Tony Luciano

Date: Not listed
From: lyingeyes98@yahoo.ie
To: hire_hitman@yahoo.com
Retrieved from the Iridium laptop at Ballybeg House

Email contents:

Im back now.

I suppose your right—I should just leave it to you and
not worry—but I do worry.

I could send the keys of the apartment to you or leave
them somewhere in Spain near the apartment for you to

collect. There is a further complication about Spain though—he has a boat and could arrange to be away on it at any time. Its impossible for me to say where he will be until much closer to the time. In any case, I suppose we could stay in touch by text if he and I are on the boat. But If im on the boat I wouldn't want anything to happen to him there. I guess if he were to get news about his sons, he would immediately return to the apartment to pack anyway.

I definitely have photos of my husband and I think I have one of the guys, but I will have to look tomorrow and email them to you.

I know you say—not to worry about the cash and that they wont have time to find out, but I have to consider what would happen if you couldn't get near the guys here in Ireland next weekend. And If I was to transfer the money to you on or before Wed, they could notice on Thurs or Fri before you've had a chance to get to them. This is a major concern for me. I cant get them suspicious of me in anyway. I'm already walking a very fine line here. Believe me. If it would do you, I think I could get approximately 13,000 Euro without too many problems before Wednesday (not money that would be missed)— how would it be if I sent that and paid a little more than the quoted fee after the job is done? I m not sure how much cash there is in Spain, but I think it is a considerable amount and would to a long way towards paying the total fee. Once my husband is taken care of, id be 'bringing him home' and any balance can be sent immediately, once I'm back here. (a matter of days) Whatcha think??

If this is totally unacceptable to you, please confirm that you will be willing to do this job at a later date when ive had a chance to get the money together.

Kind regards,

S.

Date: Friday, 11 August 2006. 8.54 p.m.
From: hire_hitman@yahoo.com
To: lyingeyes98@yahoo.ie
Retrieved from the Iridium laptop at Ballybeg House

Email contents:

Here's the deal you can send $15,000 by Wed and after we arrive we can have the $30,000 which is the balance of the deposit it will be the 18 of aug … and the rest of the Money which is $45,000 no later than 72 hrs after the job done … this is our contract or you will be our target … sorry to say that but this is our policy … now we need the pics names and address for all of them …

One thing I want to tell you don't think what people think what you thinking, think they know nothing and I guess you are not gonna worry…

Let us do our job and just relax … cause if you worry you make a mistake and we both gonna be in trouble … is that a deal

Date: Not listed
From: lyingeyes98@yahoo.ie
To: hire_hitman@yahoo.com
Retrieved from the Iridium laptop at Ballybeg House

Email contents:

Sorry for taking so long getting back to you

Tony, im not trying to be difficult about the money. If you can get me out of the unbearable situation that im in and I don't get into trouble for, then its money very well spent, as far as im concerned. What you suggested in your last email is very fair, but as I said before, im going to spain on Wednesday and Id have to take the cash and leave it somewhere for you. But if I do, the sons could notice it gone after I leave and tell him my husband. Then the shit would hit the fan for me. I know you'd be taking care of him on Sunday, but im afraid he would say it to someone.

He's got close friends with him in Spain (in the apartment next door)—he might tell them.

I have to tell you I have absolutely no intention of being your next target by not paying the balance of any money I owe you after the jobs are done. You most definitely will be paid within 72 hours. Ive got children of my own and intend on being around for them. That s another reason why I want to be as careful as possible that I don't end up in jail. I want to be absolutely sure that when I start this thing by paying you the 'booking deposit', ill be in a position to finish it by paying you what I owe. In addition, there may possibly one more person I might add to the list a little later, but ill get this job done first.

Ive been thinking about it all earlier today and I wonder if you wouldn't mind giving me some advice. Tell me honestly—would it look more 'believable' if one of the sons were to go first, followed by a few months later by the other and then immediately by the father (as planned this time). The reason why I wanted to get it all done together was I thought I could take all the money to pay afterwards and no-one would be around to notice, but maybe it's the wrong way. I know it would be a more expensive way to do it, but please let me know if it would be better. What Im thinking is, maybe I could borrow the $50,000 to pay for the others. Im not very brave, am I? but then again, you do this all the time—ive never in my life considered anything like this.

Another thing I need advice with is this—I used the computer at work (we all work together) to surf the net for a hitman. If the cops seize the computer, could they find evidence of my search?

As this is the weekend, I wont be able to talk to the bank about a loan until Monday, so there's no way I can confirm if this thing will be on for next weekend until the bank sanctions a loan, but I will keep you informed all the way of my progress.

I'm hoping I will be able to talk to you later, but in the

meantime, would you email me back and let me know what you think about the above.

Date: Not listed
From: Hire_hitman@yahoo.com
To: lyingeyes98@yahoo.ie
Retrieved from the Iridium laptop at Ballybeg House

Email contents:

First I don't know your name … my plain is we will get close to your 2 step son we can do that this is our arrange … after we finish I will fly to Spain by myself like I said before if you arrang to give me the key or not I will be in to his apartment … and I will take him out to his boat and we will do it there … so that not gonna be any miss … but I have to pay the guys in Ireland to do there job … that's why I have to have some money by Wed … so, Monday to have to get 15000,00 Euro and send it by Fedx for next day delivery … so it will be here by Wed … or you can go to other bank and transfer the money … without that sorry we can do it … i know you will pay us later that's why we give you a break for the deposit … we trust you for that … but this people have to get pay too before the job … put yourself in my shoes too …

You understand what I said just come down and let people think what you think … be yourself and don't ever ever worry about anything … just tell your step I need the money for your girlfriend just for a weak or any reason and tell them don't tell anyone about … or give them any reason and the money will be back in you bank
Let me know asap … If I will send this people or not also about the pic … we have to have asap too thanks Baby Tony luciano

Date: Saturday, 12 August 2006. 3.49 p.m.
From: Hire_hitman@yahoo.com
To: lyingeyes98@yahoo.ie
Retrieved from the Iridium laptop at Ballybeg House

Email contents:

That's what I said we need 15000 by wed and I will get the rest after the 2 son is gone

And about your husband I change my plan to his app just let him jub it depend about when … this is after we talk together over there let me know more info when he get the news … i want do it the same day whedn he get the bad news …

So, 15000 by wed and 30000 by sun the 20 aug and the rest after the husband … you still didn't get me the pic I have to have it … we don't wont to get wrong people and the last thing what's your name?
Thanks
Tony

Date: Saturday, 12 August 2006. 10.14 p.m.
From: lyingeyes98@yahoo.ie
To: Hire_hitman@yahoo.com
Retrieved from the Iridium laptop at Ballybeg House and computer at Essam Eid's home in Las Vegas

Email contents:

Gee, you got back to me fast … Thanks.

Let me get this straight. Are you saying that if I Fedex 15,000 Euro to you on Monday, to pay the people in Ireland, that you will do the rest and wait for the balance til after my husband is done? This is possible for me. But maybe I mis-understand. Please confirm.

You didn't say whether you think it is the best way to do it … all of them like this or one first and the other two later.

About the boat. I most explain. The boat is not in close proximity to the apartment and when you leave the apartment block, there are lots of shops and vendors all around. They are open until very late and they know him well. I think it would be difficult to get him out without raising suspicion and remember, I need it to look like he has committed suicide after hearing about his sons. Also, the boat is quite big and perhaps, difficult for you to handle, if you are on your own.

I think it is important that I tell you exactly the way it is there. And also point out any complications that might arise. OK?

The apartment is on the top floor of a 14 storey apartment block. It has a private terrace and plunge pool on the roof. An Irish couple, with whom he is very friendly, own the apartment next door. They are in Spain now too, but I think they have tenants in it for the summer—I'm not sure, but I can find out later. This couple also have a boat here, near his boat and if they are not in their apartment, they will be living aboard their boat—another reason why you might find it difficult to get away with taking him out on it.

My husband is planning to go on a boat trip for a few days when I get there—but I don't know when this is or where. I really don't know that until we are going. But I think, wherever it is, when he gets a phonecall about his sons, he will immediately return to his apartment to pack to come home. Unless, he decides to go directly to the airport from the marina. If he does this, then I don't know how you would get him.

I will be there, as you know. How do you suggest we stay in touch, so im not there when you get there. Also I will need to let you know when he gets the news about his sons and what he is doing then.

My husband has a bad heart—maybe when he gets the news about his sons—you wont need to do anything at all (except get your money!), but I feel I should point out all the pit falls to you beforehand. Another complication could be his friends—they might come back to the apartment with us to sympathize with him. The Irish are like that! And there are lots of Irish friends of his out there.

In your experience, when you show up to 'take care of' someone, do they ask you who sent you? Do they offer to pay you to kill that person instead of them? Just wondering …

S.

Date: Not listed
From: Hire_hitman@yahoo.com
To: lyingeyes98@yahoo.ie
Retrieved from the Iridium laptop at Ballybeg House

Email contents:

About the computer don't ever used the work computer … you have to delete every think … thanks

Date: Saturday, 12 August 2006. 11.31 p.m.
From: lyingeyes98@yahoo.ie
To: Hire_hitman@yahoo.com
Retrieved from the Iridium laptop at Ballybeg House and computer at Essam Eid's home in Las Vegas

Email contents:

Yeah, I'm worried about that. I was told by a guy in the computer company that services our computers that even if you delete stuff, it can be still accessed. One of my husbands sons had been accessing porn on the net and deleted it, but when the computer went for repair, the guy told me that they had found it all. He asked me 'whos been downloading all the porn'? of course, I knew who it was and I had deleted anything that I found myself, but it was still there.

Id have to take the computer from the office before I go. I better think of an excuse to do that.

Im just wondering now, if it might be easier to wait until we return from Spain to do my husband. After all, you plan to do his sons on Sat 19th, right? He ll get a call about it immediately and go home as soon as he gets a flight. Even if you hit him on Mon 21st, I still have time to pay you, don't I?

Its just an idea. The only thing is, one of my sons lives here with us and will be here, as will i. not sure how that would work. Again, Tony, it must look like suicide for him. Or natural causes. This vital. And the body cant disappear. It must be there.

S.

Untitled email retrieved from computer at Essam Eid's home in Las Vegas

Email contents:

Ok so do you intend for us to talk on the phone in Spain or to meet face to face?

The money. Am I to give it to you in cash? Its all going to happen within a few hours, right? As far as I know, my husband has enough cash there for me to give you the equivalent of $30,000 in Euro. Ill be able to check how much cash he has when I get there on Wed and let you know. I wont be able to take it while he is there, but if you are going to be in the apartment, I can give you the combination to the safe and you can help yourself. Is that ok? He always like to have a lot of cash with him, so im not sure if he would take the cash from the apartment while we are gone and you can check the money to satisfy yourself that it is there. But I would ask you not to touch it until he is gone ... we can talk about it anyway. With everything going on—he will be upset, therefore, I don't see a problem. I could Fedex the keys of the apartment with $15,000 on Monday.

Do you have any idea how long it would take for the authorities to release his body from Spain? Ill need to get home asap after you ve done your bit to send the rest of the money to you. Will I have to stay there until they release the body or do you think I could leave without causing too much suspicion and let them forward the body to Ireland afterwards? Perhaps you would know how this works?

Photos, I don't have a scanner here to send the photos. Ill have to source one tomorrow and send them to you then.

My name. Tony, if you knew me—I wouldn't harm a fly—seriously. Ive just been put in such an impossible situation—that I feel I really have to take drastic action. Theres no point in going into the details of it with you, unless you need to know. Anyway, I want to sleep on it tonight and decide for once and for all if I will be able to live with myself afterwards. Im a real softy and there was a time when I really loved my husband, but he has truly killed that. But eventhough I cant stand him now and have been wishing him dead for a long, long time, I found it really upsetting when I read your emails and saw it there in black and white. The reality is fairly startling, especially for an un-violent person like me. I know he has asked for it and would do the same himself, if he was in my position, but that doesn't make it easy for me.

I will let you know tomorrow for sure and will give you my name then—if I must! My son is around at the moment, so I wont be able to talk on the phone tonight as I had hoped, but we will have to talk tomorrow. Is that ok?

Date: Sunday, 13 August 2006. 03.27 a.m.
From: hire_hitman@yahoo.com
To: lyingeyes98@yahoo.ie
Retrieved from the Iridium laptop at Ballybeg House

Email contents:

Hello
I want tell you that we are professional people here … we don't give a chance to any one to make a deal with us especially the target … Even if they offer us 10 mil euro we honor our contract … so, don't ever worry about that.

So I want you Monday send the key the pic and the money plus the combinations for the safe and the address for all of them … If you have the address for the two guys which is the party add that be great.

Also I want ask you if your husband have a gun or maybe we can used to kill himself or if we not we let him jump from 14th floor … I want you stay with him till you leave spain with his body don't leave him it will be suspicious … that we recommend … I need your phone number in spain too … we can contact you there after we done in Ireland … we don't call each other by phone maybe is dangerous … just e-mail us and we reply fast
Thanks
Tony Luciano

Date: Not listed
From: lyingeyes98@yahoo.ie
To: hire_hitman@yahoo.com
Retrieved from the Iridium laptop at Ballybeg House

Email contents:

The telephone number is the one I gave before 00 353 86 xxxxxxx. I'll email you when I can talk. Is that ok.

Ive been trying to think of an excuse for removing the computer from the office. Its my husbands business and his sons work there too. I think it would be a good idea not to leave it there in case anyone decides to check it out.

I also have been thinking about getting the cashiers check. Here in Ireland, any time you buy a bank draft or cashier's check, the bank keeps a record of who you are and you have to do it at your own bank. Its regulation. Anyway, it there is any question of it at a later date, I can say that I got it from your husband—that he told me to. And if im asked what he wanted it for, I can say he didn't appreciate being asked questions. He always told me not to question him, just do what I was told. (which is true, actually)

In addition, if theres a FedEx record of the envelope, – again, I will say that I was asked at work to send it. I don't know what it was. What do you think?

Might never come to that anyway. Hopefully not anyway.

Date: Sunday, 13 August 2006. 1.46 p.m.
From: hire_hitman@yahoo.com
To: lyingeyes98@yahoo.ie
Retrieved from the Iridium laptop at Ballybeg House

Email contents:

Let me know when we can talk … we have no time it will happen this weekend which 6 days left … just send Fedex thru your company like you said and the cashier check don't right any name we will do that in our secret account … but we will give the address that you can fedex it to … You have to … I mean you have to trust us and the job will be done … dont worry or panic and act normal … like nothing happen
Thanks
Tony

Date: Not listed
From: lyingeyes98@yahoo.ie
To: Hire_hitman@yahoo.com
Retrieved from the Iridium laptop at Ballybeg House

Email contents:

Ok then, im 90% decided to go ahead with it.

I know you want me to leave to you and not question you, but I cant help it.

Date: Sunday, 13 August 2006. 1.52 p.m.
From: Hire_hitman@yahoo.com
To: lyingeyes98@yahoo.ie
Retrieved from the Iridium laptop at Ballybeg House

Email contents:

No, that's the best way we can do it we used our own stuff to do it so. There push him out one time so, there is no fingerpring or any evidence

Date: Not listed
From: lyingeyes98@yahoo.ie
To: Hire_hitman@yahoo.com
Retrieved from desktop computer at 7A Westgate Business Park, Kilrush Road, Ennis (The Howards' family business)

Email contents:

Im still caught here with my sister and her husband. I was hoping that you could ring me tonight, but I don't want them to see me checking emails and I don't want to seem impatient with them. As you said, I want to act normal.

Can you email me your telephone number and I will ring you when I can.

Date: Sunday, 13 August 2006. 11.01 p.m.
From: Hire_hitman@yahoo.com
To: lyingeyes98@yahoo.ie
Retrieved from desktop computer at 7A Westgate Business
Park, Kilrush Road, Ennis

Email contents:

Sorry I had somethink to do with my daughter just get
back … my phone is 586 xxx xxxx … You can call me any
time Sharon

Date: Not listed
Retrieved from computer at Essam Eid's home in Las
Vegas

Email contents:

If you're going to Spain, you will have to fly to Malaga. I
forgot to tell you that.

Anyway, I was just talking to my husband.

The couple with the apartment next door to ours, will
not be in their apartment. They will either be on their own
boat or gone home to Ireland. Ill know when I get there on
Wed night.

My husband plans for us to take a boat trip to Puerto
Banus on Friday and stay there until Sunday or Monday.
In any case, he will surely have to return to his apartment
after he gets the 'sad' news of his sons!

I will be able to give you my Spanish mobile phone
number and if you get yourself a Spanish phone when you
get there, you will be able to text me and then I'd be able
to tell you what we are doing. I probably wouldn't have
access to internet most of the time

Date: Not listed
From: lyingeyes98@yahoo.ie

To: hire_hitman@yahoo.com
Retrieved from computer at Essam Eid's home address in
Las Vegas and desktop computer at 7A Westgate Business
Park

Email contents:

Im still not in a position to talk on the phone, but
hopefully in a while. I have visitors staying in the house
and I need total privacy to talk.

Im assuming your people will put that substance in the
guys drink. Is that it?

Tony, as I said before, nearly every weekend, those guys
fo to Kilkee, on the west coast of County Clare. They
spend a lot of time in a bar there and they also go boating.
But there is absolutely no guarantee that they will be there
next weekend. Occasionally they go to visit cousins of
theirs at the other side of the country. I cant think of the
name of the place right now, but ill come to me. The
country is small, so no matter where they are, it's only a
few hours away. I assume this will not be a problem? I will
do my best this week, to find out what they intend doing
and will email you as soon as I can, so your people can
make alternative hotel reservations.

Do you still intend travelling to Spain yourself? Its quite
a distance for you to have to travel. I don't think there are
any direct flights between the US and Malaga.

Date: Sunday, 13 August 2006. 11.05 p.m.
From: hire_hitman@yahoo.com
To: lyingeyes98@yahoo.ie
Retrieved from desktop computer at 7A Westgate Business
Park

Email contents:

I was in Malaga befor and I know how to get there … from
Madred or Barcelona im planning on it so, don't worry

about that for now … Im so exciting to talk to you on the phone
Tony Luciano

Date: Monday, 14 August 2006. 1.38 a.m.
From: hire_hitman@yahoo.com
To: lyingeyes98@yahoo.ie
Retrieved from desktop computer at 7A Westgate Business Park

Email contents:

Im sorry to call you wrong time … but time is running out we have to know where we at … so, im going to do some business and I will be back …

    Waiting for your call
Thanks Tony

Date: Monday, 14 August 2006. 1.45 a.m.
From: hire_hitman@yahoo.com
To: lyingeyes98@yahoo.ie
Retrieved from desktop computer at 7A Westgate Business Park

Email contents:

If you cant send the Money today forget about it … it will be to late. My people not wait … plus I will pay them the rest from my pocket till you pay me after the job done … now its up to you … sorry but I have to give them the green light and I cant if no Money sorry the pressure on me
By the way you have a nice voice … sorry to say that

Date: Not listed
From: lyingeyes98@yahoo.ie

To: hire_hitman@yahoo.com
Retrieved from the Iridium laptop at Ballybeg House and
desktop computer at Westgate Business Park

Email contents:

I will be sending the money later today. Its 11am here now
so once I get the envelope to Fed Ex by 5pm today, we're
ok.

  Will you email the address for delivery.

  Im at work right now—have to behave as normal and
when i'm sent to the bank later, I will sort out the money.
Don't worry ... im going to do it. Ive decided.

  I also need to spend some time here with one of the sons
to find out what he will be doing next weekend. Will let
you know as soon as I do.

  Thanks for your phone number—will you email me the
correct prefix.

Talk later.

Sharon

Date: Monday, 14 August 2006.5.50 a.m.
From: hire_hitman@yahoo.com
To: lyingeyes98@yahoo.ie
Retrieved from desktop computer at Westgate Business
Park

Email contents:

Here is the address you can Fedex to u.s.a. T. Engle ...
6108 Camden Cove st. north Las Vegas ... Nevada 89031
and here is the account nbr Bank of America xxxx Camina
Al Norte North Las Vegas, NV 89031

  The bank under name of Essam Eid routing number
122xxxxx and the account number is 00 5011xxxxxx

  Just let me know either way so, I want know what we are
looking for ... I will talke to you later sweetie

Date: Not listed
From: lyingeyes98@yahoo.ie
To: hire_hitman@yahoo.com
Retrieved from the Iridium laptop at Ballybeg House

Email contents:

Ive decided to parcel up the money and send it that way. I will probably put something else in with it to make it look like a present.

Ill also put in the photos and the keys

Ill email you the address, combination and directions etc.

Just busy at work right now and under pressure to get everything done so I can get away early to send off parcel.

Will email you later and let you know tracking number etc.

Date: Monday, 14 August 2006. 6.34 a.m.
From: hire_hitman@yahoo.com
To: lyingeyes98@yahoo.ie
Retrieved from the Iridium laptop at Ballybeg House

Email contents:

Ok … just be careful. Talk to you later then

Date: Not listed
From: lyingeyes98@yahoo.ie
To: hire_hitman@yahoo.com
Retrieved from the Iridium laptop at Ballybeg House

Email contents:

Tony,
I told you that you could ring me, but my son came home unexpectedly—wants to spend some quality time with me this evening, as im going away on Wed, so I put the cell

phone away and put it on silent.

When he goes to bed later tonight, ill let you know.
Sharon

Date: Monday, 14 August 2006. 2.32 p.m.
From: hire_hitman@yahoo.com
To: lyingeyes98@yahoo.ie
Retrieved from the Iridium laptop at Ballybeg House

Email contents:

I guess from your voice no one can touch you and I guess
you are beautiful too … sorry to say that there is no way
to me or any one killing you … I hope we resived by
thruday … and go there … I will call the guys even if I pay
them from my pocket … we are still on … just act normal
we gonna be ok … im leving Friday from here to be in
Spain by Sat after noon … I will text msg you and let you
know that im there …

I will try to email you my pic too but don't make fun of
me … lol.

Date: Not listed
Retrieved from computer at Essam Eid's home in Las
Vegas

Email contents:

Finally I have a chance to email with no one breathing
down my neck.

Again, I must apologize for not being able to take your
calls tonight. I thought id be on my own, but my son, who
is 20 came home much earlier than I expected. He's a good
kid and said he wanted to spend some quality time with
me, as im going away on Wednesday. We were watching a
movie and chatting, and at the same time, I was trying to
email you, but, as I said, we are always always having

problems with internet connections at the house, so I lost the very long email that I had hoped to send you.

Anyway, what I was saying was—thank you for the photos. Your daughter is beautiful and clearly loves her dad and you're very handsome yourself. Italian of course!!

I had to smile when I saw your photos—for as long as I can remember, I ve been saying that I would love a sexy, yellow sports car … and as Ive always wanted to visit Las Vegas … maybe, you'll take me for a ride in yours, if I ever get there!! Now, that's cheeky isn't it?!

Anyway, I was sitting with my son last night and thinking if he only knew what his mother was planning. He definitely would wonder if he ever knew me at all. My boys would be devastated, if they thought I would do such a thing. My other son is nearly 23 and works in Dublin. I miss him a lot. We are very close. In fact, my boys are everything to me. I got married (for the first time) when I was 19. it was a disaster. There was no divorce in Ireland at the time, but I got an annulment from the Church and when divorce was introduced I got one. I didn't have to resort to extreme measures at the time … i can get on quite well with my ex-husband now. I think its important for children that parents try to get along, even when the relationship breaks down. Otherwise, the children question their own worth.

I suppose you think I want to be rid of my husband so I can get what he has? Well, I do want to inherit—I want my home and an income, of course if do. But there's a lot more to it than that. For one thing, he resents any time I spend with my boys and tried to keep me away from them. That's a reason why my son wanted to take advantage of being with me last night, while my husband's in Spain. My husband wants to control every moment of my life and has a dreadful temper. And he make sure I have no money of my own. But the main reason im doing this is because he is continually trying to force me to go out and pick up a stranger for sex. He finds the idea of it exciting and insists I must do it or Im out and he will make sure that I have absolutely nothing. Well I will not do that. No way! That mother of my boys is not a slut. I think its disgusting that a man would want his woman to be with another man. He never, ever stops pushing for it. Frankly, I don't care what he does. I don't mind if he has sex with hooker or transvestites (of which he is particularly fond) everyday, but leave me out of it. He has gone so far that im at the stage now, when I would be happy if I never had to hear of sex again. I would be perfectly content on my own now with no man. I certainly will never marry or live with someone again.

You might ask yourself why I don't just leave and sue him, but it wouldn't work, believe me. Im in a very vulnerable situation. And, because of the way he has thing tied up, im afraid his boys are going to suffer now—and I really regret that. I wish so much that it didn't have to be like this, but then again, I know that if may husband was dead and they were still here, they'd screw me anyway. In fact im sure of it. So now I want to protect myself and my boys.

Gee, Tony, I must be boring you out of your mind. It's the last thing you need to know. Sorry—I do go on.

To get back to business. I still haven't found out where the guys will be this weekend. They probably don't know themselves yet. More than likely, though, it will be Kilkee.

Date: Tuesday,15 August 2006. 2.37 a.m.
From: hire_hitman@yahoo.com
To: lyingeyes98@yahoo.ie
Retrieved from desktop computer at Westgate Business Park

Email contents:

Thanks for your comment … i bet you look so beautiful too … Maybe after we done the business … mayb it will

be my pleasure to have dinner with you … you gonna pay
for it?????? Hahahah

Date: Not listed
From: lyingeyes98@yahoo.ie
To: hire_hitman@yahoo.com
Retrieved from desktop computer at Westgate Business
Park and the Iridium laptop at Ballybeg House

Email contents:

Tony
As I said, im not sure which photos were which, while I
was sending them.
    You'll be able to tell which one is my husband … And
im the devil in the red dress!
    The photo with the guy on the left is the younger one
and the one on the right is the older.
    Im with them now, so email later.
Sharon

Date: Tuesday, 15 August 2006. 6.32 a.m.
From: hire_hitman@yahoo.com
To: lyingeyes98@yahoo.ie
Retrieved from the Iridium laptop and desktop computer
at Westgate Business Park

Email contents:

Hello Sharon … You look so great I cant wait to see you
ok lets talk business … we agreed before %50 down which
is 45000 … and we went down to 15000 and now you tell
me after all done … sorry Sharon we don't know each
other yet to dot that … and im sorry …
    I did trust you for the 30000 and now I feel you take
advantage … that's what I feel
    So if I didn't not receive the money or some of them
(1500) by Thur forget about it well! E-mail me the tracting

number or let me know wither one hr what you gonna do thanks

Date: Not listed
Retrieved from computer at Essam Eid's home in Las Vegas

Email contents:

Now I know for sure you sleep as ive just been ringing you. Well, im glad—ill need you at your best …
What I really need to know urgently is where to leave the keys of the office for your people and what name to put on the envelope.

I will not put the address in the envelope with the keys—I will give it out to you after you receive the money and confirm that the job is still on.

But I will give you some details for getting into the office:

If they leave it until late, there will be no-one around (there is a cleaner who comes on her own time, but not at night)

There is an alarm, so they must do the following—two locks on the outside door. Its not a very secure door anyway. Light switch to the right of the door. Straight up the stairs and into the reception. Sometimes the door at the top of the stairs is locked, but the key is always in the door lock. Light switch to the left of the reception door, just inside reception area. Walk behind reception. There are two doors behind the desk and also an opening to a small area behind the desk. The alarm is just inside this opening on the wall. The code is xxxx. This turns the alarm on and off. The computer that I am concerned about is the one at the reception desk. No need to take the monitor or key-board etc, just the hardware left on the floor under the desk.

It would be a good idea if the alarm was turned on again

when they leave. same code xxxx. And leave the door locked as before.

There's a safe in the office, but there is never much money in it. Just a few hundred euro. I don't want it touched. I just want it to look like one of the sons took the computer themselves for repair or something.

Ive just saved everything important for work on a CD and have it with me. If I don't hear from you, in time, I will decide myself where to leave the key and let you know.

There is something else I want done—I want a email sent to my husband's email address. I will give you the details tomorrow.

No time now. Trying to get ready for trip.

Sharon

Date: Tuesday, 15 August 2006. 11.27 a.m.
From: hire_hitman@yahoo.com
To: lyingeyes98@yahoo.ie
Retrieved from the Iridium laptop at Ballybeg House

Email contents:

I guess we have a problem to talk on the phone

I just wondering if all info in the package … what's there beside the Money?

is everything we need inside?

Don't get mad when I see you in Malaga if I like you I will kiss you …

If I don't you do it … I just joke

Thank

Tony

Date: Tuesday, 15 August 2006. 11.33 a.m.
From: hire_hitman@yahoo.com
To: lyingeyes98@yahoo.ie
Retrieved from the Iridium laptop at Ballybeg House

Email contents:

You gonna have your laptop with you in Spain? … in case
if I want contact you.

Date: Not listed
From: lyingeyes98@yahoo.ie
To: hire_hitman@yahoo.com
Retrieved from the Iridium laptop at Ballybeg House and
desktop computer at Westgate Business Park

Email contents:

Oh by the way, Tony, I know you were ringing me earlier,
but I wasn't in a position to talk at the time.

Funny now, I ve managed to send several short emails,
but before that, when I was trying to send a long message,
I lost it every time—4 times to be exact.

Now I don't know what I've said and what ive left out. I
would be able to talk on the phone at approximately 1.30
a.m. my time, if we cant get everything sorted by email,
before we meet in Spain …

Did you get my message from earlier today, regarding
someone who works in 'security' here. Is there any chance
that he could have any connection to your people in
Ireland?

Am I driving you mad with questions and suggestions?
Ok, ill wait until I hear from you before emailing again.
Sharon.

Date: Tuesday, 15 August 2006. 5.23 p.m.
From: hire_hitman@yahoo.com
To: lyingeyes98@yahoo.ie
Retrieved from the Iridium laptop at Ballybeg House and
desktop computer at Westgate Business Park

Email contents:

Call me later on when you have a chance … Or I will call
you
Tony

Date: Not listed
From: lyingeyes98@yahoo.ie
To: hire_hitman@yahoo.com
Retrieved from desktop computer at Westgate Business
Park

Email contents:

I can talk now or anytime for the next 2–3 hours. I realise
it is just after midnight here now. So, if you are in a
position to talk, please ring.
Sharon

Date: Wednesday, 16 August 2006. 1.07 a.m.
From: hire_hitman@yahoo.com
To: lyingeyes98@yahoo.ie
Retrieved from desktop computer at Westgate Business
Park

Email contents:

Hello baby
I tried to reach you several times but no answer … i guess
you are not like me you sleep a lot and im not … you can
call me any time im always up … Bye baby.

Date: Not listed
From: hire_hitman@yahoo.com
To: lyingeyes98@yahoo.ie
Retrieved from computer at Essam Eid's home in Las Vegas

Email contents:

Hello Sharon … here's the deal please don't call me a lot we will call you when the job is done … we cant find the guys at all so we gonna do it at there office … sorry it take time than we thought but the job will be done just relax … We will let you know as soon we done it …

We change our reservation at the hotel in Malaga to El Puerto costa del sol I don't know how its but we don't care … other hotel we will stay at Clare Inn Newmarket on Fergus Dromoland in Ireland I don't know how fare form the office

But we don't care either … Just let you know where we stay at … After the job done like we agree that we gonna get pay Max the 3rd of Aug … I will let you know where and how … 11000,00 euro and $74000,00 USD. If we need info we will call you … just relax be yourself and lets do our job
Thanks
Tony

Date: Not listed
From: lyingeyes98@yahoo.ie
To: hire_hitman@yahoo.com
Retrieved from computer at Essam Eid's home in Las Vegas

Email contents:

You can get an Aer lingus flight out of Cork airport every morning at around 7 a.m. if you could get to the guys today or tonight, you or your guy—or both of you—could be on tomorrow mornings flight and everything could be done by tomorrow.

Too ambitious??

Talk soon

Sharon

Date: Thursday, 17 August 2006. 7.42 a.m.
From: Ennispeople06@yahoo.com
To: hire_hitman@yahoo.com
Found during garda analysis of the computers

Email contents:

The people you want information about are as follows: The family name is Howard.

There is PJ Howard (57) and his two sons Robert (27) and Niall (23).

PJ Howard spends most of his time in the Costa del Sol in Spain. He has an apartment in Fuengirola, approximately 20 minutes from Malaga Airport on the motorway. The address—Apartment No xxxx (14th Floor) Torre III (Tower 3), Las Palmeras. This is a hotel and apartment complex. The entrance to which is beside the bus station and then ask the taxi driver to continue straight on to Calle Jac into Benevente. There is an entrance between Coyote Dance (disco) and KARAOKE Video Café (bar). There are a lots of shops in the entrance, with their merchandise on display as you walk through. When you go past approx 3 shops, turn left and the door to the apartment block is in the right. Any of the shop owners can direct you to Torre III.

PJ Howard also has a boat in Benalmadena and spends most weekends there on the boat.

Robert Howard and Niall Howard live in Ballaghboy, Doora, Ennis Co. Clare. To reach their house, drive out the Doora Road (beside the bus and railway station). Turn left at the first (?) crossroads. The house is the 3rd or 4th on the right. It is painted yellow with a dark green trim. Robert lives in the house, and Niall lives in the apartment accessible from the back of the house (basement). His girlfriend lives there most of the time with him. They own a Doberman dog. There are two other people living in the house with Robert. They rent a room from him.

Niall drives a BMW (small one) and Robert drives a Land Rover. They also have a house in Kilkee on the west Coast of Co Clare. The address is 9 Byrnes Cove, Kilkee. They usually go there at weekends and often have cousins and friends stay with them. There is a possibility that they might go to a seaside resort called Ballybunion in Co Kerry this weekend. Will find out and let you know.

The Howards have a company called Downes and Howards Ltd. The office address is 7A Westgate Business Park, Kilrush Road, Ennis, Co Clare. Driving from Ennis Town in the Kilrush direction, go through traffic lights at shop called Coote, go past Seat Car Sales on the left. Then turn right into Westgate Business Park—it is opposite another car dealer (not sure of the name of the dealer). There is a sign for John O'Dwyer Hardware and other businesses in the Business Park. Then turn right. Various shop units there on left—go as far as Aids to Independence, which is the last shop in the first block and there is a gap. The door for Downes and Howard office is to the side of Aid to Independence. It is not marked—no sign. Just a timber double door.

There is a house on the Clare Road (Limerick Road) in Ennis. Leaving Ennis town, heading in the Limerick direction, there is a filling station and car sales called Estuary (Francie Daly is the proprietor and his name is on a sign). Immediately after this there is a turn right—don't take it—immediately after that there is a blue house, then a yellow house, with a 'Sale Agreed' sign outside it. The seller is Era Leyden Auctioneers. No-one lives in the house. Behind the house, beside the central heating boiler, there is a concrete block and keys under it.

I will forward any further information that you need as soon as I have it.

Will ring you later.

Date: Thursday, 17 August 2006. 10.58 p.m.
From: lyingeyes98@yahoo.ie
To: hire_hitman@yahoo.com
Found during garda analysis of the computers

Email contents:

The people you want information about are as follows:
The family name is Howard.

There is PJ Howard (57) and his two sons Robert (27) and Niall (23).

PJ Howard spends most of his time in the Costa del Sol in Spain. He has an apartment in Fuengirola, approximately 20 minutes from Malaga Airport on the motorway. The address—Apartment No xxxx (14th Floor) Torre III (Tower 3), Las Palmeras. This is a hotel and apartment complex. The entrance to which is beside the bus station and then ask the taxi driver to continue straight on to Calle Jac into Benevente. There is an entrance between Coyote Dance (disco) and KARAOKE Video Café (bar). There are a lots of shops in the entrance, with their merchandise on display as you walk through. When you go past approx 3 shops, turn left and the door to the apartment block is in the right. Any of the shop owners can direct you to Torre III.

PJ Howard also has a boat in Benalmadena and spends most weekends there on the boat.

Robert Howard and Niall Howard live in Ballaghboy, Doora, Ennis Co. Clare. To reach their house, drive out the Doora Road (beside the bus and railway station). Turn left at the first (?) crossroads. The house is the 3rd or 4th on the right. It is painted yellow with a dark green trim.

Robert lives in the house, and Niall lives in the apartment accessible from the back of the house (basement). His girlfriend lives there most of the time with him. They own a Doberman dog. There are two other people living in the house with Robert. They rent a room from him.

Niall drives a BMW (small one) and Robert drives a Land Rover. They also have a house in Kilkee on the west Coast of Co Clare. The address is 9 Byrnes Cove, Kilkee. They usually go there at weekends and often have cousins and friends stay with them. There is a possibility that they might go to a seaside resort called Ballybunion in Co Kerry this weekend. Will find out and let you know.

The Howards have a company called Downes and Howards Ltd. The office address is 7A Westgate Business Park, Kilrush Road, Ennis, Co. Clare. Driving from Ennis Town in the Kilrush direction, go through traffic lights at shop called Coote, go past Seat Car Sales on the left. Then turn right into Westgate Business Park—it is opposite another car dealer (not sure of the name of the dealer). There is a sign for John O'Dwyer Hardware and other businesses in the Business Park. Then turn right. Various shop units there on left—go as far as Aids to Independence, which is the last shop in the first block and there is a gap. The door for Downes and Howard office is to the side of Aid to Independence. It is not marked—no sign. Just a timber double door.

There is a house on the Clare Road (Limerick Road) in Ennis. Leaving Ennis town, heading in the Limerick direction, there is a filling station and car sales called Estuary (Francie Daly is the proprietor and his name is on a sign). Immediately after this there is a turn right—don't take it—immediately after that there is a blue house, then a yellow house, with a 'Sale Agreed' sign outside it. The seller is Era Leyden Auctioneers. No-one lives in the house. Behind the house, beside the central heating boiler, there is a concrete block and keys under it.

Please ring if you require any further information.

09 | A MAMMOTH INVESTIGATION

W hat had initially appeared to be a simple investigation into an office burglary subsequently ballooned into an enquiry into allegations of conspiracy to murder and culminated in one of the biggest and singularly the most bizarre investigation ever conducted in Co. Clare.

As the details began to unravel, the gardaí investigating the case could hardly believe what was before them. The main investigators, Superintendent John Scanlan, Detective Inspector Kevin Moynihan, Detective Sergeant Michael Moloney and Detective Garda Jarlath Fahy, between them have decades of experience in An Garda Síochána. Yet, as the pieces of the jigsaw were fitted together to unravel the mystery, not one of them could have predicted the level of planning and intent that went into the plot.

At the end of an extremely challenging and sometimes tense investigation, they concluded that Sharon Collins had just one reason for hiring a hitman over the internet—so that she could inherit PJ Howard's wealth, estimated to be up to €60 million.

Lurid allegations from Collins about PJ's sexual demands of her and suggestions that he had inflicted his black moods on her were never taken seriously by gardaí as a possible motive behind the cunning plan. Collins wanted to inherit and she believed the only way she could succeed was to wipe out PJ, who was in poor health, and his sons Robert and Niall, the potential inheritors of his millions.

PJ had declined to marry Collins so she had gone behind his back and had obtained a Mexican proxy marriage certificate online. She had then used this document to obtain a passport in the name Sharon Howard and gardaí believed this was a dry run to ascertain if the marriage certificate would stand up. Collins, who was self-taught in computers, believed her aim of obtaining a marriage certificate was successful, but ultimately, she took her forays online too far and was caught spectacularly in the end.

As her fascination with the internet intensified, she hired what she believed was a hitman, online. She was confident in her belief that he would kill the three Howards and she would then be sitting pretty on PJ's millions. Those close to the investigation believed that Collins was fully confident that she would get away with the plot. 'She was deluded. If the three were killed, if Essam Eid had done his job as he was supposed to and had got rid of the computer and she had got rid of her computer [the Iridium], it would have been a huge job to prove anything,' said a source close to the investigation.

Those involved in the Prosecution firmly believed that she chose the internet and not a local hitman because he would be gone out of the country very soon after carrying out the hit. 'Put it out there at arm's length, a stranger, gone out of the country. Gardaí wouldn't look to Las Vegas. This was well thought out. The whole thing went pear-shaped when Eid decided to extort money from Robert Howard,' said a source. Ironically, the first time that Sharon Collins met her co-accused Essam Eid was on 26 June 2007, in the tiny courtroom in Kilkee, west Clare, when they were both charged with conspiracy to murder. In the courtroom that day, Eid took one look at the petite blonde woman and muttered, 'I was cheated.' That day, Collins wept in court, shocked and angry that she had been caught. Her plan had collapsed and she was going to pay.

This unique investigation was every garda's dream in many

ways and presented a fantastic challenge. Yet, on the other hand, it was frustrating in parts, such were the complexities of piecing together the evidence, bringing the case to court and succeeding with a conviction, all in the face of potential challenges by the defence to eliminate key evidence. 'It was one of those cases where something new showed up every week. It was incredible. To find a computer six or seven months later in the grounds of a hotel was incredible,' said a source.

These four senior gardaí, together with Garda Peter McNamara and Garda Annette Ryan—whose work in the case paid off as she was promoted to the rank of sergeant during the lengthy investigation—worked full-time on the case from April 2007 to the conclusion of the trial in July 2008. Superintendent Scanlan, who headed up this investigation, was no stranger to working on highly complex cases. He had been involved in many top-level investigations during his years in Limerick, including an investigation relating to another case of soliciting to kill in 2005.

Patrick Rafferty (38), from Ballina, Co. Tipperary, solicited an undercover garda, Detective Garda Patrick Crowley, to murder his wife Mary Rafferty, on 7 February 2005, in an area between Nenagh and Castleconnell, Co. Limerick. Rafferty was jailed for seven years, in January 2007, after he admitted offering €15,000 to the undercover garda to kill his wife by faking a road accident.

Superintendent Scanlan, who was based in Limerick at the time, was heavily involved in that probe. And while both cases involved soliciting to kill, the complexities and bizarre nature of the Collins/Eid case were unprecedented and could not have been matched anywhere in the country.

Superintendent Scanlan arrived in Ennis at the height of this investigation in March 2007 and his predecessor Superintendent John Kerin had also played a key role in the case.

Overall, more than 50 gardaí from Co. Clare were involved in the investigation at various stages, while two gardaí, Detective Sergeant Michael Gubbins and Detective Garda Peter Keenan were drafted in from the Garda Bureau of Fraud Investigation, based at Harcourt Square, to analyse the computers at the centre of the case. The gardaí also liaised with Interpol and the FBI.

The FBI was investigating Essam Eid and Teresa Engle over a similar incident in the US at the same time, and they liaised with gardaí in Ennis.

Such was the sensitive nature of the Collins/Eid investigation that its inner details were never disclosed publicly. While the town of Ennis had been brimming with rumours relating to the case, those involved in the investigation remained tight-lipped throughout and as the gardaí beavered away, they kept their information to within the team.

This investigation had everything that an ambitious, industrious garda would thrive on. A challenge, laced with complexities. A tale dominated by several fascinating elements. A highly sensitive case, yet a case that would result in convictions and success for those involved in the investigation. A man's millions, his lover's greed, the high life enjoyed by the two, two men in their 20s poised to inherit millions through the property business, an internet trawl for a hitman with a view to wiping out a family, a mysterious author who could not be traced and an Egyptian gangster.

Over 100 interviews were conducted by gardaí, 11 computer hard drives were analysed, while records for several mobile phones were checked. And what was beneath it all? A cold, callous plot by an evil, deceitful housewife who was determined to get her hands on her lover's millions. The level of detail was gripping, but there was one huge risk and gardaí knew it—the majority of the evidence was circumstantial and it could have been difficult to prove. Much relied on computer evidence and phone records, which those investigating believed proved that Collins and Eid were in contact. But was the jury going to believe this or was the jury fearful that there were too many inferences in the case? Would they believe Collins's story that she was set up or that Eid was caught up in all of this innocently?

Both Collins and Eid were on free legal aid and hired reputable legal teams who would examine and text the admissibility to prevent parts of the evidence from going to the jury. The case came close to collapsing on one occasion, when the judge ruled that the ricin evidence could not go to the jury. However, the

Prosecution never looked back after the judge eventually allowed it to be admitted into evidence. And while there were several anxious moments for the investigation team during the case, gardaí were extremely pleased with the outcome in the immediate aftermath of the jury's verdicts.

The garda involvement in this case had all started on the morning of 26 September 2006. Ennis garda station had received a call about a burglary at the Downes and Howard business premises. Not an unusual occurrence as Clare, like other rural parts of Ireland, has been plagued by burglaries over the years because of the actions of greedy criminals eager to get their hands on valuables.

Detective Garda Jarlath Fahy had gone to investigate. Immediately, he smelled a rat. This was no random burglary. There were no signs of a break-in to the premises. The person who had entered the office had had keys and had known the alarm code. The alarm had been deactivated at 9.24 p.m. the previous evening. Missing from the office was a Toshiba laptop computer, the hard drive of the Advent desk computer, computer cables, a wall poster of old Irish money and a digital clock.

Detective Garda Fahy had spoken to some of his colleagues and their vast experience had led them to believe that this was no ordinary break-in. Members of the Scenes of Crime Unit in Co. Clare were dispatched but found nothing substantial of an evidential nature. Gardaí viewed CCTV footage of the immediate area and while the camera at the side of the building where the office was located had been disabled, two other cameras had shown a car entering the area at 9.24 p.m. and parking in front of the business park. It was, however, impossible to see who was in the car or even how many people there were.

Given the privacy that the wealthy Howard family enjoyed, very few people even knew that their office was located at Westgate Business Park, a new business block located in a housing estate, just one mile from Ennis town centre. Only six people had keys to the premises and knew the alarm code; PJ, Robert and Niall Howard, Sharon Collins, their handyman Dan Fitzgerald and their cleaner Kathleen McMahon. PJ and Sharon were in Spain when the burglary took place.

Garda suspicions were confirmed later that evening, when they were again contacted by a member of the Howard family. Robert Howard had received a call on his mobile phone and a visit by a man calling himself Tony Luciano. Ennis Garda Station was notified and Garda Beatrice Ryan was dispatched to his house, at Ballaghboy, Doora, on the outskirts of Ennis town.

Garda Ryan was to hear that Robert had received a call on his mobile phone at around 10.30 p.m. The caller, a man, had said to him, 'I heard you lost a few computers,' followed by, 'I'll be at your house in five minutes.'

Robert Howard said he didn't know if the call was a hoax and he did not know if anyone was going to show up at his house. However, the knock duly arrived at the door at 10.35 p.m. The man standing there told him his name was Tony. He handed him the blue Toshiba laptop that had been stolen from the family business the previous night and then told him there was a contract on his life and the lives of his father PJ and younger brother Niall. He said that the contract was worth €130,000, but that he didn't want to carry out the hit and wanted Robert to buy out the contract for €100,000.

The man had a computer printout of photographs in his hand—one of PJ Howard and Sharon Collins and the other of PJ on a boat in Spain—along with directions to the Howards' properties in Clare. However, he did not mention Sharon Collins's name to Robert.

Robert Howard was acutely aware that something was amiss and acted quickly. He snatched the printout of the photographs from 'Tony's' hand and urged his brother Niall—who was inside the house, keeping watch—to phone the gardaí. The visitor left his house in a hurry and efforts by the Howards to follow him failed. But his disappearance didn't spell the end of the road and the mystery intensified when Robert's phone rang again, some two hours later. It was 12.30 a.m. and 'Tony' was curious to know if Robert had started to get the money together for him.

Robert played along and told him he had. But what the man didn't realise was that Robert Howard was well tuned in and had made contact with the gardaí.

The following day, 27 September 2006, 'Tony' again contacted Robert Howard and suggested meeting at the bus station on the Quin Road in Ennis. At this stage, Robert had been liaising with gardaí, and was advised to meet the mystery man in a public area.

The Queen's Hotel, just a stone's throw from the garda station in the heart of Ennis town centre, was the chosen location and Robert went in and sat at the bar. But he wasn't the only man in the vicinity as an extensive garda surveillance operation was by now in full swing. Several plain clothes gardaí were located in a 360 degree circle around the hotel, while two female gardaí, Beatrice Ryan and Michelle Holian, sat in the bar of the hotel. While Robert Howard was in the bar, he received another phone call from 'Tony', telling him to go to the bathroom of the hotel, where he would meet a lady who would count the money.

He immediately contacted Detective Garda Fahy, who was one of the gardaí involved in the surveillance operation and was standing outside, just yards from the hotel. Detective Garda Fahy advised Robert to go to the lobby of the toilets and meet the woman. He did that and described the woman as being dark-haired, in her late 40s or early 50s and wearing a leather jacket.

They spoke briefly, but on seeing a plain clothes female garda walking by, the woman sped off. A short time after Robert Howard met the woman in the hotel, both Essam Eid and Teresa Engle were arrested by gardaí nearby. That evening, neither Eid nor Engle had mobile phones at their disposal. Gardaí believed there was one of two possible reasons behind this: it meant that they could not be traced in Ireland, or, it was simply a basic error by them. They therefore had to depend on line of sight to keep in touch with each other in Ennis town centre that afternoon. But the surveillance operation was in place and their moves were being closely monitored.

Later that evening, an identification parade was set up at Ennis Garda Station by Sergeant Noel McMahon, who is attached to Shannon Garda Station. Nine men, including Essam Eid, were included in the line-up and both Robert and Niall Howard picked Eid out as the man who had called to their home the previous evening.

Wednesday, 27 September 2006 had been a long day and one of the most intriguing during the investigation. Those events triggered the extensive garda inquiry that was to follow and continue for a period of almost two years.

Eid was brought before the district court in Ennis the following morning and charged with the extortion of €100,000 from Robert Howard. He was also charged with burglary and two counts of handling stolen property. He was remanded in custody to reappear in court the following morning, Friday, 29 September.

Teresa Engle was released without charge and returned to America. But this was not the end of the garda inquiries as they now had to get to the bottom of the case. Why had the Downes and Howard office been broken into and what had prompted this man 'Tony' to call to Robert Howard and make a claim about a contract on the lives of the three wealthy businessmen? Given that he had a printout of photographs of Sharon Collins and PJ Howard, surely there must have been some substance to his dramatic claims?

The investigation continued and intensified over the months, gathering pace as each new piece of information emerged. When Eid was initially arrested, gardaí had no idea that Sharon Collins was involved. In his initial interviews, Eid told gardaí that he had been having an affair with Collins. While he later retracted this, gardaí were intrigued as to how he knew her mobile phone number off by heart and they felt he had a lot of detail about her and PJ Howard that shouldn't have been at his disposal. Every possibility was explored and between the end of September 2006 and February 2007, the investigation team carried out Trojan work. This included the analysis of 11 computer hard drives— eight in Ireland and three from the US. This analysis was ultimately to prove crucial and presented compelling evidence that played a key role in the case being brought.

Over those months, the gardaí liaised with Interpol and the FBI and were made aware that FBI special agent Ingrid Sotelo was carrying out her own investigation—independently of the Collins/Eid case—in relation to a similar incident in the US, involving Eid and Engle. Agent Sotelo had arranged to carry out a search of Eid's home address in Las Vegas. During this search, various materials, including personal details relating to Sharon Collins, were found.

This significant information, along with details of the FBI analysis of two Gateway computers that had been retrieved in the US, was relayed to gardaí in Ennis in February 2007. At that stage, a huge pile of evidence had been amassed and the investigation was upgraded to a conspiracy to murder probe. Sharon Collins was arrested for the first time on 26 February 2007, while Essam Eid, who was still in custody awaiting trial in the Circuit Court, was also re-interviewed at this time.

While the analysis of various computers had been ongoing at this stage, the Iridium laptop was seized from Ballybeg House— the home Collins shared with PJ Howard—on the date of Collins's arrest and this was later analysed and invaluable material was retrieved.

The investigation had gathered considerable momentum over time, but what was to come could not have been predicted by even the most experienced of garda officers. On foot of a tip-off from the FBI, it came to the attention of the gardaí that the lethal poison ricin could be found in Eid's cell in Limerick prison, in a contact lens holder. Teresa Engle had told investigators that she and Eid had made the poison in their home in Las Vegas, prior to flying over to Ireland to carry out the hits.

A search of his prison cell was carried out and the contact lens case was retrieved. It was analysed at Sarsfield Barracks in Limerick and then taken to the UK for further analysis. Of tests carried out on three sub-samples, one of them returned positive results.

This was alarming, but it wasn't the only significant information retrieved around this time. Further information obtained by the gardaí led them to return to the Two Mile Inn hotel in Limerick, also in April 2007. This was where Eid and Engle had stayed the previous September. There they found the hard drive of the Advent computer that had been stolen from the

Downes and Howard business at Westgate Business Park, Ennis, the previous September.

Christy Tobin, who worked in maintenance at the hotel had found the computer under bushes in the hotel grounds during the autumn of 2006. He had put it into the boiler house to dry it out, as it was wet. Little did he know at the time that this was going to play a crucial role in the investigation of a case that would grip the nation.

While these crucial pieces were information were being retrieved, the garda analysis of the computers was ongoing. Detective Sergeant Gubbins spent several hours analysing the computers and little by little, the email trail between lyingeyes98@yahoo.ie and hire_hitman@yahoo.com was recovered, email addresses the Prosecution alleged belonged to Sharon Collins and Essam Eid, respectively. Not only were the Irish computers analysed, but the analysis of the computers carried out in the US was duplicated in Ireland, ensuring that no stone was left unturned. This was thorough and while the defence had computer experts at their disposal, they did not call them to give evidence during the trial. Detective Sergeant Gubbins' work was exact.

As this information was being uncovered, gardaí followed up every lead. A reference to money being sent from Ireland to Las Vegas, via FedEx, in one of the emails, prompted this aspect to be investigated. This culminated in Collins admitting that she had sent money via FedEx to stop a blackmailer. The FedEx element played a significant part in the investigation, when taken in conjunction with the crucial emails.

The gardaí went on trips to Spain, the US and the UK and a lot of work went into piecing together exactly what had happened. They also reacted to information divulged by both Eid and Collins during their interviews. Collins had claimed that she had been blackmailed, after she had written personal information about herself and PJ Howard in an email to Maria Marconi, a woman she had claimed had been tutoring her to become a novelist, via the internet. Gardaí followed this up, but could find no trace of any woman of that name and after lengthy investigations, concluded that Marconi was nothing more than a figment of Collins's imagination. They pointed to the fact that Collins had claimed that she had been in regular contact with Marconi, but yet she was unable to provide a phone number, email address or postal address for her.

'She was supposed to be ghost writing a book with her. Ironically enough, no-one met her. She says she was in the office at 7A Westgate Business Park and that she used the internet. How could you bring someone around and not meet anyone? You'd meet somebody,' said a source. The Prosecution's case was if Marconi did exist, then why wasn't she called by the Defence, during the case?

On 2 October 2006—after the burglary—Collins had told gardaí that her emails and address books on the computers had been deleted. However, it wasn't until some days later that her profile was deleted from the Iridium laptop computer. Gardaí believed that she had deleted that profile, in the mistaken belief that it could not be retrieved.

Collins had an impeccable record and had never come to the attention of gardaí previously and would not have been familiar with the system in which suspects are interviewed. Any expectations by those involved in interrogating her that she might crack under pressure were dashed as she showed no sign of yielding, despite being put under intense scrutiny in several interviews in February and June 2007.

Collins was put under pressure during cross-examination in the trial to name who she believed had set her up, but she declined to name anyone. According to those close to the case, she similarly danced around the issue while being interviewed, but never boldly named who she thought it was.

Phone records have, in recent years, played a key role in major criminal investigations in Ireland and have been used as proof of suspects' locations and their communications. In this case, gardaí obtained phone records relating to a mobile phone in the name Sharon Collins, another in the name Sharon Howard and two mobiles and a landline in Essam Eid's name. These proved that there had been telephone contact between the two people, as up to 70 phone calls had been made between the numbers.

'Whoever Sharon Collins said she was talking to, her Spanish mobile has contact with Essam Eid's phone number. She left Ireland on 16 August 2006 and went to Spain. On that day, the contact moves to Spain. In her interviews [with the gardaí], she acknowledges that the phones were hers and she admitted in the witness box that only a few people had access to all of the computers and the phones. However she said in her interview that she may have spoken to someone twice, but when you break it down there were about 70 calls,' said a source close to the investigation.

Yet, despite the collection of such a huge volume of evidence, there was always the danger that there was too much evidence and that it was largely circumstantial, or that the Defence would succeed in getting key evidence ruled inadmissible.

'We were continuously trying to get that little piece that was conclusive, but we never did get that,' said a source close to the Prosecution. 'There was such a volume of evidence I don't think the jury could have come to any other conclusion. The only difficulty that surrounded this case was did we have too much evidence and the jury could be confused? However they [the Defence] were trying to exclude evidence all the time. We didn't know what the judge would exclude and it could have gone the other direction,' he added.

At that heart of this argument was the crucial ricin evidence. If it had been ruled inadmissible, as had appeared to be on the cards on the 11th day of the trial, it would have led to the jury being discharged. In opening the case, senior counsel for the Prosecution, Tom O'Connell, had spoken about the ricin element to the jury and if it was ruled inadmissible, then the jury would have to be discharged as they had been told about it. The trace of ricin found on the contact lens case was miniscule and gardaí believe that if Teresa Engle was correct in her statement that she

and Eid had travelled to Ireland with the lethal poison in a
contact lens case, then the remainder of it must have been flushed
down a toilet.

'The amount made, if she is right, could have killed hundreds
of thousands of people. Its only one function in life is to kill,' said
a source.

Given that the 'lyingeyes' and 'hire_hitman' email addresses were
set up on yahoo, a representative from yahoo in the US was
invited by the Prosecution to give evidence in the trial. However,
yahoo declined the offer and because they are based in the US, the
Irish authorities did not have the power to compel them to testify.
This could have proved a major headache for the Prosecution,
but, in the end, it didn't hinder the progress made.

Gardaí also met a stumbling block in that the internet cafés that
Collins had used in Spain didn't retain records and a lot of the
material had been overwritten. But given the huge volume of
material retrieved from computers in Ireland and the US, this,
ultimately, didn't hinder the Prosecution either.

The credibility of Teresa Engle's evidence was also going to be a
factor in the case. She coolly explained how she and Eid had
manufactured ricin together at their home, before flying to
Ireland. She described how she had sat in the car while Eid went
to the door of Robert Howard's home in Ennis and she was
insistent that this was a 'hit' and not a shakedown. While gardaí
believed her and she was granted immunity from Prosecution in
the case, the defence did not believe her story and branded her a
bare-faced liar who had a vested interest in giving evidence. If her
evidence was to be believed, it would have put Eid in the frame
for conspiracy to murder, but the jury was not convinced by her
and could not decide on those charges. According to those
involved in the case, Engle quickly turned her back on Eid and co-
operated with gardaí from October 2007 even though she didn't
have immunity at that stage.

Gardaí believed she was willing to give evidence from the
outset and despite her own lawyers advising against this, she kept

to her word and took the stand on the 13th day of the trial. Engle was granted immunity on a recommendation from the gardaí to the DPP, James Hamilton, on condition that she gave evidence in the trial. Gardaí made this recommendation after concluding that in reality, there was no prospect of her being prosecuted. The likelihood was if this case was brought to trial, there would be just one bite of the cherry and the Prosecution wanted to present its strongest possible case, with Engle as the chief witness for the State.

Engle told gardaí that she had visited Ennis weeks earlier, at the end of August or beginning of September 2006, where she had met Ashraf Gharbeiah, a friend of Eid's. She said he was supposed to kill Robert and Niall Howard, but pulled out. Mr Gharbeiah, a part-time police officer, was interviewed in relation to this case, but there was insufficient evidence to bring charges against him and he was not prosecuted.

Gardaí were also acutely aware that PJ Howard's evidence would have a bearing on the case, but what influence would this have on the jury? Mr Howard, who was a witness for the Prosecution, told the trial that Collins was not a greedy woman and that the allegations against her did not make sense. He told the ninth day of the trial, 'It is totally out of character. I find it very, very, very hard to believe.' He said she had never asked him for anything and had looked after him through his illness. After giving evidence he stepped down from the witness box, walked over to her and planted a kiss on her lips, before leaving the courtroom. How was the jury going to view this and how far up the scale would it feature during deliberations? There was every possibility that some of the jurors, at least, could have felt sympathy for Collins if one of the men she was accused of conspiring to kill was still infatuated with her.

The evidence given by John Keating would also play a role, but to what extent? Mr Keating was called by the Prosecution on the ninth day of the trial, to give evidence about changing locks for the Howards at their family business at the end of September 2006. But he told the trial, during cross-examination, that he had spent the morning of 16 August 2006 with Sharon Collins, driving around Ennis. This revelation created a bizarre twist. That was a crucial date in the case, as the Prosecution had alleged that emails had been sent by lyingeyes98@yahoo.ie that morning. After giving evidence, Mr Keating was interviewed by gardaí and his records were checked. He was later recalled to the witness box and was adamant he had spent that morning with Collins.

Collins's legal team said that he had been treated appallingly by gardaí who interrogated him in the aftermath of his earlier evidence, but what was the jury going to read into his evidence?

Both the investigation and the trial presented numerous headaches for the gardaí involved in the case. Not only did several gardaí spend much time overseas carrying out investigations in the year leading up to the trial, but many members of the investigation team travelled from Ennis to Dublin every week for the eight-week duration of the trial, at an enormous personal inconvenience. The complex nature of the case meant that they were on the edge of their seats each and every day of the trial, right up until the dramatic finale at the end of the 32nd day.

Various theories have surfaced, particularly in Ennis, prior to, during and after the trial and several opinions have been expressed on what actually swung the case towards the convictions on most of the charges. Those involved in the investigation put it down to two things: the weight of the evidence and Collins presenting two very different demeanours in the witness box. She appeared bold and brazen on the first day and teary and sad the next.

'The sheer weight of the evidence swung it, along with her [Collins] getting into the witness box. Some would say she gave the jury the opportunity to see what she was like. She was like chalk and cheese,' said a source close to the Prosecution.

Those involved in the case have also looked back at the turning points of both the exhaustive investigation and the subsequent trial, factors that influenced the entire case. They point to a number of key factors that contributed to the case being as strong as it was. These included the search of Essam Eid's home in Las Vegas; Eid's initial interviews with gardaí during which he showed some knowledge of Sharon Collins and PJ Howard; the analysis of the computers both in Ireland the US; the recovery of the ricin in the prison cell; and the recovery of the Advent computer in the grounds of the Two Mile Inn hotel. The Prosecution said that Essam Eid's decision to approach Robert Howard—when he couldn't get in contact with Sharon Collins— and offer to sell him the contract, was also crucial in the whole scheme of things and was a major turning point.

While it was impossible to recover every single email—only part of the email that Sharon Collins wrote to the *Gerry Ryan Show* was retrieved—those involved in the case were particularly pleased with Detective Sergeant Gubbins's retrieval of emails on three key days in particular, 2, 8 and 16 August 2006. These dates were outlined to the jury on the opening day, in Mr O'Connell's lengthy speech, as being central to the case.

On 2 August, the email account lyingeyes98@yahoo.ie had been set up on the Advent desktop computer at the Downes and Howard business. Searches for a hitman had also been carried out on that date. Six days later, on 8 August, lyingeyes98@yahoo.ie had established contact with hire_hitman@yahoo.com in what was the first of several emails exchanged between the two addresses. On the morning of 16 August, the progress of the FedEx package had been checked, through its tracking number, from the Iridium laptop at Ballybeg House (the computer from which a large proportion of the emails were retrieved). This was the day after Collins had sent €15,000, via FedEx from Shannon, to Eid's home address in Las Vegas.

'There was a history of everything on the relevant computers on those dates and that was where FedEx came up, her checking FedEx. The net analysis of those dates was crucial,' said a source.

Collins came up with an explanation about the €15,000. She introduced the name Maria Marconi and claimed she had been blackmailed. Gardaí followed up this claim, and senior investigators say this explanation would not be the thinking of a seasoned criminal, who would have said nothing, when probed about this.

A reference to a fourth hit was made in one of the emails sent by lyingeyes98@yahoo.ie to hire_hitman@yahoo.com and this, too, was investigated by gardaí, but while various theories exist, they did not come to any conclusive conclusion as to who this person was and it was not referred to again.

As the investigation opened up new avenues, various keyword searches were carried out along the way as part of the analysis. For example, when gardaí were made aware of a reference to a FedEx package, a keyword search was carried out for FedEx. The tracking number was found and this was crucial in many ways in the Prosecution case as Collins was traced checking out the movement of the package.

Gardaí asked themselves many questions during the investigation, including, if it was possible for somebody to plant all of the information on computers and have it sitting there. However, the analysis showed that this was not possible. The analysis also led gardaí to make contact with Brian Buckley, a Dublin-born soldier who told the trial that he had contacted the website www.hitmanforhire.net because he thought it was a joke. The website had advertised contract killings and he had been searching for cheat codes for the Hitman computer game when he had stumbled on the site. He filled out the application form, using the email address judas69@gmail.com on 29 July 2006. On 10 August, he had received a reply from Tony Luciano which stated, 'I have a job for you if you are interested. Two males in Ireland. One in Spain. asap. Let us know. We will try and call you.' He said he had received several phone calls from a man calling himself Tony Luciano, but would not talk to him.

The email contact between judas69@gmail.com and the 'hitman' website had been retrieved during analysis and gardaí had located Mr Buckley at his Dublin home and he gave evidence for the Prosecution.

On foot of the new evidence that had come to light, Sharon Collins was arrested for the second time on 25 June 2007. This was the day before Essam Eid was due to on trial at Ennis Circuit Court, accused of extortion, burglary and handling stolen property. However, that morning, a *nolle prosequi* was entered in court on those charges. Eid was released from custody, but re-arrested minutes later outside Ennis Courthouse. He was brought to Kilkee District Court, where he and Collins were both charged with conspiring to murder Robert and Niall Howard. Both were remanded in custody and while Eid was to remain in custody up to his trial, Collins was granted bail in the High Court within days. As part of bail conditions, she was prohibited from communicating with the Howards and she then moved from PJ Howard's plush home, Ballybeg House, to Nenagh, Co. Tipperary, to live with an old school friend.

Eid was later charged with extortion, burglary and two counts of handling stolen property. Both were later returned for trial to the Central Criminal Court and the trial date of 21 May 2008 was fixed. The week before the trial, the additional charges—relating to conspiracy to murder PJ Howard—were added to the indictment. A legal issue had arisen because the proposed hit on PJ Howard was to be carried out in Spain and this was why his name was not included in the initial charges that had been brought in June 2007.

The huge amount of evidence, contained in a nine volume Book of Evidence, was presented throughout the 32-day trial, but such was the technical, complex nature of the case, that it was impossible to predict the eventual outcome. Conspiracy to murder cases are not common in the courts in this country and the Prosecution had to prove that a tacit agreement was in place between Collins and Eid. The jury had an extraordinary amount of evidence to sift through and there was every possibility that some of the 12 jurors would either take pity on Collins or take the view that the details were so ludicrous, it was impossible to convict.

But the jury took its job seriously and considered the evidence in great detail, before convicting Collins of soliciting and of conspiracy to murder the three Howards. They could not decide if Eid had conspired to murder the three Howards and acquitted him of burglary. But they convicted the Egyptian of demanding €100,000 from Robert Howard to cancel a contract on his life and the lives of his father PJ and brother Niall and also convicted him of handing stolen property.

Privately, gardaí were pleased with the outcome and had always firmly believed that Sharon Collins was lyingeyes98@yahoo.ie. They believed that she had planned everything and that the Eagles song 'Lyin' Eyes'—which she had used in her email address set up for the purposes of the plot—fitted perfectly. However, given the sensitive nature of the investigation and the affect the entire case had had on so many people in the close-knit community in Ennis, gardaí declined to make a public statement on the matter.

10 | SHARON COLLINS IS LYING EYES

Cold, callous, calculating, deceitful, arrogant, manipulative. The list is endless, but all were used to describe Sharon Collins over the course of the trial. But, in stark contrast, Collins presented herself as being a doting mother and a caring and compassionate lover who was innocently caught, when she was set up by a blackmailer. She sat daintily in the courtroom day after day, often smiling and whispering to her sons, Gary and David, and nodding in accordance with the various pieces of evidence presented in the case. Like an angel. She confidently walked into court every one of the 32 mornings, carrying her file of notes and bottle of water, and in the early days a supply of chewing gum that would keep her going throughout the day. Always impeccably dressed in black trouser suits—either plain black or pin-striped with white or cream coloured blouses or low cut tops—Collins consistently wrote notes throughout the case, which she or one of her sons passed to her legal team while the evidence was being heard. Those were written on white paper during the early days but she changed to yellow post-it notes as the case wore on.

Sitting extremely close to her sons every day, Collins portrayed herself as being a loving mother. She had separated from her husband Noel Collins in 1990 and had become very close to their sons Gary and David—both in their 20s—over the years. When she became romantically involved with PJ Howard in 1998, she quickly moved in to his luxurious home and brought her two boys with her. Like any mother, she had sorely missed Gary when he had travelled to Australia in 2007, while she had helped David to buy a house on the Clare Road in Ennis. She organised the purchase of the house and dealt with the auctioneers. The sale had been finalised towards the end of 2006 and the house is now rented out.

But, ultimately, she was not like any caring, kind mother, as her greed tragically transformed her into an evil woman who would stop at nothing until she got exactly what she wanted. After months and months of investigations, the Prosecution presented her as an evil, conniving gold-digger whose dark ambition was to rid the world of PJ Howard and his two sons, Robert and Niall. She had claimed that PJ's sexual demands and black moods had made him unbearable to live with, but the gardaí investigating the case say she had one motive only—she wanted all three dead so that she could get her hands on PJ's millions. That was the conclusion that detectives had come to, after spending almost two years working on the case. They trawled through computers, investigated telephone records and interviewed dozens of people in a complex investigation that spanned the world. Given the bizarre, unpredictable nature of the case, gardaí would not leave a stone unturned and investigated in detail every single lead that emerged. The jury agreed that Collins was not the woman she claimed to be and did not believe her story that she had been blackmailed. They indicated this in their decision to convict her on all of six charges on which she stood accused.

Born on 11 May 1963 and christened Sharon Martha Coote, she was the youngest of three sisters. Her older siblings were Suzette and Catherine. They lived in a house in McNamara Park, which is just off the Kilrush Road on the outskirts of Ennis town. Her parents, the late Charles (known in Ennis as Lucas) and Bernadette (Ber) Coote separated several years ago and Sharon was very close to her mother, who still lives at the home in

McNamara Park. In fact it was her mother who attended court with her when she was initially charged with conspiracy to murder Robert and Niall Howard, at Kilkee District Court on 26 June 2007. Her mother is a glamorous woman in her mid-70s. Her maiden name was Cronin. Ironically, Sharon Collins used the name Cronin on the application form on the 'hitmanforhire' website. She told the trial that a lot of people in Ennis would know her as 'the girl of the Cronins'.

Sharon Collins had grown up in Ennis where she was described by locals as a confident, self-assured young woman. In general terms, growing up, she was no different to other teenage girls her age. She thoroughly enjoys socialising, while she also has an interest in music, reading and writing, has expensive taste in clothes and is always keen to look well. Throughout her life, keeping trim and looking well has always been a priority. Collins is an attractive, ambitious woman, with a great fondness for men. She loves going overseas on holidays and has a particular affection for parts of her native Clare, not least Seafield beach in Quilty, which she visited as both a child and adult and has indicated a desire to have her ashes spread there.

After completing her second level education in Ennis, she studied computers at the National Institute for Higher Education (now known as the University of Limerick). She was just 17 at the time and, two years later, she married her sweetheart Noel Collins in 1982. Collins was from a local village Newmarket-on-Fergus and they enjoyed many happy times together, during which they had two sons, Gary and David. The marriage had lasted for just eight years and they separated in 1990 when she was 27, and later divorced. She stayed in the family home in Maiville, a private housing estate—which is just a stone's throw from her mother's home—on the Kilrush Road in Ennis, for several years and had custody of their sons, whom she adores.

Those who know her say that Collins always enjoyed good relationships with men and had various partners over the years. But she did not settle down again until PJ Howard crossed her path. Collins had spotted him in their native Ennis when she was a young schoolgirl, aged no more than nine or 10. At that stage, he was in his mid-20s and he was making shapes in the business world. Their paths crossed again in November 1998, when he had walked into a furniture shop she ran at the time in Ennis. They soon became an item and within weeks, she and her two sons moved from their home in Maiville into his posh home, Ballybeg House, on the Kildysart Road, just a few miles from Ennis.

According to her, PJ had invited them to stay over the Christmas period, but they had effectively remained there permanently. She felt that his house was big and isolated and it seemed a lonely place for him to be on his own for Christmas. 'We went there with a view to moving back home after the Christmas, but, in reality, we only went back to our own house for a few days in February, around the first anniversary of Bernie's death [PJ's partner, Bernie Lyons]. He wanted to be alone for those few days. We then moved back in with him, permanently. I didn't take the move lightly,' she wrote, in one of her letters to the DPP. She said that a very short time after they met, PJ had asked her if she thought they could make a life together and they decided to stay together. 'I loved him and still do,' she wrote, in March 2007. 'If I am to be honest, though, I would have liked [it] if marriage was on the cards. However he made it clear to me that it wasn't,' added Collins. She said that by the time she became aware that his views on marriage were definite, she was well settled into his house 'so there was nothing for it, but to accept it and make the most of what was a very good and close, loving relationship, not without its ups and downs, but certainly not worth throwing away.'

But her wealthy partner didn't just provide her with a home. He gave her opportunity to live a champagne lifestyle and also provided her with employment. This pretty young woman who had lived quite an ordinary life in Ennis suddenly found herself checking in and out of airports on a regular basis, always on the go and thoroughly enjoying it. 'I didn't spend a lot of time in the country,' she told the jury. She worked as a part-time receptionist in PJ's company, Downes and Howard, and was fortunate enough to have had the opportunity to work inconsistent numbers of hours as money wasn't an issue for her. Robert would phone her when she was needed. 'Sometimes I spent an hour there a week. Sometimes I spent five or six hours,' she said. She took home around €850 per month from that job. PJ Howard gave her €1,000 a month and looked after her expenses.

Her only other source of income was her rental income from her properties, which was used to pay the mortgages on them. Along with the family home in Ennis, she has a retail unit in Tullamore and an apartment in Limerick. She was granted free legal aid for her trial, after her solicitor had told Ennis District Court on 29 June 2007—just days after she was charged with conspiracy to murder Robert and Niall Howard—that she would be 'very lucky' if she has 'anything left' after the case. That was Collins's second court appearance and her then solicitor Mary Larkin made a successful application for free legal aid.

Ms Larkin said that her client, who had not been employed for 'quite a considerable amount of time,' owned properties to the value of €725,000. On that occasion, the solicitor presented a statement of means to the court and said her client's bank balances showed two debits, and a small credit of less than €1,000 in one of them.

Judge Joseph Mangan then asked where she was living. Superintendent John Scanlan replied, 'Prior to this event, she was living at Ballybeg House. That address will not be available to her arising from this case.'

Ms Larkin said the family home, at Maiville, Kilrush Road, Ennis, would be available to Collins. 'The fact of the matter is that my client has no income … Leaving aside the family home, she has assets of €273,000.'

Collins, she said, would have to pay Capital Gains Tax of 20 per cent on the two properties she would have to sell to attract money. 'She has no income at all and defending yourself on very serious charges, both leading to a life sentence,' she said. She said computer experts may have to be acquired at a cost of up to €60,000, and investigations in the US, may form part of the case, which would be expensive. 'If she has anything left, she will be very lucky,' said the solicitor. Supt Scanlan said he accepted what the solicitor said and pointed out that there was an international element to the case.

Judge Mangan granted free legal aid and remanded Collins—and her co-accused Eid—in custody, but days later she was granted bail in the High Court and her status did not change until the end of the trial.

Love played a significant role in the saga. Though Collins was keen to marry PJ Howard, the feeling wasn't mutual and they never wed. It had been discussed between the two but PJ's solicitor advised him against it, as it would affect his healthy assets. But, tragically for PJ, Collins was adamant that she would get her claws into his assets, whether he was opposed to the idea or not. The issue was discussed betweeen the two and was raised again after PJ's estranged wife Teresa died suddenly from a brain haemorrhage, in February 2003. According to Collins, in the aftermath of Teresa's death, she began to realise that it would now be possible for her and PJ to marry. 'Well, to be honest, people were quick to point it out and I admit, I had thought of it too. I know that sounds terrible, but it's true,' wrote Collins, to the DPP. She and PJ spoke about it and in January 2004, he proposed to her while they were in Spain. However, the excitement didn't last as PJ was advised by his solicitor that a pre-nuptial agreement did not have any standing in Irish law. Much to her disappointment, everything was put on hold and while they pledged themselves to each other in Sorrento, Italy, in 2005, they never married.

But that was not the end of the matter, in Collins's eyes at least. Towards the end of 2005, she obtained a Mexican proxy marriage certificate on the internet, which stated that they had married. She arranged for this document to be sent to her book-keeper Matt Heslin in Kilrush. His statement was read to the jury during the trial. In it, he said that Collins told him in 2005 that she and PJ Howard were going to get married and they would be having a big wedding in the plush surroundings of Dromoland Castle in Co. Clare. He said that when he met her she was wearing an engagement ring and a Rolex watch. However, the wedding invitation never arrived. He contacted her and was told they would not be having a wedding in Ireland. 'She told me PJ's sons were not in favour of them getting married, so soon after the death of their mother,' he said.

Mr Heslin said that she asked him to receive the proxy marriage certificate as she was afraid it would arrive when she was away and 'the two boys would open it and perhaps damage it.' He said he felt that PJ was aware of it and he himself believed they were genuine documents.

Early in 2006, Collins used the proxy marriage certificate to obtain a passport in the name Howard—a move the Prosecution said was done as a dry run to see if it would stand up in the future. She told gardaí that she obtained the passport in his name as a gesture to him. 'I thought he would like it. I liked the idea. I wanted to belong. There was nothing sinister about it. I wanted it for myself,' she said.

But, significantly, the proxy marriage certificate was obtained without PJ's knowledge and was the first part of her prolonged internet activity that would gravely affect him. Gardaí believe that this was the first step in a carefully planned plot to have PJ and his two sons, Robert and Niall, killed. She wanted to inherit and could see that this was not going to happen if things remained the way they were. Collins had lived a high life with PJ, where holidays, boat trips, parties at five star hotels and castles and friendships with well-to-do people were the norm, but this was not enough. She wanted everything and set out to find somebody who would wipe them out, once and for all. This woman had gone from living an ordinary life in the town of Ennis to living a life of luxury, due to her association with PJ Howard. Over the years, she had engaged in several 'get rich quick' schemes and now she wanted her ultimate goal—to get her hands on PJ's millions and she would sit pretty forever.

Previously, Collins had operated a fitted furniture business in Ennis for a few years—which had closed in 2002—and had taught aerobics to children for a short period. She was also involved in a pyramid scheme—or as she referred to it as a multi-level scheme—with her accountant Matt Heslin, but denied this was a method of making cash quick. In fact, the deposit she sent to 'hitman' was money she had received from selling her franchise of the childrens' fitness programme to a friend.

Collins trawled the internet for an assassin and believed she had found one. So, why did she not make efforts to hire a local hitman, instead of travelling into the unknown? It begs the question, was she foolish to think that her footprints on the web would not be traced?

Gardaí believe it was not a foolish plan; they say she was well aware of what she was doing at all times and had all the pieces fallen into place for her, there would have been no solid evidence against her. If 'hitman' had disposed of the computers, as he had been ordered to do, and carried out the hits, then the Howards would be in their graves. There could be mountains of speculation and Collins would have been a suspect, but there would not have been any firm evidence to convict her. 'Hitman' would have been long gone, across the Atlantic. That was the way she saw it.

'She is not a stupid woman. She is a woman who wanted to get rich quick all her life. She was involved in pyramid schemes, and had her own fitted kitchens business at the pinnacle of the boom, when there was money to be made,' said a source close to the Prosecution.

The significance of the email address lyingeyes98@yahoo.ie is particularly sinister. The email address was set up in the name B. Lyons. Bernie Lyons was PJ Howard's former partner, who died in 1998. The '98' part of the email address was also relevant as it marked the year Collins and PJ Howard became an item, while the song by the Eagles 'Lyin' Eyes' was about a rich old man who fell for a beautiful young woman, who cheated on him. One of the verses of the song reads, 'My, oh my, you sure know how to arrange things, You set it up so well, so carefully, Ain't it funny how your new life didn't change things, You're still the same old girl you used to be.'

In the midst of Collins's stream of lies, she claimed that she was not familiar with the song, but it suitably fitted her malicious plan. She had arranged it all perfectly. Or so she thought.

Collins told gardaí that money didn't float her boat but they were cynical about this claim. Collins came across as an intelligent, articulate woman both in the witness box and in her writing, through her letters to the DPP and her emails to 'hitman'. She has had an interest in writing books and said PJ Howard had encouraged her to do this. But, while she claimed she was being tutored to write novels, all the time she was writing away to her heart's content, but alarmingly the writing was of a very different variety. While the contents of her emails could well form the basis of not only a novel but a film, her claim that she was learning how to write novels couldn't have been further from the truth. But, the jury could have decided otherwise and could have had sympathy for her. Her emails were very detailed and descriptive and ran into thousands of words. The level of detail and her inclination at times to treat 'hitman' almost like a pen-pal, allied to her allegations about PJ's treatment of her, could have presented her as a lonely, desperate woman, who had been neglected.

Collins had a void in her life after she had drifted from her best friend—who had become preoccupied with her own life—and, apart from PJ, she didn't have anyone to confide in. She claimed Maria Marconi became like a pen-pal and she started to divulge personal information to her. She even presented very detailed information to gardaí on a visit she claimed that Marconi had made to Ennis. She said that she had taken her on a tour around Clare and had showed her various houses and had taken her to her home, Ballybeg House.

Collins wrote about the time they had spent together with great attention to detail, in one of her letters to the DPP. She said they had gone to the seaside resort of Lahinch, in north Clare. 'It was summer. I stopped and got ice-cream cones there—a small one for me as I was dieting. I told her how popular the place was. There were quite a few people around on that day. We drove up to the top of the hill and I parked the car in a position that PJ and I often park while we ate the cones,' she wrote.

She described how they returned to Ennis, after their tour around the county, and she took a detour around Ballyea, so that she could show Marconi where they lived on the Kildysart Road. 'She thought it was fabulous and unique. We live on a lake shore. I could see she was impressed with the house and surroundings.

She remarked that I should do well in a divorce or in the event of my husband's death and I replied that I would never divorce my husband and that I was only interested in my home and a reasonable income if anything were to happen to him. I told her that anything more would be too much like hard work for me,' she wrote.

But gardaí investigating the case did not buy into the Marconi story and say it was all concocted by Collins who was desperate to retain her innocence.

Collins also presented herself as being quite spiritual, with a strong belief in God. She went to Lough Derg in Donegal on pilgrimage several times. Monsignor Richard Moran testified to this in the trial, giving evidence that she had visited for two days, between 9 and 11 August 2006. He said the records there suggested that she had been there eight times previously. Collins said, in one of her letters to the DPP, 'I have always tried to ensure that I prayed daily—much more than that these days, mind you, as it gives me comfort and hope. I'm sure that there are a lot of good things I could have done and didn't do in my life, and also a lot of things I could have done better, but I never did anyone any harm and never would, nor would I wish anyone any harm. I firmly believe that you reap what you sow in life and I am at a loss to understand why I'm being punished so severely at the moment with the threat of what might happen hanging over me. I can only put my faith in God and pray for everything to work out for the best—and also write to you.'

Collins accepted that she had been stupid for divulging personal information to Marconi—which she said had got her into the mess—but said apart from that, she had lived her life to the best of her ability. She described herself as being family-orientated, maternal, very soft and that she felt deeply for people. Allied to this, her neat, ladylike approach in the courtroom every day, could have fooled many, but not the jury.

One word that came up several times during the trial in reference to Collins was 'manipulative'. She was accused by the Prosecution of being manipulative by smiling at the jury, while her letters to the DPP, asking not to be charged, were also criticised. Collins had asked the DPP James Hamilton in her letters not to have her charged as a trial would have a devastating effect on all of her family, particularly her youngest son David, who was just 21 at the time. She said she had reached breaking point and had contemplated suicide after she was questioned by gardaí in relation to the matter. She wrote:

> What am I to do Mr Hamilton? You are the only person who can decide if our lives are to be destroyed. My life is very much in your hands. I'm quite desperate for all this to stop … Please not have me charged, please let us get on with our lives. I've told the truth about everything. If I am charged, my relationship with PJ will be over.
> … I'd rather be dead than subject myself to this. My life is in shambles. My husband has been told by gardaí I've paid money to have him killed but he does not believe it.
> … The thing is, being charged is unbearable for me. I do believe someone out there has the capability of setting me up and it had to be done for financial gain. Who would want a family killed in one go? It doesn't make sense to me.

But, gardaí put all of this down to Collins's wild imagination. Sources close to the Prosecution believe that as time wore on, she even began to believe her own lies; such was the conviction with which she told her stories. It also begs the question, what truth lay in her stories about PJ Howard's sexual preferences? This was a woman who claimed she loved PJ Howard, yet was adamant that he would die and had calmly discussed possible causes of death— suicide or natural cases—via the internet, with 'hitman'. It was imperative that it did not look like a hit, she had said.

But who believed her lies? Apart from her sons, her former husband Noel Collins and his wife Fiona, she did not have any friends to call upon in court during her trial. Her six defence witnesses were 2FM dj Gerry Ryan, his producer Siobhán Hough,

Collins's sisters Suzette and Catherine, her former solicitor Mary Larkin and a furniture dealer John Kenny. Apart from her sons, she did not have any shoulder to cry on in the courtroom during the trial—no school friend, neighbour or cousin that she could confide in.

When Collins set out to put a premature end to PJ, Robert and Niall Howards' days, she was gripped by determination and consumed by greed. She thought she had struck gold when she met PJ, the millionaire who had everything. She believed she was invincible when she set about her evil plot to inherit everything he had. She had hopes and dreams of living off his millions. Not content with enjoying his money in his company, she wanted the massive chunk all to herself.

Tom O'Connell, in his opening speech to the jury, made it quite clear that the Prosecution case was, 'Lying Eyes is Sharon Collins.' Significantly, the jury agreed. And, on the evening of 9 July 2008, it all came crumbling down as her hopes of a fairytale future were dramatically dashed. Her lies and deceit came back to haunt her and she transformed from 'lyingeyes' to crying eyes.

Collins the ambitious, charming young woman had, over the years transformed into a bitter and twisted gold digger, and she was dramatically caught out in the end. Her lavish lifestyle with a man who was besotted by her was quickly replaced by an unenviable lifestyle in the women's section of Mountjoy prison, her dream of becoming a millionaire well and truly dead.

11 | THE EGYPTIAN GANGSTER

The Prosecution claimed Essam Ahmed Eid was a hitman, but his legal team painted him to the contrary. His lawyers claimed he was not somebody involved in a conspiracy to murder and ultimately the jury could not decide and recorded verdicts of disagreement in relation to the three conspiracy to murder charges he faced. He denied demanding €100,000 from Robert Howard to cancel a contract on his life and the lives of his brother Niall and father PJ on 26 September 2006.

Eid denied entering as a trespasser Downes and Howard Ltd, Unit 7A, Westgate Business Park, Kilrush Road, Ennis, and stealing a computer, a laptop, computer cables, a digital clock and a poster of old Irish money, on 25 September 2006.

He was also accused of handling stolen property. These were keys to the Downes and Howard office, a digital clock, a poster of old Irish money and computer cables, at the Two Mile Inn hotel, Limerick. On 27 September he was also charged with handling a stolen Toshiba laptop at Ballaghboy, Doora, Ennis, on 26 September 2006.

Essam Ahmed Eid was born in Egypt on 22 October 1955. He grew up in Egypt and moved to America at the age of 25. Most of his family still lives in Cairo. His address in Egypt was 30 Ismail, Serry, Cairo. He has a daughter, Aiya, who is now aged 20, of whom he is very fond. However, she lives overseas and did not attend the trial. In 2006, Eid lived at 6108 Camden Cove Street, Las Vegas, Nevada, USA, with his wife Teresa Engle and a woman he had previously married, Lisa Eid, née Meress. He admitted to gardaí that he had two wives, that it was not against his religion. He said he didn't care what the US authorities thought about that as, 'I have to do it on account of my religion.'

He worked as a poker dealer in a casino in Las Vegas called Casino Bellagio, where he earned $6.15 an hour. He was known as 'Sam' in the US.

Eid, a Muslim, cut a lone figure during the trial, but seemed to actually enjoy the whole experience. He sat near his legal team every day and except for an Egyptian man living in Dublin, who frequented the trial on occasions, there was no sign of any support for him. He always appeared pleasant, smiled and chatted with prisoner officers and slapped them on their backs. He smiled at journalists, always saying a friendly 'Good morning' and spoke of his ill-health, and waved to photographers as he was led in and out of the Four Courts daily. His smiles and waves became a feature of the publicity surrounding the case in the newspapers, as he appeared like a man who hadn't a care in the world. However, gardaí involved in the case describe him as cunning and devious. His English is poor, but gardaí say he is a very intelligent man. Apart from his communications with his legal team and prison officers, his talk to the media was Essam Eid's only brush with humans during the lengthy case. He did not have any defence witnesses at his disposal and did not go into evidence himself.

Various pronunciations of his surname—efforts ranged from Ed to Eye-eed to Ide—by those on their feet in the trial yielded the odd grin from the man himself.

He even sat back and smiled as the verdicts were brought in throughout the final day of the trial.

During the trial, he wore black Levis jeans and black runners and had two shirts at his disposal, one white and the other pink. He also alternated between two striped ties, one based on red and the other predominantly blue. During the cold, wet conditions during part of the (summer!) trial Eid wore a black Nike sports jacket with the word 'Nikeshox' on the back. Despite his lack of contact with family members during the trial, Eid never appeared to become despondent and in the latter stages of the jury's deliberations, he took out his Quran and began to read it. That seemed to give him solace.

His wife, Teresa Engle—who has turned her back on him—flew back to America shortly after her arrest and subsequent release in Ennis in September 2006 and only returned to Ireland to give evidence in this trial.

Eid had been in custody in Limerick prison since his arrest directly across from the Queen's Hotel in Ennis on 27 September 2006. During this time, he had been in ill-health—he suffers from diabetes and has a pacemaker fitted. He was granted free legal aid for the trial.

Eid travelled to Ireland on 24 September 2006 and stayed at the Two Mile Inn hotel in Limerick, with Teresa Engle. He told gardaí he was here on holiday and said it was the longest holiday of his life, but the Prosecution argued that his motives were far deeper and more sinister than a mere holiday.

It was the State's case that he operated the website www.hitmanforhire.net and had conspired with Sharon Collins, through email, to murder PJ, Robert and Niall Howard. However, while the jury convicted him of demanding €100,000 from Robert Howard to cancel a contract on his life, along with the lives of his father and his brother, it could not decide on the three conspiracy to murder charges against him.

It was the State's case that he was the man behind the email hire_hitman@yahoo.com and used the alias Tony Luciano, claims that he vehemently denied at all times.

Eid initially appeared before Ennis District Court on Thursday, 28 September 2006, charged with the extortion of €100,000 from Robert Howard. Eid, who was 50 at the time, was also charged with burglary and two counts of handling stolen property. He was remanded in custody to reappear in court the following morning. On that occasion, his then solicitor Tara Godfrey applied for free legal aid. However, Inspector Michael Gallagher, prosecuting, said that issue would have to be checked out by gardaí as Eid was living outside the jurisdiction. Judge Joseph Mangan deferred the application, after hearing that Eid had an average weekly income of €1,000 and also had a mortgage, relating to a property in Nevada. Ms Godfrey said her client had no savings. She said he only had €200 on him and did not have the means to pay a solicitor. The solicitor also applied for bail and pointed out that her client had no previous convictions either in Egypt or in the US.

'Given his age, he is not at risk of re-offending,' she said.

However, Inspector Gallagher objected to bail and Eid was remanded in custody for a fortnight. Eid later applied for bail in the High Court, but was refused and made several appearances before Ennis District Court over the following months. In that court on 24 November 2006, Inspector Gallagher said that good progress was being made in the case and he sought a further remand in custody for a fortnight.

However, Ms Godfrey said her client had been refused bail both in the District Court and in the High Court. She said she had not seen any evidence in relation to 'what the substantive matters are about'. Judge Joseph Mangan agreed with the request to remand Eid in custody. Eid was later returned for trial to Ennis Circuit Court, where he was due to go on trial on 26 June 2007.

However that morning, the State entered a *nolle prosequi* and indicated in court that it was not going to go ahead with that case and Eid was released from custody. He was re-arrested minutes later outside Ennis Courthouse and immediately brought to Kilkee District Court, charged with conspiring with Sharon Collins to murder Robert and Niall Howard.

Detective Sergeant Michael Moloney told Kilkee court that he arrested Eid at Lifford, Ennis, that morning. He had nothing to say, in reply to the charges and was remanded in custody.

Several District Court appearances in Ennis followed and Eid was in custody throughout.

During one court appearance, on 13 August 2007, solicitor Siobhán McMahon (who is employed by solicitor John Casey, who represented Eid during the trial) expressed concern about the length of time it was taking for the Book of Evidence to be prepared.

Inspector Gallagher said the case was a complex one and the investigation had extended to the US and Mexico. He said that as part of the investigation, five computers were being examined at garda headquarters. However, in court two weeks later, 27 August 2008, the State was accused of 'buying time'.

The remark was made by solicitor John Casey, after Inspector Tom Kennedy sought an adjournment of the case, to allow for the Book of Evidence to be completed.

Asked by Mr Casey what stage the Book was at, Inspector Kennedy replied, 'It is in the process of being prepared … more than half way to being available. Quite a number of extensive enquiries in relation to the charge before you come into play.'

He pointed out that while Eid was initially charged in September 2006, the charge he was currently facing did not come before the court until June 2007.

'The main plank of Mr Casey's argument is this is going on since last September, when he was first charged. That is not the case,' said Inspector Kennedy.

The solicitor said he could not consent to an adjournment and said his client had been in custody for almost a year. 'Now they are only half way through the Book of Evidence. Two months have passed. He is a non-national. He doesn't have contacts in this country. Bail is proving extremely difficult. How long is a piece of string?' he asked.

'Is the State buying time? Mr Eid is languishing in Limerick prison,' he said.

He said the accused was in ill-health and his manner had deteriorated, over the previous 12 months. 'It cannot be open-ended. It's not fair to him. He is innocent until proven guilty,' said Mr Casey. However, Judge Leo Malone remanded Eid in custody.

At Ennis District Court on 26 October 2007, four other charges were brought against Eid. He was charged with demanding €100,000 from Robert Howard to cancel a contract on his life and the lives of his father PJ and brother Niall. He was also charged with burglary and two counts of handling stolen property.

Detective Sergeant Michael Moloney told the court that Eid made no comment when charged. However, John Casey said that the new charges were 'a delaying tactic by the State because they knew they would not have the Book of Evidence on the conspiracy to murder charge in court today'.

'He has nobody, no friends, no relatives. Under the Criminal Justice Act 1999, the State is allowed 42 days to prepare a Book of Evidence, but since Mr Eid was charged with conspiracy to murder last June, he has been in custody 122 days—that is 80 days more than the 42 day limit,' said the solicitor.

'There has been an inordinate delay in preparing the Book of Evidence and the State has objected strenuously to every bail application by Mr Eid. The State cannot have it all their own way and it must abide by the rules. Judge, is it time that you blew the whistle on the State as this cannot go on indefinitely,' he said.

State solicitor for Clare, Martin Linnane sought a two-week adjournment to allow the Book of Evidence to be fully completed, after explaining that an error in his office had resulted in most of the Book of Evidence being deleted.

'There are over 100 witnesses in the case with 44 exhibits and there is 1,000 pages in the Book of Evidence. 850 pages were deleted. I brought the computer to a computer expert in Dublin in order to retrieve the Book of Evidence, but to no avail. I have been working around the clock on this as I am aware that Mr Eid is in custody,' said Mr Linnane.

He said he was totally rejecting the accusation that the new charges were a 'delaying tactic'. Judge Joseph Mangan extended time for service of the Book of Evidence and remanded Eid in custody.

The Book of Evidence was later served and Eid, along with Collins, was returned for trial to the Central Criminal Court, where the date of Wednesday, 21 May 2008 was fixed for the trial.

Eid agreed to take part in an identification parade at Ennis Garda Station on 27 September 2006, where Robert and Niall Howard identified him as the man who had called to their house the previous night, demanding €100,000 from Robert in order to cancel a contract on his life and that of his father and brother.

Details of Eid's interviews with gardaí throughout the investigation were included in the Book of Evidence and introduced as exhibits during the trial. The Prosecution argued that he assumed a 'flippant' tone during those interviews, first claiming he had an affair with Collins, but later retracting the statement.

During the first of those interviews, conducted at Ennis Garda Station on the evening of 27 September 2006, he had been quizzed by Detective Garda Jarlath Fahy and Garda Beatrice Ryan. This was shortly after his arrest close to the Queen's Hotel, which is situated on Abbey Street, just yards from Ennis Garda Station. In that interview, Eid had explained that he was married and 'came from Egypt to visit my wife. I go there every year for my Green Card and I go back to my country Egypt.' He told gardaí that he had arrived in Shannon airport on 24 September 2006 on a US Airways flight for a holiday and was going back on 1 October. He said he had visited Ireland with his 'friend' Teresa Engle. Asked was she his wife, he said, 'Ya, like partner wife. I see her once a year.' He said they had got married three years earlier and did not have any children together. He had an 18-year-old daughter with his first wife and she was in college.

He said that he worked in casinos in Las Vegas and also in Egypt. He explained that he and Teresa Engle were staying in Room 208 at the Two Mile Inn hotel in Limerick. They were due to leave that day and had planned to visit Dublin for three days after that. He had never been to Ireland previously, but had visited England, Spain and other European countries. He was asked when did he go from Egypt to the US and said, 'About three or four weeks ago. I don't remember the dates. I stay about month to two month and then go back.'

He said they had rented a light blue car from a company at Shannon airport, after arriving in Ireland. He said that was his second day in Ennis during his holiday. They had gone to Ennis for a look around and for something to eat. He said they had visited a 'very expensive shopping store Dunnes Stores' in Limerick the previous night.

Eid was asked if he had phoned anyone in Ennis that day and said he had not. He said he had tried to call his wife in Egypt from a public phone at the Square (also known as 'The Height') in Ennis. He was asked did he ever use the name 'Tony' and said, 'No, I use Sam in America as they have a hard time saying Essam. It's easier to say Sam. Why is Tony for?' Asked did the name Robert Howard mean anything to him, he replied, 'No, is it for America?' He said he knew a Robert in America.

He was then asked where he was the previous evening, 26 September 2006, between 10 p.m. and 10.30 p.m. He said he was in Dunnes Stores, as far as he could remember. They then went into Limerick and had a meal in a Mexican restaurant. Asked was he in Ennis the previous night, he replied, 'No, I don't think so. I in Limerick last night.' He was asked did he return a stolen laptop to Robert Howard the previous night, and replied, 'No, if somebody stole something, why give it back. Nice guy.' He was then asked, 'Robert Howard who lives in Ennis, had a stolen computer returned to him last night by a man who fits your description. Are you saying that was not you?'

He replied, 'I'm positive. I'm positive. A lot of people look alike. I'm positive.' He said he did not know anybody in Ennis. It was his first time in the town, 'looks like last time too', although his wife had been there the previous month.

Eid was interviewed again the following morning, 28 September 2006, by the same two gardaí. It was put to him that in the identification parade the previous night, Robert Howard had identified him as the person who had returned his stolen computer on Tuesday, 26 September.

Eid replied, 'He knows me before I came in the line maybe. I don't know. I complete different from two days ago. Shaven face. I had baseball cap two days ago. I completely different night before he pick me up within a second he no look at the line like he know me before he comes in.' He said he had never met Robert Howard before.

It was also put to him that Niall Howard had picked him out in the identification parade and Eid said he had never met him before either. During that interview, Eid was shown two photographs, which Robert Howard said 'Tony' had with him, two days earlier. Looking at one of them, he said, 'I know this lady. It's Sharon … Sharon, I don't remember her last name. Lane or Connor or something like that.'

He said he didn't know the man in the photograph. One of the gardaí then said to him, 'After the identification parade last night, I brought you for a cigarette. You were still under caution and you told me that you knew a PJ Howard.'

Eid replied, 'Ya, I know him. I heard about a PJ Howard. Ya, I used to date his wife.' He said that was the woman in the photograph. He said he had dated her for two or three years, on and off. The last time he had met her was on a boat in Malaga in June and they talked on the phone a lot. He said he had spent about six days in a hotel in Malaga and had been in and out on a boat with her. He was shown a photograph of PJ Howard and said he had never met him. He was asked about the other computer that was missing from Downes and Howard Ltd and replied, 'You kidding. I don't know that 'til now.'

He was asked had he told anyone he was visiting Ireland and replied, 'Ya Sharon … I was to go to Malaga to meet Sharon, but my wife said she come with me. I cancelled my trip and come here with my wife.' He said that Sharon had known for months about his trip and she had paid for the flight tickets on a credit card. 'Generous lady, Sharon, is she?' asked the garda.

Eid replied, 'Ya, she is very nice, but I tell her I pay her back for the other ticket.' He said that Sharon had phoned him twice. 'Sunday I call her and give her the room number and she called me twice after that.'

It was put to him in that interview that he had broken into the Howards' office on Monday of that week, 25 September. He replied, 'Na. No sir. There is no reason to break into anybody's house or office to get computer.' He also denied calling to Robert Howard's house and denied demanding money from him. He said he never spoke to Robert.

'€130,000 is not worth it to kill family. I used to be a fighter. I used to be black belt. I think my daughter see me hit somebody. I big heart. You have no idea. I shocked when my lawyer told why kill somebody for this … If you make this kind of deal with someone, you don't give them five to 10 minutes to get it. You give them week, two weeks or two months to get it. How he get money at night? I don't know about you guys, but our bank close at 5 o'clock,' he said.

It was put to him that he had arranged to meet Robert Howard at the Queen's Hotel the previous day, 27 September and was arrested directly across from the hotel.

He replied, 'Yesterday was your lucky day. Maybe he know I coming there around the area there. Somebody track me down.' He said his wife was having coffee in the Queen's Hotel.

It was put to him that he was telling lies, but he denied this.

'No I'm not. I am not lying. I don't know how to explain to you. I brought up different to you. If I live if you steal money from anybody, even a penny, it like poison in my kid's mouth. I come here with my wife for good, then why I bother with asshole like that. Sorry for my language,' he said.

As the investigation continued, Eid was remanded in custody to Limerick prison. He was interviewed again several months later, on 1 March 2007, by Detective Sergeant Michael Moloney and Detective Garda Jarlath Fahy, two of the chief investigators in the case. During those interviews, Eid retracted his earlier claim that he had had an affair with Sharon Collins and said Teresa Engle had told him to say it, when they were together in the cell at Ennis Garda Station. 'I never met the lady. I have never, never been in Spain,' he said.

He said that Teresa Engle and Sharon were in regular phone contact but he did not speak to her. Eid also said that Teresa Engle had paid for the flights and accommodation for their holiday in Ireland. He denied all knowledge of the email addresses tony luciano2001@yahoo.com and hire_hitman@yahoo.com. He said he had never received an email from lyingeyes98@yahoo.ie.

During that interview, Eid was told that the FBI had carried out a search of his home in Las Vegas on 4 December 2006, during which a number of items were seized. Among the items were an address book, which contained a mobile phone number for Sharon Collins. 'How could a phone number for Sharon Collins, County Clare, end up in the address book of Essam Eid in Las Vegas?' he was asked.

He replied, 'I have no clue.'

Phone records were also referred to, where it was pointed out to him that a phone call from his landline was made to Sharon Collins's mobile number. He denied making that call.

'There are nearly 70 calls to Sharon Collins from your landline and your mobiles. Can you explain that?' he was asked.

He replied, 'I have no comment … I can say I never spoke to this woman at all.'

It was put to him that the email accounts essameid@yahoo.com and hire_hitman@yahoo.com were accessed from the same computer one minute apart, on 24 June 2006.

Eid replied to this, 'It is not me.'

He said he was working on this date. It was then put to him that the two email addresses were accessed again in less than a minute of each other on Monday, 28 August 2006, which was during his day off from work. 'That means to me that you are 'hire_hitman',' said the garda.

Eid replied, 'Maybe I'm not there.'

It was then put to him that both of those email addresses and tonyluciano2001@yahoo.com were all accessed within minutes from his computer, also on 28 August 2006.

'Essam Eid, Tony Luciano and 'hitmanforhire' are all the one person. Do you accept that? Does it seem logical?' asked the garda.

Eid replied, 'Well somebody use it so it seems logical.'

Details of an email sent from hire_hitman@yahoo.com to lyingeyes98@yahoo.ie on 20 September 2006, were read to him, but he said this didn't mean anything to him.

The garda investigation intensified over time and Eid was again interviewed on 20 June 2007. He had been arrested in Limerick prison that morning, on foot of new information and evidence gathered by the investigation team. On that date, he told gardaí he had four cell phones, but he could not remember the numbers. Asked what had brought him to Ireland, he said, 'For a holiday. Big mistake. Big mistake.'

He said he would have no reason to demand €100,000 from Robert Howard.

When it was put to him that it may have been for money, he replied, 'Money, I make $94,000 a year. I have my house. I have my boat.'

He was asked to explain how an email recovered from the Iridium laptop at Ballybeg House was also recovered from a printout at his house, Camden Cove, and he said, 'I am not responsible for what came into my house.'

He was told that Robert Howard had identified him as the man who had called to his house, calling himself 'Tony.' In reply to this, Eid said, 'Is this guy mentally ill? Is he gay? The way that he came in, don't write this. Oh shit. I don't know if you write it.'

During one of those interviews on 20 June 2007, Eid said to gardaí, 'You know from day one I'm framed for this and I'll prove it to you. I'm not this kind of person. I have kids.' Eid told gardaí his trip to Ireland was the 'longest holiday of my life'.

He was shown four photographs and it was put to him by a garda that they were sent to him by Sharon Collins.

Eid replied, 'I believe if I play the lottery I win. I never see any of those.'

He was then asked, 'It is also my belief that the reason they were sent to you and reason being so you could identify three targets you had to kill?'

He replied, 'Wow, you smart man, that completely wrong.'

The ricin issue was then put to Eid, brought on by a question relating to his sight. He was asked if he had ever worn contact lenses and said he never had as he was too scared to put anything into his eyes. It was then put to him that when his cell in Limerick prison was searched on 25 April 2007, he was asked if he had a contact lens holder.

'You said yes and you showed the gardaí where to find it,' said the garda.

Eid replied, 'I told the gardaí where my clothes at. I never say where contact lens. If you don't believe me, ask the Governor. I never wear contact lens. He was there same night and he handcuffed me.'

The garda said, 'Our information was that you had a contact lens holder in your cell and when Mr Fahy asked you where it was, you told him where it was and when he went into the cell, he found it and that is what happened.'

Eid's single-word response was, 'Wow'. He denied that the contact lens case was his. He said that the men who had searched his cell were dressed in attire 'spaced like going to the moon'.

It was then put to him, 'They were all suited up with biological gear, the reason being they were told it contained ricin.'

Eid replied, 'So eight months later I had it. I have no idea what ricin was 'til I read it next day in the paper. Everybody make phone [fun] of me, saying don't touch him.'

He was told it was lethal and replied, 'If I had something like this, how come I not die?'

Eid was then told that when his computer at Camden Cove Street, Las Vegas, was examined, a document on how to make ricin from castor beans was retrieved.

He replied, with a question, 'How everything on computer in my house point to me?'

The garda told him that the contact lens cover in his cell contained the ricin poison. 'It is lethal and has only one function, but to kill,' said the garda.

Eid replied, 'Absolutely. That is what you said.'

The garda asked him, 'And you had it?'

Eid replied, 'Congratulations.'

It was put to him, 'And here on your computer at home, you had the recipe to make it?'

Eid replied, 'How nice.'

Asked how he had made it, he said that he hadn't made it.

'Did you bring ricin poison into Ireland with the intention of killing PJ Howard, Robert Howard, Niall Howard?' he was asked.

'Hurt innocent people, never, never. I never, ever hurt anybody. Their father almost my age, would not hurt his kids. I never that way,' he replied.

He was asked to explain how ricin was found in his cell and answered, 'No comment sir. Next question.'

He was then asked why text about poisoning, ricin poisoning, about people that were killed from it, cyanides, potassium, poisons and deadly poisons were found on his computer but, again, he refused to comment.

The garda then said, 'I know why. You came over to Ireland with ricin to kill the Howards?'

Eid replied, 'Beautiful next question.'

Asked how much money he was getting to kill the Howards, he replied, 'Newspaper say €15–20,000.'

Asked what he had got, he said, 'Nothing.'

Asked if he had received any of the €15,000 sent to his address by Sharon Collins, Eid replied, 'No, sir.'

He was then asked if he had conspired with Sharon Collins to kill PJ, Robert and Niall Howard and replied, 'No comment, sir.'

Eid was again interviewed the following morning, 21 June 2007 at Ennis Garda Station. The search of his cell in Limerick prison was the focus of some of the questions. Detective Garda Jarlath Fahy asked Eid if he remembered being searched by him and another person.

Eid said he did remember being searched and said the garda looked like 'space, spaceship' because of the clothes he was wearing. It was explained to him that they were dressed like that because they thought they might find the ricin poison. It was put to Eid that he told gardaí on the evening of the search of his cell that he did wear contact lenses.

He refused to comment.

'You told me that you did but you lost them in the prison cell about two months after you had been there. Did that happen?' asked Detective Garda Fahy.

Eid refused to comment.

'When you were asked that evening, you stated that you did, that it was off-white in colour and that it was in a box under the centre of your bed in your cell. Is that correct?' asked the garda.

Again, Eid refused to comment.

The garda continued, 'When I left you, I told that to the army man, who was also dressed in a biological suit. He went into your cell first, went to the box under the centre of your bed and took out a contact lens holder. Is that your contact lens holder?'

Eid did not comment.

Asked if he had known how to make the ricin poison, he said, 'No.' He also denied ever buying a castor bean plant and did not comment when asked if he had ever purchased castor bean seeds. He also refused to comment when asked if he had put the ricin poison into a contact lens cover.

'Some time after your arrest, you managed to dispose of the ricin poison, but you held on to the contact lens cover?' asked the garda.

Again, Eid did not comment on this.

'Essam, you have been shown a lot of evidence during your detention, phone records in relation to contact with Sharon Collins, emails, some found on your computer and from the laptop owned by Sharon Collins and from the business desktop at 7A Westgate Business Park, Ennis. When you were arrested on 27 September 2006, your room at the Two Mile Inn was searched and property stolen from 7A Westgate Business Park was found in that room. Do you have anything to say about all that, Essam?' asked the garda.

Eid's short reply to the long question was, 'No comment.'

(Detective Garda Jack Duffy had told the seventh day of the trial, Tuesday, 3 June 2008, that during a search of Eid's room at the Two Mile Inn hotel, on 27 September 2006, gardaí had recovered several items including two wigs, a pair of black leather gloves, a 'Halloween mask', a black balaclava, a digital clock, a poster of old Irish money and two keys. He told the court that the keys found in the hotel room 'fitted the lock Robert Howard brought to Ennis Garda Station' on 28 September. 'I believe it was from Robert Howard's business premises at Westgate Business Park, Ennis,' he said.)

It was then put to Eid that when he was first arrested, he told
gardaí that he was having an affair with Sharon Collins and had
spent a week on a boat with her and knew her phone number off
by heart. He was asked how could he explain this.

Again replied, 'No comment.'

Towards the end of that interview, Eid was asked if he regretted
getting involved in 'all of this'.

He replied, 'No. Never regret. No comment. No.'

Essam Eid did not give evidence in the trial, but the memos of his
interviews with gardaí were read to the jury. In his closing speech
to the jury, Eid's barrister David Sutton sc said the evidence
produced by the State in the case pointed only to fraud and not
conspiracy to murder.

He said there were 'inconsistencies and lack of evidence' in the
State's case. 'This is a case where there is a number of possibilities.
It's dressed up to look like the most important case on earth,' he
said.

He said the Prosecution had claimed, during the trial, that
nobody else apart from Sharon Collins could have sent the
emails. 'But the State has never said there was anybody other than
Tony Luciano who sent those messages,' said Mr Sutton.

He said that no-one was there to murder anybody. 'They were
there to do a shakedown, nothing else,' he said. He said that a
similar event had occurred in California, but no conspiracy to
murder charges had been brought in that case.

'Maybe the FBI take a more hard-nosed approach and they
don't get carried away,' said Mr Sutton. He said that the gardaí
knew in their 'heart of hearts that what was going on here was a
shakedown. What was going on here was soliciting, not a
conspiracy. They know that the conspiracy to murder charge is a
bridge too far. Simple as that and nothing Teresa Engle would say
could change that. She says the intention was murder. She hasn't
a notion as to how this murder was to happen. Was she going to
follow the Howard boys around Kilkee with a bottle in the hope
that they would get thirsty? It's at that ridiculous level.'

Mr Sutton told the jury that the evidence was just not there and it could not be 'welded together by self-serving perjury' from the mouth of Teresa Engle. To the amusement of the courtroom, with the exception of Sharon Collins who exhibited a very serious expression, Mr Sutton said the 'hitmanforhire' website was a 'clownish operation run by clowns in the hope of hooking fools'. He said the State over-egged the pudding for Eid, because they wanted to get Sharon Collins, 'and what patsy are they carrying along? Mr Eid. Clearly it was nonsense because they were trying to get Ms Collins. That's who they are after. We are only a prop in the operation,' he shouted to the silent courtroom.

He said it was a plot worthy of the Coen brothers and warned the jury not to 'join in the dots for the State. If the State can't do it, the judge can't do it. You can't do it.'

Mr Sutton's closing speech was on the 29th day of the trial, Friday, 4 July. The previous day, Robert and Niall Howard had briefly returned to the courtroom for the closing speech by Úna Ní Raifeartaigh for the Prosecution. Neither they nor their father PJ had attended the trial since PJ had finished giving evidence on the ninth day of the trial, almost a month earlier. Their presence did not go unnoticed and Mr Sutton made reference to it in his closing speech. 'Yesterday, who was brought in to the back of the court, the Howard brothers, here to eyeball you. Two live exhibits, because no-one was killed here,' he said.

The jury listened intently and did convict Eid of demanding €100,000 from Robert Howard to cancel a contract on his life, along with the lives of his father PJ and brother Niall, at Robert's then home, Ballaghboy, Doora, Ennis, on 26 September 2006. The maximum sentence for this offence is 14 years in jail.

However, after deliberating for almost 11 hours, the jury could not reach a decision on the three conspiracy to murder charges Eid faced and verdicts of disagreement were brought in on those.

He was acquitted of burgling at the Howards' family business, Downes and Howard, Kilrush Road, Ennis, on 25 September 2006.

However, he was convicted of handling a stolen laptop at Ballaghboy, Doora, and handling keys to the Downes and Howard office, computer cables, a digital clock and a poster of old Irish money, at the Two Mile Inn hotel, Limerick.

And, as he had done throughout the trial, Eid smiled and sat back in his seat as the verdicts were read out to the court. Shortly after, he was remanded in continuing custody to Cloverhill prison, where he had remained throughout the trial, to await sentencing.

12 | THE MILLIONAIRE BUSINESSMAN

It was a simple question, but it said a lot about the man. The date was Thursday, 22 May 2008 and the venue was courtroom number 16 in the Four Courts building. PJ Howard was seated on a bench along the wall in the packed courtroom, when his PR advisor Caimin Jones invited me over to introduce me to the millionaire businessman and his two sons. Robert and Niall shook my hand and said a few quiet words, but PJ had one question on his mind.

'Will this be of much interest in Clare?' he asked meekly.

I smiled and said, 'I'd imagine it will.'

I had been dispatched by my employer, *The Clare People*, to cover the trial, in the knowledge of the huge appetite for this story in Co. Clare. When the decision was taken by the newspaper to cover the entire trial in great detail, I was aware of many of the allegations that were going to come out, but the lid had not yet been lifted on several parts of the bizarre tale. PJ Howard would also have been acutely aware of many of the allegations that would be brought to light during the trial, but his naivety—in the shape of that question he posed—suggested he did not anticipate that the trial would make not only local but also national headlines every single day of its duration.

PJ Howard has amassed millions—estimates range from €12 million to €60 million—but has done this far away from the limelight. Even his company's office, at Westgate Business Park on the Kilrush Road in Ennis, is cut off from the hustle and bustle of town and most people would not be aware of its existence there. He has never courted publicity and is an intensely private, aloof man.

Although PJ is known as a shrewd, tough businessman, very little is known about his private life and that is the way he has always liked it. Unlike Collins, who loves attention, PJ Howard always got on with his life in a quiet away, mixing with other businessmen, away from the bright lights and public glare. He believed, or at least hoped, that this trial would come and go and that his privacy would remain intact. How wrong he was and how public his personal life would become over the following weeks, not least through bizarre allegations made in relation to his sexual interests. Allegations about his sex life, written by Collins in a letter to the *Gerry Ryan Show* on RTÉ's 2FM, would emerge during the trial. And while Mr Howard himself never publicly defended himself against those claims, two of his close friends did come out in the aftermath of the trial and strongly refuted what Collins had claimed.

PJ (Patrick James) Howard has enjoyed a life of luxury and it was his fortune that was at the centre of the case. Ironically, he turned 59 on Tuesday, 8 July 2008, when the jury was deliberating his partner's fate. By that stage, he had become extremely recognisable, having previously kept out of the public eye all his life.

PJ Howard owns a multimillion-euro home a few short miles from Ennis, off the Kildysart Road, called Ballybeg House, which is located on a lake shore. He also owns a plush penthouse apartment in Las Palmeras, Fuengirola, Spain—where he spends part of the year—and owns up to 70 properties, mainly in Clare and Limerick. These are a combination of commercial units and residential properties. For many years, he has been heavily involved in property and owns two businesses, Downes and Howard Ltd and Waymill Ltd. Mr Howard also owns a luxury yacht in Benalmadena, Spain—located six miles from Fuengirola—called *Heartbeat*. He chose this name on the recommendation of a friend, after suffering heart trouble and undergoing a quadruple bypass in 2000.

He was interested in boats and in travel all his life and has a strong affinity with the seaside town of Kilkee in west Clare. His connection with the town first arose when he had visited there with his parents, as a young boy. They had owned a caravan there in the 1950s and 1960s. As a child, he had gone there on holidays and had fallen in love with the town. His sons Robert and Niall also have a fondness for the town. They own a holiday home there, at Byrne's Cove, and spend much of their spare time socialising in the town, where the Greyhound Bar, on O'Curry Street, is a firm favourite of theirs. They also own a boat in west Clare.

PJ's eldest son Robert had lived in his home at Ballaghboy in 2006, but moved from that home prior to this trial. He drives a top-of-the range sports jeep. Standing six foot tall, Robert has the mature appearance of a man many years his senior. PJ's youngest son Niall had lived with Robert at Ballaghboy, but has since moved to another address. Niall, smaller in height than his older brother, drives a sports car. Both sons play an active role in running the lucrative family business as poor health has prompted PJ to take a back seat. However, the sons live their lives as their father has, away from the public eye.

But the Howard empire did not miraculously appear overnight. A combination of hard work and good fortune over the years made PJ the wealthy man that he is today. The firm Downes and Howard, a car sales operation, was set up in the 1950s on the Mill Road in Ennis, by PJ's late father Jack and a man called Denny Downes. PJ eventually joined his father in the business.

Jack Howard came from the west Clare village of Kilmurry McMahon, while Mr Downes hailed from Kilmihil, also on the western side of the county. The business quickly became a resounding success and was operated on that premises for two decades.

In the 1970s, they acquired a site directly across the road and expanded their business. Along with selling cars, they then operated petrol pumps and car repairs. At that stage, it was one of the biggest businesses in Ennis and was thriving, as this was the main Galway/Limerick road and was a hive of activity.

They built a forecourt on the site and operated the car sales part of the business from a prefabricated office. At the time, Downes and Howard held the only franchise in Clare for Fiat cars. Then, two decades on, in the 1990s, the original garage was knocked to the ground and was replaced by several shop units and an apartment complex. Now leased to another businessman and named Liddy's Costcutter Express, the shop and petrol pump business continues to thrive. Car sales no longer feature in the business, but there are a number of business units on the site, including a pizza restaurant, a Chinese restaurant and a wine store, while there are apartments in the immediate vicinity. The Howard empire on the Mill Road has expanded over the years as they have acquired several residential and commercial units on that busy stretch, which are rented out.

Just over a mile down the road, the Downes and Howard Ltd business has operated from an office in the Westgate Business Park, on the Kilrush Road in Ennis, since 2004. That property firm was registered on 12 January 1978 and is run by PJ, Robert and Niall Howard. PJ is both a director and secretary of the firm, while his two sons are company directors. PJ is also a director of Waymill Ltd, which was set up in 1986, and deals with the management of real estate. Robert is also a director of this company.

Despite his power and wealth, PJ Howard had one major weakness, which ultimately could have cost him his life and could have abruptly ended the days of his young sons. He has a penchant for beautiful, blonde women and after his wife and his subsequent partner had died, he fell for the charms of Sharon

Collins, who was almost 15 years his junior. His hopeless love for her blinded him to the extent that he could not believe she was capable of plotting to kill him.

PJ married Teresa Conboy, a woman from Co. Leitrim, in 1974. They had two sons together, Robert and Niall, but the marriage fell apart and they parted company in 1992. They were legally separated. Teresa continued to live in the family home on the Kilrush Road in Ennis, with Robert and Niall. An attractive, bubbly blonde-haired woman, Teresa was well-liked and worked in Tesco in Ennis for several years. She tragically died as a result of a brain haemorrhage in February 2003. Her youngest son Niall had arrived home from work at lunchtime one day and had found her gravely ill in her bed. She died some hours later.

After his separation from Teresa, PJ formed a relationship with Bernie Lyons and this lasted for some years, before she died from cancer in February 1998. A short time after her death, in November of that year, PJ Howard met Sharon Collins and it was this fateful meeting that would ultimately destroy his life and rip his privacy to shreds. When they met, PJ was 49 and Collins was 35. It was a chance encounter, but Collins felt it was destiny.

She had noticed him several years earlier when she was an innocent schoolgirl and he a successful businessman. PJ was taken in by her charm and within weeks of their meeting, he had invited her to stay at his home, Ballybeg House, along with her sons Gary and David. That invitation was intended as a short-term thing, but Collins effectively never left and their relationship became serious. Given his wealth, they enjoyed good times together, spending some of the year in Ennis and the remainder in Spain. He not only brought her into his home, but he also provided her with employment, as a part-time receptionist at Downes and Howard Ltd, and they enjoyed a lavish lifestyle together. They travelled a lot, drove top-of-the-range cars and jeeps and attended parties at the plush Dromoland Castle.

Materially, Collins had everything with PJ Howard, but she wanted to marry him. She realised after the death of Teresa in 2003 that he may now marry her, but he was reluctant. He obtained legal advice and was told that a marriage to Collins would affect his assets. But Collins was a gold-digger and was keen to get her hands on his assets. Unknown to him, she set about doing this, firstly by obtaining a Mexican proxy marriage certificate online and then planning to have him and his two sons killed, so that his millions would be hers.

But even in the face of the earth-shattering allegations against her, PJ Howard was obsessed with Collins and did not believe the claims. He made this clear in a letter he wrote to the Director of Public Prosecutions (DPP), on 23 March 2007, in which he expressed concern about the situation. He explained that he had known Collins for over eight years and had never known her to harm anyone. He said she had helped him through his by-pass operation in 2000.

'I firmly believe Sharon should not be prosecuted. This was a scam by Essam Eid, Teresa Engle and Maria Marconi to extract money from Sharon,' he said in the letter. While the short letter was referred to during the trial, it was not introduced as an exhibit and was not given to the jury when it requested it, during its deliberations. PJ's letter was sent just weeks after Collins was first arrested, as part of the investigation, and his letter was written just ten days after she had sent the first of three lengthy letters to the DPP, asking that she not be charged.

PJ's evidence in the court case was fascinating, particularly his defence of Collins and his decision to kiss her on the lips after he stepped down from the witness box, on his final day in the courtroom, on Thursday, 5 June. That emotive gesture stunned the courtroom and left Collins looking very pleased with herself. PJ did not reappear for the remainder of the trial.

He took the witness stand three times during the trial, starting on Tuesday, 27 May and resuming again on Wednesday, 4 June. His final evidence was presented on Thursday, 5 June and he spent almost two hours in the witness box over that time.

It was just after 3 p.m. on 27 May when he was first presented to the courtroom. It was put to him by senior counsel for the Prosecution, Tom O'Connell, 'You are a comparatively wealthy man.'

He replied, 'You'd wonder,' and smiled briefly. He accepted that he was financially comfortable and did not have mortgages on either his Ennis home or his apartment in Spain. He said he spends approximately half the year in Spain, where he owns a boat. He explained how he had suffered ill-health over the years and because of this, had taken a back seat in the business and had been spending more time in Spain, while Robert and Niall took a more active role in managing the business.

Given that his relationship with Collins was significant in the background to the case, much of his time in the witness box was dedicated to this. PJ explained how Collins was reasonably good at computers, having taught herself. Then he was asked had he ever married Collins.

'No', he said.

Had they discussed marriage?

'We discussed it and I took some legal advice from Michael Houlihan, a local solicitor. I was advised that a pre-nuptial wasn't accepted and wouldn't be recognised in Ireland ... stating what would happen to my assets if I died. I was informed if we had any type of a marriage, legal or church, it would affect my assets. Sharon and I discussed it. I told her the situation. We came to an agreement. I think it was in 2005. We signed an agreement, the two of us, to say we weren't married and we weren't getting married,' he said. That agreement read, 'During this trip to Italy from 6–13 October 2005, we are not partaking in any marriage ceremony with any third party.'

Sharon, he said, had drawn up the agreement and they both signed it. They went to Sorrento in Italy for a holiday between 6 and 13 October 2005 and went to a church to say a few prayers. However, he pointed out that there had not been a ceremony in Sorrento. 'None whatsoever,' he stressed. He said that Sharon had told friends that they had got married, but he didn't have any objection to this, and they had held a party after they had arrived home. He said he bought Sharon an engagement ring at the time, which she wore. Asked was she still wearing it, he replied, 'Not to my knowledge.'

He said that he had been on a lot of medication when he was ill and Sharon had looked after this 'for years'. He also said that she knew the combination of the safe in his Spanish apartment. On one occasion, in 2004, he said the safe contained a lot of cash for up to two weeks, after a friend had sold a boat.

He said that Sharon used internet cafés in Spain and also used a computer at their home. He was then asked by Mr O'Connell when he had first heard the name Maria Marconi.

'I heard it from Sharon maybe a day or two after the office was broken into. I was on the phone to Robert. Sharon probably overheard me. She told me she had something to tell me. She said she had answered a pop-up on the computer. She said she had contact with Maria Marconi over the past eight or nine months. She thought it might have something to do with the break-in. She said she was in correspondence with Maria Marconi and she was tutoring her to write a book,' said PJ Howard.

The couple had been in Spain when the Maria Marconi revelation had emerged, he said, and it was the first he had heard of the woman. He had never met her.

He was then asked about the demand for money that had been made of Robert. What was PJ's reaction to this? '

I found it very hard to understand. I told him to notify the guards and not to pay anything,' he said.

He said his email address was pj@downesandhoward.com. Mr O'Connell then read out details of an email sent to leonard@proxymarriages.com from an eircom email address, pjhoward@eircom.net, in 2005. The email stated, 'We have tried several times over the past couple of weeks to ring you, but the calls were diverted to an answering machine. Sharon left a message over a week ago and again last night. I have to be honest, I am very worried and getting more skeptical as each day goes by.'

However, PJ Howard said he did not send that email and never organised a proxy marriage. He said that an eircom email address had been set up in his name, but he did not think he had ever used it.

It emerged during the trial that Collins bought a Mexican proxy marriage over the internet for $1,295, towards the end of 2005, claiming she and PJ Howard were married. He was not aware of this until June 2007 and said he had never been to Mexico. Asked where he did his banking, PJ Howard said it was with AIB in Ennis. A friend of his, Gerry Keohane, had been the manager there but moved to Limerick.

During his evidence on 4 June, Mr Howard was asked by Mr O'Connell if Sharon Collins had ever visited Las Vegas. He replied that she had, on his instruction, in May or June 2007. 'I asked her to go. She went from Malaga. I asked her to employ somebody to look for Maria Marconi,' he said. She spent about ten days in Las Vegas and employed a private investigator (called Venus Lovetere), but could not track down Marconi.

PJ Howard was asked about one of the computers at the centre of the case—an Iridium laptop computer that he had at his home, Ballybeg House. He said he had bought it for his own use, in Galway. At one stage, Sharon's son David went to college in Galway, for about a year, and he had given it to him while he was there. David later returned it to him. He never saw anybody using the computer in the house. It was missing at one stage for a considerable period of time, after there had been a party in the house when he wasn't there. He said that Sharon had told him, after the break-in, that Maria Marconi had used the laptop while she was in the house, during her visit to Ennis.

The court was told that two US Airways flight tickets and accommodation with an international company were paid for on Mr Howard's American Express card in September 2006. However, he said he did not carry out those transactions and had not given anyone permission to do so. Asked who had knowledge of the account details, he replied, 'Sharon had them. Sharon kept the details of that account in her purse as she used to pay for my credit card every month [online]. I'd give her the money. I'll explain to you about the purse. Her purse was stolen the end of August, early September, in Spain, the first of September, as far as I know. I say, I have strong reason to believe that Teresa Engle took the purse. She was there at the time. She was in Fuengirola staying at a hotel. She was due to stay a few days. She disappeared after one day,' he said.

The following day, 5 June, will long be remembered as the day of the kiss. PJ Howard's open affection for Collins was on display as he leaned across and kissed her on the lips on his way out of the courtroom, having completed his evidence to the trial. But the gesture was not before he had spoken highly of her, in the witness box, during cross-examination by her barrister Paul O'Higgins sc.

Mr O'Higgins referred to the pre-nuptial agreement that had been raised and asked was that partly to ease his two sons' state of mind.

PJ replied, 'They were considerably involved in the business at the time and would have expected to be left the business. The business is too small to be divided up. It has been put across here that it was a very fast decision. This was not a very fast decision. It was decided over a number of months. We spent time discussing it. We both took legal advice. I think it was well established that we were not married.'

He was then asked if he found Collins to be a greedy person and his response was met by tears from Collins, who wept as he spoke about her. 'In the eight years I've known Sharon, she has never asked me for anything. That's one of the things I find astonishing. I often offered her things and she said, "No." If she was given three or four hundred euro for herself, the first thing she would do was make sure her two lads had enough. She'd be far from a greedy person, far from it. I made a statement to that effect,' he said.

'When I wasn't well she looked after me extremely well. She had a very good life for us. I was very happy with it. I presume she was too. We didn't feel there were any serious problems between us until this situation arose. Prior to that, we were living quite normally,' he said.

Asked about the allegations against her, he said, 'It doesn't make sense to me. It is totally out of character. I find it very, very, very hard to believe.'

PJ Howard's evidence came to an end at 11.50 a.m. on Thursday, 5 June, but it was not the last the court would hear about him.

Startling allegations that he used prostitutes and transvestites emerged later in the trial, through a letter that Collins had written to the *Gerry Ryan Show* on 2FM. Details of the letter, sent to the radio programme on 4 April 2006, were read to the court. In it, she had said that his black moods and tantrums were unbearable, that he used appalling language and that he had encouraged her to engage in 'strange sex'. 'He has even told me that he would love it if I would work as a prostitute and that this would really turn him on. I find the idea beyond repulsive. He has insisted on many occasions that we go to swingers' clubs while abroad and has been unbearable to live with afterwards as I do not want to partake in what goes on there. I've witnessed things that I sincerely wish I never had to see. Don't get me wrong. I'm no prude, but I simply do not see myself this way,' she wrote.

Collins was questioned at length about the letter to the *Gerry Ryan Show*, while in the witness box. It was put to her in cross-examination that PJ had not attended the trial since he had finished giving his evidence. Collins said he had been harmed in court. 'Had he a choice after the humiliation he's been through?' she asked.

She said she was referring to the letter she had written to the *Gerry Ryan Show* being read out. She agreed that she had written the letter, but said it was a private matter. She was questioned on whether the contents of the letter were correct and said, 'I think you know a lot of it was missing.'

She was asked if the allegations relating to PJ's sexual preferences had been true and said that some of them were. Asked if the issue of sex with strangers had been discussed between them, she said, 'That was discussed, partly in a fictional sense. I don't think I need to explain.'

She said the move that had frightened her, as had been mentioned in the email to the *Gerry Ryan Show*, was if she would leave him and start all over again, having been through one break-up previously. But Collins was not keen to talk about the letter, telling Úna Ní Raifeartaigh, BL for the Prosecution, 'To be quite honest with you, I don't want to discuss this at all. I don't see how this relates to murder.'

Ms Ní Raiferataigh then said to her that hatred could be a possible motive.

Collins replied, 'I don't hate PJ.'

But the letter to the *Gerry Ryan Show* was not the only time PJ Howard was portrayed in a bad light by Collins. In one of her many descriptive emails to 'hitman', Collins—as 'lyingeyes'—stated, 'I've no conscience about my husband, he's a real asshole and makes my life hell, but I do feel bad about the others, however, I thought about it long and hard and I realise that it is necessary or there is no advantage to getting rid of my husband other than not having to look at his miserable face again. But I must be sure that I will be ok financially.'

In another email, she said she would prefer if it was just her husband she wanted dead, but because of the way he had arranged his affairs it would be too complicated if his sons were still around.

And, as she communicated with 'hitman', she wrote coldly about how her 'husband' would die and how his body would be transported home from Spain. To her, it was nothing more than a business deal that would ultimately make her handsomely rich. The level of detail and planning that was going on in her head was nothing less than cold and callous.

Ms Ní Raifeartaigh, in her closing speech for the Prosecution, said that PJ Howard's affection, loyalty and trust was only returned by Sharon Collins's betrayal, deception and public humiliation.

As the bizarre and potential damaging allegations about PJ were repeatedly aired on the national news, he declined to refute them publicly or make any comment in relation to this or any other matter relating to the case. Despite repeated queries through his PR advisor Mr Jones, neither PJ Howard nor his sons Robert and Niall spoke publicly about any of those matters.

However, his friends have refuted the suggestions that PJ was anything other than an honourable gentleman. A close friend of PJ's, Manuel Di Lucia—who is a former mayor of Kilkee in west Clare—hit out at the claims about PJ, saying they were fabrication and lies. He said that when he was setting up the Kilkee rescue service in 1982, PJ contributed handsomely, by paying for their first ever boat. 'We were fundraising for our first lifeboat when PJ called me up and asked me were we looking to buy a boat. He said to me, "Find out how much it is and I'll fund it,"' said Mr Di Lucia. He said the boat cost £2,500 and PJ paid for it and the two men travelled together to the Manchester area to collect it. They took many trips together over the years and Mr Di Lucia said there was nothing negative that could be said about Mr Howard. 'A more decent, more honourable man you could not meet. The allegations about his sexual preferences were 100 per cent false as I know the man and I have known him for over 30 years,' he said. 'He is a very quiet, shrewd businessman. In business, he could be quite exact and tough, but outside of that, he is very down to earth. His character was completely ruined by that statement in court,' said Mr Di Lucia.

'He shunned everything, anything to do with publicity. When he bought us the boat, he didn't want to come at all to the launch, but I coaxed him to come down. That is the way he is. He shied away from publicity. She has ruined his life really and he will find it difficult to get over the hurt,' he added.

Limerick-based businessman Bob McConkey also came out in support of PJ Howard, in the aftermath of the trial, saying he was 'flabbergasted and astonished' by the revelations about him, having known him for almost 20 years. While Mr McConkey did not give evidence in person in the case, a statement he made was read to the court by the Prosecution. In it, he said that he owns an apartment in Fuengirola, next door to PJ Howard, who he referred to as a friend and business acquaintance. He pointed out that Sharon Collins frequently visited internet cafés in Spain and even recommended various internet cafés to him. He said that PJ had been in bad health and he would check up on him regularly. He said he was under the impression that PJ and Sharon were married and he had attended a party at the Admiralty Lodge in Spanish Point in late 2005 to celebrate with them. 'It was only recently PJ told me they were not married. I believe he only went along with the marriage story to appease Sharon,' he said.

PJ Howard's life will, undoubtedly, never be the same again. His association with Sharon Collins has ruined him and not only has he to get over the hurt and betrayal, but he also has to face his local community in Ennis, where his privacy has been stolen from him. He is also at the centre of mind-numbing rumours about his sex life, as claimed by Collins.

While the trial was going on, in June 2008, PJ Howard lodged an objection with his local authority, Clare County Council, against a housing development near his home, Ballybeg House, and this was widely reported in the media. Previously, this would have gone virtually unnoticed, but this is an indication of the changed circumstances he has been forced to contend with, along with his new status in his hometown.

In her closing speech, Ms Ní Raifeartaigh spoke about PJ's humiliation and, acutely aware of the effect the whole saga has had on him, asked 'Can he ever go back to Ennis?'

It begs the question, will his life ever be the same in Ennis again? The answer to the latter, sadly, is a resounding 'No.'

EPILOGUE | LIVES DEVASTATED

The game was finally over for Sharon Collins. Almost two years after she had filled out an application form on www.hitmanforhire.net, she was finally found out and convicted. Her conniving, heartless plotting and planning, which had been driven by greed, was transparent and the jury saw right through it. Not only did the jury decide that Collins had solicited Essam Eid to murder PJ, Robert and Niall Howard, but they also ruled that she had conspired to murder all three. Six convictions on gravely serious charges, each carrying up to 10 years in prison.

Essam Eid was found guilty of one major charge, extortion, which carries a sentence of up to 14 years. He was also convicted of handling stolen property, but acquitted of burgling the Downes and Howard business premises. The jury could not decide if he had conspired to murder the three Howards, after deliberating for almost 11 hours.

At the end of a pulsating eight-week trial, Collins and Eid were led away to prison on the evening of 9 July 2008; Collins to the women's section of Mountjoy prison and Eid to Cloverhill (and later to Limerick prison). And while they will be forced to pay for their greed through prison terms, it is those they have left behind who will have to live with the devastation, particularly in the case of Collins. Innocent lives have been ruined.

Undoubtedly, two families have been shattered by Sharon Collins's greed. Life will never be the same again for the Collins and Howard families, through no fault of their own. Take Sharon Collins's own family. Her elderly mother Bernadette Coote has changed from an outgoing, vibrant, glamorous woman to a devastated lady who now rarely leaves her Ennis home. Collins's two sisters Suzette and Catherine have also been wounded by their younger sibling's cruelty. Collins's two young sons, Gary and David, have also been deeply affected by all of this. Both in their 20s, the red-haired brothers supported their mother during the trial, closely sitting alongside her almost every day. Both have now moved from their native Ennis to Dublin, where their father, Collins's ex-husband, Noel Collins lives. Gary had moved to Dublin some time ago, but David recently left his job in a menswear shop in Ennis and moved to the capital. Like all young men in their 20s, both Gary and David had a great social life in Ennis, where they have dozens of friends. But this has all been taken away from them as the effect of their mother's deviousness took hold.

As the allegations against her emerged in 2007, David was inconsolable and his work was affected. He, like Gary, was very close to his mother, yet she had the gall to write about him during some of her emails to 'hitman', at one stage pointing out that he had arrived home to spend some quality time with her. 'Anyway, I was sitting with my son last night and thinking if he only knew what his mother was planning. He definitely would wonder if he ever knew me at all. My boys would be devastated, if they thought I would do such a thing. My other son is nearly 23 and works in Dublin. I miss him a lot. We are very close. In fact, my boys are everything to me,' she wrote.

Her actions have also created havoc and heartbreak for the Howards. PJ gave her his heart, but only got evil deceit in return. He believed they had a good time together, sharing a lavish lifestyle. But not in his wildest dreams did he ever believe she was capable of plotting anything so sinister behind his back. PJ was living in a dream world and did not want his dreams to be crushed. His sons Robert and Niall were also propelled into the limelight, for the first time in their lives, because of their 'surrogate mother's' actions. Men of few words, they were forced to give away something very dear to them—their privacy. Their lives will never be the same again, but ironically, they are lucky to be alive at all.

If Collins had had her way and the evil plan to kill them had gone ahead, the three Howards would now be dead. If Collins had hired a lethal hitman, as she thought she had, then Robert Howard would not have been approached for money. Rather, he, his brother and father, would have been taken out.

In her vicious emails, Collins openly discussed various methods of killing all three—men who had trusted her and had built up close relationships with her. But, to her, their lives came in the way of her needs and her gold digging. As she typed away, the language she used in email after email made it appear as though it was just a job, a business deal, but one that involved three lives.

The Howards' and Collins's privacy has been shattered as their every move is now monitored by the media. Neighbours of Bernadette Coote have been forced to hunt several members of the tabloid press and various photographers from her doorstep both during and after the trial as they tried to shield the grieving woman from the press. Gary and David Collins's trips to see their mother in jail have also been publicised, while PJ Howard has been followed to Spain by journalists and photographers. His visit to Collins in Mountjoy jail has also been noted, in dramatic fashion, both in terms of news copy and photographs in the national media.

And all of this grief brought on by an evil woman, who felt she had nothing to lose but everything to gain. Yet, in the face of being found out, she continued to lie her way through it all, presenting a story about a novelist called Maria Marconi. She claimed that her association with Marconi, via the internet, had led her to the mess that she found herself in, but not one shred of this could have been validated and gardaí came to the conclusion that Marconi was nothing more than a figment of Collins's wicked imagination.

She complained about PJ's alleged sexual preferences and his black moods, while she thought his plush home—that she had made her own—was too big. She wanted everything to be perfect. But, even if the damaging allegations she made about PJ Howard were true, she had plenty of options. Walk away from it all. But no, Collins had become gripped by greed and that was not her style. She wanted to be the queen of his millions.

Sharon Collins was a bright, attractive, ambitious young woman, growing up in Ennis. But her ambition went too far and tragically, has led to devastating consequences for so many people. Her selfishness, thoughtlessness and lack of compassion for anyone but herself have destroyed several lives. Right up until the very end, she firmly believed she was invincible, but the bitter truth was told in the end, in harrowing fashion. For now, Sharon Collins must pay the price of her actions.